THE CULTURE OF RECONSTRUCTION

The Culture of Reconstruction

European Literature, Thought and Film, 1945–50

Edited by

NICHOLAS HEWITT

Professor of French
University of Nottingham

St. Martin's Press   New York

791.43
C968

First published in the United States of America in 1989

Printed in Great Britain

ISBN 0–312–03105–X

Library of Congress Cataloging-in-Publication Data
The culture of reconstruction: European literature, thought, and
    film, 1945–50 / edited by Nicholas Hewitt.
        p.   cm.
    Bibliography: p.
    Includes index.
    ISBN 0–312–03105–X
    1. European literature—20th century—History and criticism.
2. Motion pictures—Europe—History.   3. Reconstruction (1939–1951)—
Europe.   4. Europe—Intellectual life—20th century.   I. Hewitt,
Nicholas.
PN771.C85   1989
791.43'094—dc19

                                                        88–36652
                                                            CIP

MB

Contents

Preface

This volume is based upon papers given at the conference 'The Culture of Reconstruction' held at the University of Warwick from 1 to 3 May 1987, under the auspices of the European Humanities Research Centre. I am indebted to the staff of the centre, in particular its director, Dr Tom Winnifrith, for all their help in the organisation of the conference and the preparation of the manuscript; to the University of Warwick, for its generous financial assistance towards research for the papers by Brian Rigby and myself; and to the French Embassy in London for generously contributing to the expenses of Pierre Sorlin.

N.H.

Notes on the Contributors

Keith Bullivant is Reader in German Studies at the University of Warwick. He has written extensively on various aspects of German culture in the nineteenth and twentieth centuries, and his publications include *Literature in Upheaval* (with R. H. Thomas, 1974), *Culture and Society in the Weimar Republic* (1977), *The Modern German Novel* (1987) and *Realism Today* (1987).

Michael Caesar is Lecturer in Italian at the University of Kent at Canterbury. He has written particularly on Romanticism and on twentieth-century Italian literature, and is co-editor of *Writers and Society in Contemporary Italy* (1984).

David Forgacs is Lecturer in Italian Studies at the University of Sussex. His publications include a chapter in *Modern Literary Theory* (edited by Ann Jefferson and David Robey, 1985), an edited collection *Rethinking Italian Fascism* (1986) and editions of two volumes of Gramsci's writings in translation: *Selections from Cultural Writings* (with Geoffrey Nowell-Smith, 1985) and *A Gramsci Reader* (1988).

Ursula Fries is a researcher at the University of Bochum, West Germany. She is a member of the joint research team of the Universities of Warwick and Bochum working on the project 'Urban Reconstruction and Social Change – Bochum and Coventry, 1945–1960'.

Stephen Gundle is a Research Fellow of Churchill College, Cambridge. He has published a number of articles on Italian politics and culture, and is currently preparing a book on Communism and cultural change in Italy since the war.

Nicholas Hewitt is a Senior Lecturer in French Studies at the University of Warwick. He has written extensively on the literary and intellectual history of the interwar years and Fourth Republic in France. His publications include *Henri Troyat* (1984), *The Golden Age of Louis-Ferdinand Céline* (1987) and *'Les Maladies du siècle': The Image of Malaise in French Fiction and Thought in the Interwar Years* (1988).

Michael Kelly is Professor of French at the University of Southampton. He has written extensively on literary, intellectual and cultural movements in twentieth-century France, and his publications include *Pioneer of the Catholic Revival: Ideas and Influence of Emmanuel Mounier* (1979) and *Modern French Marxism* (1982).

Colin Nettelbeck is Associate Professor of French at Monash University. A specialist on Céline, he has written widely on French literature, ideas and history in the interwar years and the postwar period. His publications include *Patrick Modiano: Pièces d'identité. Ecrire l'entretemps* (1986).

Helmut Peitsch is a Lecturer in German at University College, Swansea. He has written extensively on postwar German literature and his publications include *Nachkriegsliteratur in Westdeutschland 1945–1949*, I: *Schreibweisen, Gattungen, Institutionen* (with Jost Hermand and Klaus R. Scherpe, 1982) and *Nachkriegsliteratur in Westdeutschland 1945–1949*, II: *Autoren, Sprache, Traditionen* (with Jost Hermand and Klaus R. Scherpe, 1983).

Brian Rigby is a Lecturer in French Studies at the University of Warwick. He is the author of numerous articles on Volney, Stendhal, Hazlitt, Victor Hugo, and English and French nineteenth-century periodicals. He is currently preparing a volume on Hazlitt and France, and a volume on modern French popular culture.

Pierre Sorlin is Professor of History at the University of Paris VIII (Vincennes-Saint-Denis). He has published extensively on various aspects of twentieth-century history and has helped to pioneer, in France, the use of film by historians. His publications include *La Croix et les Juifs* (1967); *L'Antisémitisme allemand* (1969); *Lénine, Trotsky, Staline 1921–1927* (with Irène Sorlin, 1972); *Octobre: Ecriture et idéologie. Analyse filmique de l'oeuvre d'Eisenstein* (with Marie-Claire Ropars, 1976); *Sociologie du cinéma: ouverture pour l'histoire de demain* (1977) and *Générique des années 30* (with Michèle Lagny and Marie-Claire Ropars, 1986).

Christopher Wagstaff is a Lecturer in the Department of Italian Studies at the University of Reading. He has published articles on Italian avant-garde literature and on Italian cinema.

Introduction

When the Second World War ended in Europe on 8 May 1945, there was inevitably a profound sense of an ending and of a new beginning. The sheer scale of the physical devastation of the continent was such that a return to the past seemed impossible. As Derek Urwin writes:

In 1918 when the First World War ended, only the battlefields of Belgium and Northern France lay in ruins: elsewhere war damage was comparatively negligible. In 1945 the situation was entirely different. Military and technological development had made war seem universal. Very few areas in Europe had remained immune from the conflict and its consequences. The outlook everywhere was bleak. The development of air warfare had laid even the British Isles open to destruction. The devastation of northern France between 1914 and 1918 may have been more intense, but what the Second World War lacked in quality it made up for in quantity. In every direction whole regions had been virtually defoliated. Industrial production of the continent had slumped; in 1945 and 1946 it stood at only one-third of the 1938 figure. Agriculture had also suffered: agricultural production was down to half the prewar level. Cities had been severely damaged. Millions of acres of valuable farming land had been rendered useless, not only from being battlefields but also through the demands of war. Land was exhausted through overcropping, while the compensation of fertilisation was lacking because commercial fertilisers were unobtainable. Furthermore, the death rate of animals had been extremely high. In the factories and mines machinery had been crippled because it had been overworked and because it had not been maintained satisfactorily: in addition replacements were generally unavailable.

Economic reconstruction after the war started off at a great disadvantage for additional reasons. The war had disrupted and destroyed communications networks. Aiming for a speedy end to the conflict, the Allies had concentrated on the destruction of communication lines. Hence, bridges, railways, marshalling yards and shipping facilities had been targets of high priority to

Allied bombers. Again, rather than allow such valuable acquisitions to fall into the hands of the advancing enemy, the German military had attempted to destroy them wherever possible.[1]

At the same time, the nature of the war itself and the level of the physical destruction had implied an unprecedented involvement of the entire population: the phenomena of mass-conflict and total war. Whereas the civilian populations during the First World War, apart from those who happened by chance to live in the immediate areas of the conflict itself, experienced it at one remove, through the involvement of loved ones and economic effects, the Second World War brought the conflict home in a concrete way to most Europeans: the mobility of the war established battlegrounds from one end of the continent to the other; aerial bombardment menaced all cities and industrial targets; under the German occupation of Europe, all of its citizens were to some degree subject to conscription, requisition for German industry, deportation and summary punishment. These phenomena of total war and their psychological effects were compounded by the fact that the end of the Second World War also marked the end of two long-lived Fascist regimes, that in Italy from 1922 to 1943, and that in Nazi Germany from 1933 to 1945, and the end of the German and Italian occupation of France from 1940 to 1944 (1945 in some cases, such as the naval ports).

It is hardly surprising, therefore, that for contemporary participants and commentators, it seemed impossible that such traumatic events as total war, large-scale destruction, military defeat, occupation, should leave no trace on European development and should not imply some kind of radical departure, socially, politically, intellectually and culturally. In particular, the realisation of the extent of the Holocaust and of the implications of the atomic bombs dropped on Hiroshima and Nagasaki, seemed necessarily to establish new parameters of thought and to render a return to the past unthinkable. In the sphere of social and political organisation, history has not been kind to such aspirations and illusions: by the end of the 1940s, all three major West European countries, France, Italy and West Germany, had returned to recognisably traditional parliamentary regimes, and the revolutionary ideals of the French Resistance and the Italian partisans had been largely neutralised by the return to professional politics. In the area of cultural and intellectual history, however, the assumption that the Second

World War automatically produced innovation and experimentation in ideas and expression has proved considerably more persistent. There are two major reasons for this assumption. In the first place, cultural historians are often persuaded that the model of the period immediately after the First World War, which produced not merely revolution and the Weimar Republic in Germany, but also, apparently, a whole range of experimentation in the visual, plastic and literary arts, is applicable to the period following the Liberation of Europe in 1944–5. Secondly, it has proved difficult for those same cultural historians to accept any notion of the imperturbability or autonomy of cultural development in the face of traumatic historical circumstances, and to question the assumption that the events of the Second World War must automatically and necessarily have been registered in literary and artistic production. Accordingly, the cultural history of the postwar period is often described as if it were one of innovation and experiment, but such a description can often only be arrived at through a partial and selective perception of a whole body of material which is notoriously complex. In other words, the theory of an innovative cultural reconstruction of Europe is often based on isolated examples such as Neorealism in postwar Italian cinema, the work of Böll in Germany and the production of the French Existentialists, which are in their own right highly ambiguous and which are spread over a chronological spectrum that is often too broad to be historically valid. Whilst it may be true that the first fifteen years following the war, from 1945 to 1960, show evidence of considerable cultural renewal, with the development of the French *nouveau roman* and the beginnings of the *nouvelle vague* in cinema, and the work of Günter Grass in West Germany, much of the real innovation occurs at the end of this period and is by no means directly attributable to the effects of the war itself: rather, it is best seen as the result of purely autonomous cultural developments which have little to do with the superstructure of history and which have their origins before the war itself. In this context, even the model of the period following the First World War is ambiguous, since Modernism and the avant-garde movements in fact straddle the war, perhaps accentuated by it, but nevertheless continuing a cultural tradition established in the 1900s and more resilient to historical impact than at first sight appears.

In order to assess the real nature of cultural reconstruction in the postwar period, therefore, and in order to see whether that reconstruction constituted a new departure or merely a rebuilding of the old structures, it is essential to limit the period under analysis to the immediate postwar years from 1945 to 1950, when the debates on the direction in which European culture should go were at their height, and when the issues had not become clouded by later developments which often owed little to the impact of the war itself. Similarly, rather than establishing a general European model for postwar cultural development, in which Italian Neo-realism, French Existentialism and the German Gruppe 47 rub shoulders to confirm a general, but vague, impression of innovation and experimentation, it is equally necessary to undertake a detailed comparison of artistic production in the three major European countries, France, Italy and West Germany, in order to pinpoint individual national characteristics and to explore the precise nature of cultural reconstruction in each country.

Clearly, the circumstances of each country at the end of the war differ in many crucial respects, but all appeared to point towards a complete break with the past and a new beginning. Germany, as the instigator of the conflict, was punished both physically and morally and politically: it had suffered the most severe devastation of the European nations, through Allied bombing and the effects of the Allied advance in 1945: it was placed under direct Allied occupation and divided between the four victorious powers, who limited with greater or lesser degrees of severity both political activity and cultural expression; and, through the Nürnberg Trials, was made fully conscious of its responsibility, not only for the war itself, but for the war crimes against humanity committed during the conflict. The cases of Italy and France were more ambiguous. Italy had entered the war as Germany's ally in 1939 and therefore, as a member of the Axis, shared to a large extent its responsibilities. Nevertheless, it had overthrown Mussolini's Fascist regime in 1943, had suffered the rigours of German military occupation and had participated in its own liberation through the partisan war. Whilst the Allies, therefore, and particularly the Americans, considered Italy to be a defeated power and restricted severely the nation's autonomy, particularly in the field of foreign affairs, progressive forces, especially the Socialists and Communists, considered that they had helped to liberate the country and that they had a powerful voice in the establishment of a new regime, built in part, at least, on the values of the Resistance. France found herself in a similar, if apparently less ambiguous situation. Occupied by Germany after the disastrous campaign of 1940, its role as victim was considerably weakened by the establishment of the Vichy regime in the Southern Zone and its collaborationist policies which took the form, notably, of vigorous antisemitic programmes and the sending of French volunteers to fight alongside German troops on the Eastern Front. Despite Allied reservations concerning France's role as a quasi-ally of Germany, however, the French at the end of the war were able, particularly through the astute manoeuvering of De Gaulle, to impose a view of recent history in which collaboration was the work of a small minority and where Resistance was the norm. France could therefore claim to have liberated herself, both through the activities of her internal Resistance organisations and through the military intervention of Leclerc's Deuxième Division Blindée and De Lattre's First Army group, and to have a legitimate place as an equal amongst the victorious powers, particularly since she had participated in the invasion of Germany in 1945. As in the case of Italy, therefore, the stage seemed set for the establishment of a new regime, founded on progressive Resistance ideals which would also, through the process of *épuration*, rid the country of the last vestiges of guilt stemming from collaboration.

Despite these crucial differences in the individual circumstances of Germany, Italy and France at the end of the war, by 1950 they came to present very similar characteristics. In France and Italy, for example, despite the expectations of the Socialist- and Communist-dominated Resistance movements, there was an inexorable return of middle-of-the-road centre-right parliamentary regimes which had nothing to do with revolution and which, in the case of France, bore a close resemblance to the structure of the Third Republic. Similarly, the establishment of the Federal Republic in West Germany saw the elimination of extremist or marginal groupings and the creation of a two-party parliamentary system, dominated throughout the 1950s by Konrad Adenauer's CDU. In other words, by 1950, both Italy and West Germany were governed by Christian Democrat parties and whilst the situation in France was more volatile, the Catholic MRP was a consistent force in government. This return to traditional parliamentarianism is attributable on one level to the short-lived nature of post-Liberation euphoria and the relative weakness of the amateur, as opposed to the professional, politician. It was also due to the rapid marginalisation of the European Communist Parties: in the Western zones of Germany immediately after 1945, the Communist Party was always small and was rendered virtually redundant with the establishment of the DDR in the East; in the cases of France and Italy, there were brief periods of tripartism, nineteen months in Italy and seventeen months in France, in which Communists, Socialists and Christian Democrats shared power, but in both cases the Communist Parties were denied the key ministries and were rapidly placed in a position where they were forced to leave the government. This marginalisation of the European Communist Parties as effective parties of power coincided clearly with the beginning of the Cold War and the integration of Western Europe firmly into the American sphere of interest. By 1950, therefore, aspirations towards a new beginning had largely been eliminated, the major political force for radical change, the Western Communist Parties, had been neutralised, and the continent was governed by recognisable, structurally conservative regimes, which constituted less a system of political innovation than the establishment of links with the past.

This political evolution, or regression, is clearly deeply significant for European cultural production during the same period, and crucial in this respect is the role in Italy and France of the Communist Party. At the end of the war, many intellectuals, writers, artists and film-makers, emerging from the Resistance, saw the PCI and the PCF as their natural home or, at least, as a natural ally, committed to both social and artistic change, and in this respect the initial period following the war, 1945 and 1946 especially, appeared to confirm their assumptions. The Italian Party was always more open to intellectual and artistic innovation and debate than its French counterpart, but in both countries the early postwar years were characterised by a genuine flexibility and tolerance on the part of Communists with regard to pluralism and diversity, as evidenced by the range of subject-matter and contributors of the PCF's monthly review, *Action*, or the early history of Vittorini's review, *Il Politecnico*. With the onset of the Cold War, however, and the end of tripartism, both Parties adopted a considerably sterner cultural and intellectual policy, with more rigorous control of the orthodoxy of their journals and the adoption, to a greater or lesser extent, of the precepts of Zhdanovism, which elevated an always-incipient distrust of the avant-garde into a categoric condemnation of formalism in favour of Socialist Realism. In other words, the European Communist Parties, which initially played a role in favour of diversity and innovation in cultural and intellectual production, rapidly constituted a conservative force in which speculation and self-reflexiveness were replaced by adherence to a strictly materialist and realist tradition.

If Communism, therefore, represents an ambiguous force for social and cultural change in the early postwar years, so, paradoxically, does the United States. One common and recurring feature of French, Italian and West German culture of the period is enthusiasm for America and particularly for the American novelists of the 1930s and 1940s, Dos Passos, Faulkner, Hemingway, Saroyan and Steinbeck. Hemingway, in particular, was immensely popular and the translation of *For Whom the Bell Tolls* was one of the major literary events of the postwar period. At the same time, there was considerable interest throughout Europe in the American cinema of the late 1930s and the 1940s. The fruitful and rejuvenating nature of this American impact was severely diminished, however, by a number of factors. In the first place, with the onset of the Cold War and the hardening of the Communist cultural policy under the impact of Zhdanovism, American literature and cinema ceased to be a model for innovation and became perceived instead as an integral part of American imperialism, to be rejected *en bloc* by Communist intellectuals and their left-wing allies. Similarly, whilst the formal experimentation of Faulkner was condemned as obscurantist and avant-gardist, the extreme realism, often in the sexual domain, of many American novelists, was perceived as a symptom and an agent of Western decadence and corruption. In this context in France, Communists and the conservative Right joined together to pillory Henry Miller in the name of a new-found moral puritanism. At the same time, there was often general distrust amongst a large body of European intellectuals and artists of the mass culture and its accompanying technological and economic implications which America was seen to represent. Nor were European fears by any means totally unjustified: there is ample evidence of a conscious attempt to impose American cultural hegemony upon the countries of Western Europe. In the American zone of Germany, for example, not only did the authorities impose a rigid censorship, more extreme than that in the other zones, but they also, particularly in the domain of the theatre and the cinema, took care to introduce American products which presented a flattering view of American society. In France and Italy, American cultural policy was operated chiefly through the cinema, with the Americans attempting to obtain the best possible conditions for the release of their films, often the result of the five-year backlog which had built up during the war, to the detriment of indiginous products. It is quite understandable, therefore, that the Blum–Byrnes Agreement of 1947 and negotiations between the Italian Government and the Americans on import quotas for US films were widely seen as a capitulation by Western governments to American imperialist aspirations. What is important, however, is that, as in the case of the European Communist Parties, what started out as a potential influence for innovation and rejuvenation in postwar cultural life was severely limited in its impact as the effects of the Cold War began to make themselves felt.

This pattern of initial receptiveness to change followed by retrenchment is repeated in the one aspect of European cultural production which at the outset seemed the most promising: the new thematic possibilities afforded by the war itself with, in the field of literature, the concomitant swelling of the ranks of writers with those who had lived through the experience and who took to writing for the first time in order to convey that experience. The literature of the period is dominated by first-hand accounts, in the form of memoirs, autobiographical fragments, barely fictionalised transpositions, of German concentration camps, the activities of the Italian partisans or of the French Resistance. That this influx of new writers and apparently new subject-matter did not produce a durable impact on European culture is attributable to several factors. In the first place, few of the writers of first-hand accounts continued to write once their initial message had been conveyed: their work was essentially ephemeral, often fragmentary, dominated by the experience itself and rarely susceptible to extension or development. At the same time, the impact and novelty of their work depended upon the interest of their audience in that experience and as soon as that interest waned, as it was bound to as the postwar period progressed, the *raison d'être* for such work diminished. This coincides with the fact that such literature was essentially naive and depended upon an assertion of veracity and a denial of artifice: readers in the years immediately following the war wanted the 'truth' about certain hidden aspects of the conflict and assumed a direct untrammelled relationship between the lived experience of the author and its transcription. The problem, however, is that such literature comes to rely almost exclusively for its impact on the sincerity of its authors, in a situation in which sincerity alone is no guarantor of accomplishment or durability and is a minor ingredient in literary success. Nor, paradoxically, is sincerity and direct transcription the most effective means of conveying the inherent strangeness and complexity of hitherto unimagined experiences. In a survey of concentration-camp litera-ture published in 1968, A. Alvarez argues that sincere, first-hand, traditional accounts of life in the camps somehow fall short of conveying the sheer horror of the experience and that it is precisely through artifice, through a conscious stylistic and narrative subver-sion, that it may be authentically transmitted. Jorge Semprun, in *Le Grand voyage*, achieves this by adopting the issue of mere survival as the centre of his novel and making of it 'an aesthetic, creative procedure'.[2] In the same way, the Polish writer Tadeus Borowski mirrors the degradation and inhumanity of Auschwitz by narrating his stories in a 'curt, icy and brutally direct' style[3] and by con-sciously blackening his first-person narrator. Such discoveries regarding the complexities in narrating the un-narratable were comparatively rare and tended to come later. For most writers dealing with the war in the immediate postwar period, whereas the experience of the concentration camps, of torture and persecu-tion, of resistance and the partisan war, was unique and new, the method of its narration was traditional and backward-looking, drawing either on patterns of war or adventure narrative which had changed little since the nineteenth century, or, more recently, on the form of the politically and philosophically conscious novel of the 1930s represented by Silone in Italy or Malraux in France. The past still continued to exert a stranglehold on cultural innova-tion.

This was particularly true in France and West Germany with regard to the role of writers and cultural figures during the period of the war itself. Whereas in Italy there were comparatively few debates concerning the activities of writers and artists under the Fascist regime, in France and Germany, accusations and counter-accusations of complicity in Nazism or collaboration were rife, and often dominated intellectual and artistic life to the detriment of a new beginning. In Germany, accrimonious debates as to the relative merits of exile or 'inner emigration' split the cultural community and forced its members to constantly look back to the past. In France, the preoccupation with the *épuration* of writers who were deemed to have collaborated with the Germans or the Vichy regime gave further primacy to political considerations over aesthetic innovation and laid down the foundations for a system of evaluation and exclusion which were to hamper artistic and intellectual expression throughout the Cold War period. In fact, only those writers who, like Guéhenno, refused to publish at all during the Occupation or who, like Vercors, published only in the clandestine *Presses de Minuit*, were totally immune from charges of some degree of collaboration: even left-wing writers such as Sartre and Camus, who permitted their works to be published and performed under German censorship and paper-rationing regulations, could be seen as in some way contributing to the cultural 'normality' which the occupying forces wished to establish. And even the Italian Neorealist cinema owed a considerable debt to the techniques of documentary film-making which had been learned under Mussolini's regime.

In fact, claims to 'normalisation' of culture were as strong in the postwar period as they were during the war itself. In Italy, writers like Moravia may have momentarily shifted from analysis of bourgeois psychology to more social concerns, but the Left did not nevertheless cut itself off from the tradition of Crocean Idealism and liberalism. In France and Germany, some considerable comfort was derived from a notion of cultural continuity, in which the uninterrupted production of writers, whether in exile or under the domination of Nazism, was seen as the guarantor of the survival of the national spirit. In Germany, the important feature of the debate between exiles and 'inner emigrants' is not so much the political validity of the various claims to political purity as the unquestioned assumption that it was essential for German culture to continue to operate unchanged and unaffected by the Nazi regime from 1933 to 1945. Similarly, in France, even the most extreme *épurationiste* journals devoted considerable space to the writing of exiled writers and their return to France after the Liberation, and took pride in the continued production of writers under the Occupation itself. It was as if the Third Reich and the Occupation could be considered a bad dream, with no implications for change, an aberration in the general pattern of normality to which Europe could thankfully return with the cessation of hostilities. It is highly significant, therefore, that in France some of the most distinguished, and most traditional, novel-cycles, such as Georges Duhamel's *Chronique des Pasquier* or Jules Romains's *Les Hommes de bonne volonté*, begun in the 1930s, could be serenely continued or concluded when the Occupation ended. It is also significant that postwar claims to philosophical, moral or political legitimacy should be made by the invocation of past national traditions: German writers, particularly the 'inner emigrants', laid claim to the ground of German Idealism; the attempt at a postwar concensus in France was based upon a general acceptance of the notion of 'Humanism', in which Communists, Catholics and Existentialists shared, but which originated in large part in some of the most traditional elements of the Third Republic. Communists in France and Italy justified their position by reference back to the tradition of materialist philosophy which began in the Renaissance but culminated in the eighteenth and nineteenth centuries.

The postwar period in Europe began politically and culturally with a faith in 'rebirth', conveyed by the German notions of *Kahlschlag* or *Nullpunkt*, the French *Renaissance* and the Italian *Rinascita*. Within a few years, however, it became clear that what Europe was witnessing was rather a process of 'Reconstruction', a more complex and more ambiguous process in which the rebuilding of the past was inextricably mixed with the search for the new. External political events, particularly the Cold War, and the economic effects of postwar austerity, which drove out of business so many ephemeral avant-garde publications, contrived to privilege the former at the expense of the latter. But whilst these external factors are undoubtedly important and, in many respects, decisive, it is the inner workings of cultural production itself which often feature as an inherently autonomous and conservative force.

Notes

1. Derek W. Urwin, *Western Europe since 1945: A Short Political History* (London: Longman, 1969) pp. 27–8.
2. A. Alvarez, 'The Literature of the Holocaust', in A. Alvarez, *Beyond all this Fiddle: Essays, 1955–1967* (London: Allen Lane, 1968) p. 32.
3. Ibid., pp. 26–7.

1

The Communist Party and the Politics of Cultural Change in Postwar Italy, 1945–50

STEPHEN GUNDLE

In the period during and shortly after the war of national liberation, which followed the fall of Fascism, many of Italy's artists, writers and intellectuals turned to the Italian Communist Party (PCI). The reasons for this intense and largely unexpected identification are relatively straightforward. Politically, the Party emerged from the Resistance as an authoritative force that quickly proved itself capable of attracting a genuine mass base in the north and centre of the country. It embodied and represented a widespread and deeply felt need for radical change that intellectuals, who in the course of the war and the Resistance had abandoned their traditional isolation and embraced the theme of social involvement, shared in large numbers. Culturally, the PCI also represented a new factor. It was the bearer of Marxism, a philosophy which had scarcely penetrated Italy and which had been excluded for some twenty years. Moreover, the Party strongly affirmed the need for a profound renovation of the national culture to match the change that was taking place in social and political relationships. It claimed to want to deprovincialise Italian culture, overcome the great influence of Crocean Idealism and facilitate the reintroduction of democratic currents of modern thought. For artists and intellectuals determined to escape from their ivory towers and participate in some way in the rebuilding of society, these were attractive proposals that in principle accorded with their own aspirations. But two additional factors are also relevant in explaining the PCI's attraction. First, by arguing that the key to cultural regeneration lay in the sustained social and political engagement of the country's writers and artists, who were actively urged to collaborate with the Party and its various publications, it placed itself in the best possible position to capture a diffuse, but often confused, demand for change. Secondly, the international dimension of the PCI's political culture added to its appeal and enhanced faith in the prospects for a general opening-up process that would definitively overcome the closures and the stifling atmosphere of Italian culture under Fascism.

In the event, the cultural role of the PCI in postwar Italy would prove to be somewhat different – at least in the estimation of some. Twenty years after the Liberation, and one year after the death of Palmiro Togliatti, the man who led the PCI from Gramsci's imprisonment in 1926 until 1964, an article was published in a special supplement to the Party weekly *Rinascita* strongly criticising the axis on which the late leader had sought to found the project of cultural renewal between 1944 and 1947.[1] The article's author, Rossana Rossanda, argued that, by putting all the stress on a national progressive tradition to be refounded and developed, Togliatti adopted a hypothesis of cultural regeneration that cut out potentially progressive currents in much European and North American culture. Modernist art and literature, as well as innovative philosophical trends which emerged in the interwar years, were not engaged, nor was their possible contribution to the regeneration of Italian culture considered. The result was an impoverishment of the whole perspective of cultural renewal and a reinforcement of the very provincialism that the PCI claimed it wished to see overcome. To be fair, Rossanda, who at the time of writing was head of the cultural section of the PCI, did suggest that Togliatti had some good reasons for distrusting some of the more recent developments in Western thought and letters. He was suspicious of the ambiguities in their relationship to Marxism and the labour movement, of their affiliation with decadentism and the avant-garde and of their propensity towards what he considered to be irrational forms of protest against the existing society. Moreover, none of these novelties had ever made any deep or lasting impact in Italy. But she none the less maintained that Togliatti had been mistaken in dismissing some of the most vital moments in twentieth-century culture.

For her pains, Rossanda was severely criticised by various figures within the Communist establishment.[2] Her removal from high-level responsibilities and an eventual exclusion from the Party in 1969, together with other leading members of the left-wing *Manifesto* group, made it easier to bury the spectre she had raised and reaffirm the historical correctness of Togliatti's line. But

Rossanda had touched on a real issue that deserves to be investigated. To what extent did the PCI objectively act as a force for cultural conservatism in the postwar years and how far was Togliatti himself responsible for this paradoxical situation? To what extent did the Party, by using its extensive influence in the way that it did, restrict the horizons of Italian culture, confirm certain parochial tendencies, reinforce existing relationships and impede a potentially fruitful cross-fertilisation with European and international culture? These may seem strange questions to ask about a political party which not only did not enjoy a monopoly or even a very significant slice of state power, but which also commanded barely twenty per cent of the popular vote.[3] But the nature and extent of the extraordinary influence which the PCI exercised over intellectual and cultural life in Italy render them legitimate and worthy of examination.

It indeed appears that the PCI, a force which many people were convinced would have a revolutionary impact on Italian society, played a conservative role in certain important respects, by seeking to cast all aspects of regeneration within a recast national cultural tradition and by implicitly reinforcing certain given structural relationships governing the interconnections between intellectuals, the arts and society. At the same time, however, despite an unfortunate tendency towards authoritarian intervention in the cultural sphere in the latter part of the period under consideration, it would be wrong to highlight only the negative consequences of the PCI's role. Under Togliatti the Party made a genuine effort to trace and develop a cultural tendency which would go beyond, and ultimately replace, the dominance of Crocean Idealism. It encouraged intellectuals and artists to set their work in the context of the society in which they lived and address the concerns of their fellow citizens. In addition, it broadly respected and defended freedom of expression at a difficult time and, no matter how inadequately, it addressed the issue of carrying culture to those sectors of society that, for historical and political reasons, had been excluded from it. Moreover, the specific reasons behind the PCI's chosen mode of intervention need to be taken into account. The Party's cultural policy was formulated in relation to Togliatti's overriding concern to implant the PCI as a national force and root it irremovably in the life of the country. The chosen lines of that policy, and in particular the prejudicial hostility towards modern European culture, therefore need to be understood perhaps less in relation to the international alliances of the PCI and the baggage of critical judgements and preferences related to them, than in relation to the specific character of cultural life in a nation at the stage of development in which Italy found itself, the raw material the PCI had to work with and the range of possible relationships that were conceivable to political leaders largely schooled in that culture.

In the period between the fall of Mussolini in July 1943 and the liberation of Italy in April 1945, political and cultural alignments were radically redefined in a way that highlighted the formation of a new social awareness amongst significant sectors of the population. For the first time, ordinary people were drawn *en masse* into events whose outcome would shape the destiny of the nation. Workers and peasants in the north and centre of the country played an important role in driving back the retreating German army and dismantling the remaining structures of Fascist authority. In those centres where the Resistance had been strongest, and had actually taken over economic and political power for a short period, fundamental social change and even political revolution seemed distinct possibilities. But whatever the subsequent politics of the Liberation period, it was the working class and not the bourgeoisie that had played the decisive role in restoring national dignity and independence, and this fact, for many, created the basis for new meanings to be given to the concepts of nation, people and democracy. Potentially, it also raised the possibility of a new order of relations between intellectuals and the people, and between culture and society.

The war and the dramatic events leading up to the Liberation provoked a profound crisis in the prevailing modes of intellectual and artistic life in Italy. During the Fascist period writers, artists and men of letters had preserved a measure of independence and autonomy from the regime by embracing the prevailing definition of culture as a special sphere separate from politics and largely removed from the life of society. But from Italy's first involvement in the war in 1940, the aristocratic spirit of Italian culture began to crumble. For many younger intellectuals it constituted the first step on the road to a shift in consciousness that would eventually lead to participation in the Resistance and a demand for a quite different conception of the social role of culture. Indeed, between 1944 and 1947 the old ivory tower mentality was almost wholly displaced by a manifest and diffuse desire for engagement.[4] Writers and intellectuals sought to define a function for themselves in the construction of a different, politically progressive order in the country, and to this end argued that reconstruction needed to be considered not merely as a set of necessary economic measures but rather as a global project possessed of moral and cultural dimensions.[5] As Romano Luperini puts it: 'the strongly humanitarian and cultural-type accent put on the theme of Reconstruction and on the engagement necessary to bring it about formed the unitary ideological texture that was destined to become dominant in national culture between 1945 and 1947'.[6] Unquestionably, this moment was a product of the political framework of national unity within which Italy returned to democratic rule. Reconstruction was seen, and not only by intellectuals, as a national enterprise that would involve everyone, regardless of class and political distinctions, and see the consolidation of the universal values of peace, humanity and progress. But the radical connotations of the cultural developments of the period should not be underestimated. Intellectual and artistic life was infused with a new set of generically left-wing assumptions, a widespread disaffection from the dominant currents in Italian culture occurred and a conviction was almost universally shared that the arts should in some way be made popular and accessible.

The extraordinary way in which much of Italy's cultural elite came to identify with the PCI in the course of the Liberation and after can be explained by reference to the high profile of the Party's role in the Resistance and its success in presenting a general design for the construction of a progressive order embracing all spheres of society. With the liberation of Rome and then Milan, the adhesion of intellectuals, artists and writers to the Party became a phenomenon of very considerable dimensions. In a short time it could count on the support of university professors of international repute, such as the Latinist Concetto Marchesi, the archaeologist Ranuccio Bianchi Bandinelli and the philosopher Antonio Banfi, established painters including Renato Guttuso and Mario Mafai, the writers Romano Bilenchi, Cesare Pavese and Elio Vittorini, and poets of the calibre of Umberto Saba and Salvatore Quasimodo, as well as many more less-well-known figures. More than any other force the PCI seemed to possess a view of the way in which the impulse towards engagement might find a meaningful outlet. More consistently and rigorously than anyone else, it urged intellectuals and artists to mix with the people and make their aspirations and concerns the central theme of their work. It stressed the social responsibility of the intellectual and it criticised all forms of culture that divorced themselves from society, that were introspective or bound up in an inaccessible language.

Before considering the cultural role of the PCI in more detail, it may be useful to sketch in its political profile, for as it re-emerged in Italy after a twenty-year absence, the Party presented itself as a very different sort of force from the small and combative nucleus that had briefly erupted on the political scene in the early 1920s. Under Togliatti's leadership, the PCI assumed the form of a mass party, attracting some two million members by 1946,[7] and committed itself to a process of institutional change within the framework of anti-Fascist unity. It renounced any advantages to be derived from a possible revolutionary outcome to the crisis opened by the collapse of the Fascist regime in favour of a long-range perspective that envisaged a phase of structural reforms to the economy that would dismantle the power of the old ruling classes and permit the PCI to consolidate its organisational presence, form a network of alliances with Italy's heterogeneous middle classes and extend Communist influence to the South. Despite this, the PCI returned to political life with its revolutionary image virtually intact. For many of those who still possessed a deep-seated fear of Communism, Togliatti was the man from Moscow who had come to make the revolution in Italy. And so he was perceived by many of the Party's own members – men and women who had joined the PCI in the course of the Resistance in the expectation that the final struggle against the bourgeoisie was just round the corner. Moreover, the PCI still considered itself to be a revolutionary party at this time, in the sense that it was a component of the world Communist movement and heir to Lenin, and in the sense that its long-term objectives remained unchanged.

This element of continuity with the past is of significance in explaining why the cultural field was endowed with such importance by the Party leadership. As a force which, in theory, aimed not merely at the improvement or modification of the existing social and political system but rather at its overturning, the Party had to engage in a critique of the false values and ideologies that served to justify prevailing arrangements and expose their partial character. It had to undertake the task of transforming society at all levels of the social body, including that of ideas and culture. As Togliatti wrote in a key programmatic pronouncement published in the first issue of the Communist ideological journal *Rinascita* in June 1944:

> We are not capable of raising artificial or hypocritical barriers between different spheres of activity in a nation, whether economic, political or intellectual. We do not and cannot separate ideas from facts, the trajectory of thought from the development of relations between real forces, politics from economics, culture from politics, individuals from society or art from real life. In this unitary and realistic conception of the whole world lies our strength, the strength of the Marxist doctrine.[8]

From the very beginning, therefore, the PCI claimed the right to cast its policies across the whole of the social system and Togliatti himself staked its interest in influencing the cultural sphere. It would be difficult, not to say impossible, to understand the cultural policy of the PCI at the time without reference to the personal role of the Party leader. A cultivated, even erudite, man with a particular feeling for ideas, Togliatti was alert to the cultural dimensions of Party activity and to the importance of the 'battle of ideas' throughout his leadership. Like Lenin and Trotsky before him, he was one of a handful of leaders of the workers' movement with a near encyclopaedic range of interests, who prided themselves on their ability to engage in debate with the leading bourgeois adversaries of the day without the slightest inferiority complex. For this reason, the cultural policy of the Party, much more even than its politics, was Togliatti's personal fief. With the possible exception of Emilio Sereni, none of the other leading cadres who emerged from clandestinity or returned from exile possessed anything remotely resembling his expertise in this field. Togliatti not only mapped out the general lines of intervention but also followed up all aspects of Party work, often sending private notes, written characteristically in green ink, to compliment, correct or reprove a collaborator or subordinate.[9]

Prior to Togliatti's return to Italy in March 1944 and immediate proclamation of the need to make the PCI a mass party, Communists had been wary of diluting their revolutionary purity by seeking converts amongst newly politicised writers and intellectuals. Before such persons could join, it was necessary for them to accept Communist doctrine *en bloc*. Very quickly after Togliatti took charge, however, such exacting criteria were set aside. Instead, an 'open door' membership policy was adopted under which recruits were not expected to embrace Marxism as a philosophy, but merely to express sympathy with the Party's general aims. It was thanks to this move that the PCI experienced such success in winning the allegiance of bourgeois intellectuals of a Crocean, Liberal Socialist, and even Catholic schooling. But what was the purpose of attracting these people? Why did Togliatti go to such lengths in order to gather the nation's intelligentsia under the banner of the Party's social and political struggles – often to the extent of handpicking his closest collaborators from amongst its most promising younger members? To many it seemed anachronistic, and even offensive, that men who had often remained silent during the Fascist period, or in some cases actually participated in the cultural organisations of the regime, should be courted so assiduously by the Left. Following the publication of Gramsci's prison notebooks in the late 1940s, moreover, it would become clear that Togliatti stressed the function of the traditional intellectual at the expense of organic revolutionary intellectuals, whose formation was under normal circumstances to be the special task of the Communist Party. The explanation lies in the PCI's leader's perceptions of the overriding goal facing his party and of the levers required to reach that goal. Having removed the question of political revolution from the Communist political agenda, Togliatti committed his party to a policy of innovation within a context of political collaboration and institutional continuity. For this to be effective it was vital that the label of 'foreign' or 'different', which was frequently applied to the PCI, be overcome at the earliest possible opportunity. The Party had to render itself and its strategic project fully national if it was to succeed in maintaining and extending its influence within a wide coalition of forces. For this reason the cultural novelty which the PCI embodied was presented not in terms of a break in the national culture, but as a development that continued the Italian cultural tradition at a higher level. The aim of a 'rebirth of the thought and activity that follows in the great progressive current of Marxism' was seen as a national task, of interest to all and necessary for the regeneration of Italian culture.[10] It was a mission that obliged the Party to:

> call together, to assist us in this new activity, various forces not normally enrolled in our movement that are nevertheless

convinced like us of the need to break with a past first of decline then of collapse, and open the way to a radical renewal both of our political life and our culture.[11]

Before drawing out the conservative underside of this approach, which would involve the PCI in reinforcing certain given features of cultural life, it is first necessary to underline the degree of novelty represented by the PCI. For the Party was unquestionably perceived in the immediate postwar years as a force whose aim was a profound regeneration of culture. It was the force which wished to promote and extend the leadership of the working class over all sectors of life. It proclaimed the need for the consolidation of art and of intellectual activity no longer removed from the concerns of the people, but profoundly immersed in them. It was the bearer of a philosophy of world-historical significance that hitherto had made little impact in Italy. Finally, it was the channel through which many people sought to acquaint themselves with international culture. The Party's pamphlets and discussion journals were eagerly devoured by the young and not-so-young alike, as people from all walks of life struggled to fill gaps in their knowledge and gain some rudimentary familiarity with the classics of Marxist thought. Togliatti, moreover, dedicated considerable energy to an on-going polemic with Benedetto Croce, the Idealist philosopher and liberal politician who dominated intellectual life in Italy over much of the first half of the twentieth century. Although Croce's influence was much reduced by the end of the war, many converts to Marxism had studied under him and notions derived from his thought still permeated Italian culture. Referring familiarly to the elderly thinker as 'don Benedetto', or mockingly as 'il bravo don Benedetto', Togliatti sought both to ridicule his refusal to grant Marxism a patent of cultural legitimacy and to shatter the last residues of a conception of culture as separate from politics.[12]

There were, however, marked elements of Croceanism in the PCI's perspective on culture. Togliatti engaged in polemical exchanges with Croce but there was no question of Communists launching an all-out attack on the leading representatives of the Idealist tradition. Like Lenin, the PCI leader posed the question of cultural progress not in terms of an outright break with the heritage of the bourgeoisie, but rather in terms of an evolution that would selectively conserve and develop the best fruits of that heritage. Hence the polemic was also an attempt to establish a dialogue with Crocean thought that had as its ultimate aim the appropriation of the latter's pre-eminent place in Italian culture. Yet the continuities were more than mere residues; they derived from Togliatti's determination to read the novelty represented by Marxism back into the national past. This was a sophisticated operation that served the Communist leader's aim of 'national-ising' the PCI, but which would not be free of retrograde conse-quences. A more general revival of the Enlightenment tradition and an attempt to trace the threads of a current of democratic commitment and civil engagement in Italian culture provided the context for the reintroduction of Marxism. The nineteenth-century literary critic Francesco De Sanctis was held up as an example of an intellectual who had interpreted the literary culture of the nation in relation to the democratic ferments of the bourgeois revolution. Set next to Carlo Cattaneo, De Sanctis was seen in a perspective leading not up to Crocean Idealism but to Antonio Labriola, the founder of Italian Marxism, to Gramsci and to the contemporary struggles championed by the Communists.[13] References were also made to the secular, materialist tradition of the French Enlighten-ment (Togliatti himself publishing a translation of Voltaire) and to the democratic Russian thinkers of the nineteenth century, whose engagement with social and political issues was highlighted.

This undertaking had the merit of inserting the PCI's project in a broader and more familiar framework than that offered by the theorists of the international Communist movement. But it also meant that Marx, Engels and Lenin tended to be displaced from the centre of the PCI's elaborations. Together with Stalin and Dimitrov, these featured regularly in the pages of *Rinascita*, and pamphlet versions of their work were made widely available to the base of the Party. But they were amply balanced by names from a progressive Italian pantheon. Togliatti himself scarcely referred to Marx or Lenin in the mid-1940s, whilst he discursed freely on the merits and demerits of such figures as Giolitti, Salvemini, Dorso, Einaudi and Gobetti. What this meant was that Marxism was presented less as a viable theoretical corpus and more in terms of the practical impact it had made on the world through its material distillation in Soviet society.

The immersion of the Communist cultural project in a national tradition, albeit one alternative to the dominant one, conferred a somewhat establishment air on the Party, by identifying it un-equivocally with high culture or, to be more precise, with the culture of an earlier bourgeois era. In the context, this lent the PCI a certain credibility and distinction. It also perfectly suited the temperament and tastes of a man of classical education like Togliatti, who did nothing to hide his pronounced conservative views on literature and his distaste for Modernism.

Togliatti's personal tastes set the tone in the Party as a whole. But in the 1944–7 period, there was no attempt to impose a set of aesthetic judgements on artists and intellectuals in the Communist sphere of influence. Nor was there any attempt to indicate preferred themes, forms of expression or methods of work. The Party insisted only on the need to recognise the indivisibility of reflection and action, and of consciousness and life. It encouraged artists and writers to debate and discuss the problems of their work in the pages of the PCI press, but without ever officially promoting a specific doctrine. Indeed, in answer to a precise question on the matter put by the painter Mafai, Togliatti denied that an official view on artistic questions could exist. The Party, he said, limited itself to arguing for the elimination of all Fascist and reactionary influences. It was up to the artists themselves to decide how this might best be put into practice in their work.[14]

What lent a certain menace to Togliatti's personal preferences was the way in which these seemed broadly to coincide with prevailing approaches within the international Communist movement. In the immediate postwar period, there was little trace in Italy of either the substance or the style of the philosophy of the arts formally adopted following the Soviet Writers' Congress of 1934, at which Gorky and Zhdanov had unveiled the aesthetic doctrine of Socialist Realism and defined the role of the artist as one of service to the people, to the Party and to the cause of Socialism. Togliatti scrupulously avoided all forms of militant aesthetic criticism and edited *Rinascita* in an open, tolerant way. At no time between 1944 and 1947 was any Italian writer subjected to the sort of opprobrium and public vilification that was common currency in the USSR. Yet the attempt to keep Zhdanov out of sight was not wholly successful. The theory of Socialist Realism was, to borrow Nello Ajello's phrase, like 'a huge iceberg at the centre of Communist cultural policy' that would progressively reveal more of itself towards the end of the decade.[15] But even early on there was evidence of a creeping substratum of cultural orthodoxy in the reports that appeared in the Party press of the assault launched by the French Communists on the decadentism and alleged moral indifference of the art and literature of the interwar years. Special attacks, moreover, were made on Gide and Sartre and *Rinascita* even indicated a positive model of the contemporary intellectual in the former Surrealist Louis Aragon, whose unctuous dedication to the PCF and its leader Maurice Thorez found no equivalent at all in Italy.

By the end of 1946, the PCI could count on the support of a very significant proportion of the country's intellectual and artistic elite. But this is not to say that its project for cultural regeneration based on a recast national tradition was universally shared, either in general or in the specific ways in which it was articulated by the Party leadership. For some intellectuals, the emphasis needed to be placed less on tradition and more on innovation and experimentation. Encapsulated in the formula of 'new culture' this idea had first been advanced by the cultural front of the Resistance movement. The aim was to resuscitate a progressive current in Italian culture by introducing and debating all the novelties in contemporary thought, literature and art that Fascism had suppressed or excluded. This design represented the programmatic codification of a *de facto* tendency, particularly strong during the Fascist period, to perceive cosmopolitanism as dissent. Under the regime, intellectuals and writers had looked abroad in search of alternatives to official cultural models and new sources of inspiration. Writers such as Cesare Pavese and Elio Vittorini eagerly translated Faulkner, Melville, Hemingway and Caldwell, finding in their novels evidence of a freer world where life could be lived more directly and authentically. The films of Renoir and Carné offered an idea of cinema totally at odds with the epic pot-boilers and home-made sophisticated comedies of the Italian cinema of the thirties, as, in a different way, did the Russian film classics for the few who were privileged to see them at Rome's Scuola sperimentale di cinematografia. Even jazz, detested as it was by the regime, seemed to open up a different panorama, not only of sounds but also of human relations and experiences. Well before Marxist texts began to circular in Italy, this pattern of impulses and stimuli opened the way for writers and artists to look at the country in a new light following the collapse of Fascism.

It will now be shown how the idea of a new culture to be formed through renewed contact with the progressive currents in European and North American culture constituted an alternative hypothesis of cultural regeneration that found a key reference point after the war in *Il Politecnico*, a journal founded and edited between September 1945 and December 1947 by Elio Vittorini. It will also be shown how the PCI intervened sharply to curtail this hypothesis and fix the national contours of cultural renewal. For even though *Il Politecnico* never commanded a wide intellectual following, its presumptions jarred with both the immediate priorities and the underlying purposes of Communist cultural policy. In the second part of the section, it will be argued that the PCI's encounter with, and adaptation to, the cultural perspectives of Cold War Communism in the post-1947 period saw not so much a displacement of the Party's national anchorage as a marked reinforcement of its commitment to a concept of literature that was both traditional and, increasingly explicitly, provincial in outlook.

Let us first look at what *Il Politecnico* represented in postwar Italy. In the words of Vittorini, the journal was not: 'an organ for the diffusion of an already formed culture, but a working instrument in a culture in formation'.[16] Whereas *Rinascita*, in line with Togliatti's aim of introducing Marxism and Communism into national life, devoted much space to the re-elaboration of the national tradition, *Il Politecnico* sought to renew Italian culture by subjecting it to an intensive international refresher course. Vittorini and his collaborators were motivated by an almost pioneer spirit in their desire to reinsert the national culture in a European and world context, to the extent that the journal seemed, in its first few issues, to have something new to say about everything. It sported a striking red and black layout that stood out from the rather dull appearance of other magazines and newspapers of the period, and this immediate sensation of novelty was confirmed by the very wide variety of often unorthodox political, cultural and social topics that were tackled in its pages. Articles on psychoanalysis and Existentialism (known only by name in Italy at this time) were published alongside surveys of working-class and peasant life in Spain, Japan, France and the USSR. The Hollywood cinema, jazz and comic art were all given serious treatment and, next to political commentary and declarations of cultural principle, many foreign authors were translated into Italian for the first time. Among these was Ernest Hemingway, introduced to readers by Vittorini as 'the greatest living writer in America and the whole world',[17] whose novel *For whom the Bell Tolls* was published in serialised instalments from the first issue.

In the great cultural and political ferment of the post-Liberation period, *Il Politecnico* struck a non-conformist note, particularly for a publication that was founded with the encouragement and moral support of the PCI. For some, especially the student and lower-middle-class reading public, whose thirst for novelty would be satisfied by the huge number of foreign works put on the market by commercial publishers in the late 1940s, it was Vittorini's magazine that 'finally spoke, or stuttered, the language of cultural liberation'.[18] But at the level of cultural politics, it is not at all clear that Italy was ready for such a heterodox and original presence. That Vittorini never succeeded in attracting mass support for his project of regeneration is evident in the fact that barely eight months after it was founded, *Il Politecnico* was compelled to convert from weekly to monthly publication. Sales, moreover, settled at a mere 22,000 copies, whereas a total of 100,000 per issue was required to break even.[19]

What was perhaps even more significant, though, was Vittorini's failure to win the allegiance of other groups and individuals who might have been expected to support his cause. Pavese, for example, who like Vittorini had found comfort and inspiration in the American literature of the 1930s, preferred Togliatti's national line, which he considered to be more consonant with the experience of the Resistance and the tasks of national reconstruction. *Società*, another journal founded on the fringes of the PCI, whose editors would themselves be accused towards the end of 1946 of making irrelevant excursions into modern European philosophy, also remained diffident. Although it disapproved of Togliatti's failure to break off all links with Croceanism and adopted an openly sceptical attitude towards certain aspects of the national culture, *Società* argued that the transformation of the values and modes of expression of Italian writers and artists would inevitably be a slow and painstaking process, not the result of any sudden change in stylistic models and cultural reference points.

At first Togliatti welcomed *Il Politecnico*, as he did other collateral initiatives that sprung up alongside official Party publications. Neither the cosmopolitan curiosities of *Società* nor the internationalist vocation of Vittorini's journal dovetailed very well with his own project of acclimatising Marxism to Italian conditions, but their possible role in extending Communist influence was seen to compensate for any initial lack of harmony in approach. The potential for conflict implied in this rather instrumental commitment to pluralism was always present, however. The heterodoxy of a small and somewhat academic journal such as *Società* was a relatively minor nuisance compared with *Il Politecnico*, though. For it became clear relatively quickly that Vittorini was advancing not merely a cultural policy that was different from that of the mainstream Left, but one that had the reform of the Left as one of its principal objectives. In setting the anti-bourgeois sensibilities of a Sartre, Kafka or Gide *en bloc* against an official Party line geared towards the appropriation of high bourgeois culture, he fixed his sights not merely on the break-up of the provincial isolationism that had characterised the latter part of the Fascist period, but also on the opening-up of the Left which, through its national orientation and aesthetic conservatism, tended to confirm provincialism. As Franco Fortini, one of Vittorini's closest collaborators, would admit in 1953, the latter's demand for intellectual autonomy was in reality a political demand 'for a certain cultural policy that was to be imposed on the political leaders'.[20] The PCI's rejection of this alternative was not just motivated by the need to reaffirm political control, however, although this would be an important factor in the dispute with *Il Politecnico*. Vittorini's modernist preferences conflicted with both Togliatti's personal tastes and, more importantly, with the formal observance the Party maintained of the cultural policy of the Soviet Communist Party. To this extent, he overstepped an invisible mark and opened *Il Politecnico* to the risk, as Togliatti himself put it, of 'engaging in or giving credit to fundamental errors of ideological approach'.[21]

The first leading Communist to advance criticism of *Il Politecnico* was one of Togliatti's closest collaborators, Mario Alicata. Writing in *Rinascita*, he suggested that the magazine had failed to approach coherently the twin task that had faced it at the outset. It had been charged first with the re-establishment of 'a "productive" contact between our culture and the interests and *concrete* problems of the popular masses in Italy', and secondly with 'creating a vast movement of common moral and practical interests between the middle classes and intellectuals' that would bridge 'the breach that has always separated these categories as a whole from the democratic movement of the mass of workers' and which had been responsible for their past capitulation to reactionary forces.[22] The problem was that the central themes tackled in *Il Politecnico* seemed neither to have very much to do with pressing social problems nor to concord with the PCI's aim of using the national culture as a vehicle for the creation of a new social bloc. Vittorini merely sought to inform his readers of everything that had been excluded from Italy during Fascism, without first applying a critical filter to developments within international culture. His language, therefore, was 'abstract' and 'exterior'. As Togliatti would put it, the original promise was replaced 'little by little by something different, by a strange tendency towards a sort of encyclopaedic "culture" in which an abstract pursuit of the new, the different and the surprising took the place of coherent choices and meaningful inquiry, and in which mere news and information had the better of thought'.[23]

Alicata concluded that *Il Politecnico* could have contributed to an enrichment of taste, by weaning Italian culture of some of its provincial encrustations and introducing a more lively and modern sense of the possibilities of creative expression.[24] But the Party could have no particular interest in promoting a cultural modernisation of this sort for its own sake. From its own point of view, what was needed was the development of a type of art that aimed at the conquest of truth and that aided men in the struggle for justice and freedom. To leading Communists, Hemingway could scarcely be considered an adequate standard-bearer for such a project. According to Alicata, *For Whom the Bell Tolls* provided 'final proof of Hemingway's incapacity to understand and judge (that is, in other words, to *narrate*) something that goes beyond the self-centred sensations of his own elementary and immediate experience'. It was also questionable whether 'an old and superficial journalistic reportage of the October Revolution', such as John Reed's *Ten Days that Shook the World*, also serialised by Vittorini, would be considered 'useful' or 'revolutionary'.

It would be wrong to deduce from judgements of this type that the PCI opposed the deprovincialisation of culture *per se*. At the Fifth Congress of the PCI, held in Rome between the end of December 1945 and early January 1946, Alicata himself declared: 'We must conduct a struggle for the deprovincialisation of Italian culture. . . . There is an old culture in Italy not simply because there has been a crisis of humanistic culture, but because in Italian culture there are the ideological residues of the backwardness of Italian society'.[25] The real issue concerned the way in which cultural internationalism was to be understood. In the age of imperialism, the PCI felt it was necessary to defend the organic relationships that could be created within a national culture and through selective international exchanges against the political and cultural rootlessness of wholesale cosmopolitanism.

The marked distaste for much American and contemporary European culture which came fully to light during the dispute over *Il Politecnico* assumed a prominent place in PCI cultural policy in the Cold War period. The policy of the Party did not undergo a fundamental change in the late 1940s, but the very different political situation – both domestically and internationally – necessarily led to significant modifications. The exclusion of the left-wing parties from government in 1947, and the subsequent conquest of an overall majority by the Christian Democrats in the bitterly fought elections of April 1948, put an end to all hopes for the construction of a progressive democracy rooted in national unity, and made the whole cultural project of the PCI much more problematic and less straightforward to put into effect. Writers and intellectuals who had envisaged that they would be able, through their enrolment in the Party, to participate in a far-reaching process of national reconstruction began to have second thoughts and, in some cases, to retreat from politics. In contrast to the eclecticism and relative openness that marked the PCI's dealings with artists and intellectuals in 1944–6, much more rigid policies prevailed after 1948. What had previously been indications assumed the weight of directives, and what had been left loose and undefined in its approach was firmed up. For the first time, the preference for a national rooting of progressive culture took on the explicit characteristics of a defensive battle to be waged against cosmopolitanism and its false mask of progress.

It would be easy to conclude that the PCI buckled under to the demand for greater homogeneity and orthodoxy in the Communist world in 1947 and 1948. With the formation of the Cominform, the period of flexibility and potential originality that had followed the dissolution of the Comintern in 1943 came abruptly to an end. In a way that it had managed to avoid before, the PCI aligned itself explicitly with Soviet artistic and cultural policy and even defended the repressive measures that were applied to independent creative activity in the Soviet Union. At the Sixth Congress of the PCI in 1948, overall responsibility for the Party's activities in the cultural field was put in the hands of Emilio Sereni, one of the few Italians to embrace wholeheartedly the directives of Zdhanov, whose writings he personally edited and introduced into Italy.[26] Even Togliatti, who had earlier denied the existence of Party doctrines on the arts and promised respect for intellectual autonomy, intervened to stress the need for ideological direction. Under the pseudonym of Rodrigo di Castiglia, he regularly wrote brief notes for *Rinascita* in which he inveighed against the degenerate manifestations of bourgeois art in terms that betrayed not only political hostility but also personal distaste of the most profound sort.

Yet all this did not lead the PCI to abandon the national referent it had established in 1944. On the contrary, the encounter with the very rigid, closed type of cultural policy associated with Zhdanovism served not to cancel but to accentuate in a doctrinaire way certain already existing characteristics. This was because Zhdanovism in its pure form was too heavy and too crude to be absorbed whole by a Party that in the preceding phase had pursued a very different sort of approach. Thus, adaptation to it tended to occur through the medium of domestic equivalents to Soviet aesthetic canons. In 1948, for example, the PCI launched a battle for realism in the arts, yet practically this took the form of adhesion, not to Socialist Realism, but to the more domestic brand of Neorealism. Moreover, De Sanctis, Labriola and, above all, Gramsci, were most often cited in critical support, rather than Zhdanov or Stalin. The treatment of the Sardinian Communist in postwar culture itself constitutes something of a case study in this connection. For obvious reasons, Gramsci was presented in the same breath as Lenin and Stalin in the late 1940s, as a contributor to orthodox Marxist–Leninist thought.[27] Yet in rendering public his prison notebooks, which were published by Einaudi between 1948 and 1951 in six thematic volumes, the PCI leadership undertook a bold act that buttressed the progressive national tradition outlined by Togliatti and guaranteed its continued existence. The rub arose, however, in the way in which the notion of the national popular, that Gramsci had employed to trace the role of the working-class movement in promoting the cultural unity of people and nation, was deployed, not as a general indication of method, but as a criterian of realist aesthetic judgement by Communist art and literary critics in their dealings with left-wing artists and writers.[28]

The greater rigour in the PCI's cultural perspectives did not isolate it from the intellectual and artistic community in Italy in the late 1940s. On the contrary, the decision to set up a Cultural Commission of the Party in 1948 was widely seen as a necessary step towards greater cohesion. Moreover, apart from the occasional heavy-handed intervention, the theoretical and practical debates in which Communists engaged at this time were always closely related to real needs and tendencies within Italian culture. But there can be no doubt that despite this, the Party's close links with intellectuals came to hinge on an ever more traditional and parochial conception of culture. The penetration of such currents as neopositivism and pragmatism, together with the growing role of Hollywood capital in the fragile structures of the Italian film industry, furnished the PCI with a pretext for a campaign in which a provincial defence of tradition and an indiscriminate rejection of modern bourgeois thought were dressed up as a struggle to safeguard the progressive cultural heritage of the country.

Founded in 1948 by the Socialist and Communist Parties, the Alliance of Culture had as its declared aim the defence of the national culture against unwelcome foreign influences. Because Marxism had been portrayed as a current of thought which continued critically a cultural tradition in which all liberal and progressive intellectuals could recognise themselves, the PCI was able to oppose, in the name of all, those novelties which tended to break that continuity with the national past. But in order to attract the support of a wide range of forces in this struggle for authenticity, Sereni was obliged to refurbish the very corporate spirit of Italian intellectuals and obsession with the autonomy of culture that the PCI had so strongly criticised in 1944–6 and which it effectively denied its own militants. The Alliance of Culture, for example, was open to all, regardless of ideological or political differences and it had as its goal the struggle, as Sereni himself put it, for 'the unity of Italian culture . . . for the defence, the safeguarding of Italian culture' against the 'extravagant and artificial pursuit of the new and the original'.[29]

At the end of the war there was a spontaneous trend towards realistic representation in the Italian cinema, in literature, in the theatre and in painting, as the nation's artists sought to transfer the pain, misery, sacrifice and heroism of the period directly into art. Stories taken from life, the trials and tribulations of ordinary people, autobiographical experiences and a sort of oral history all filled the first books, films and short-stories to appear after the Liberation. *Rome Open City*, *Paisà* and *Bicycle Thieves*, together with the theatre of Eduardo De Filipp and the novels and tales of Calvino, Fenoglio, Pavese and Pratolini constitute the key co-ordinates of the culture of postwar Italy. At the time, Neorealism was a way of being left-wing, of showing a sense of social awareness and political responsibility. In more recent years, however, it has been suggested that it was rather an expression of populism – a form of exterior cultural identification with the people that satisfied the desire of writers and film-directors to rediscover themselves and understand the tragedy they had survived, but which scarcely received any input from, or made any impact on, the sharp conflicts of a political character that marked the popular condition in reality at that time. The fact that the industrial working class, as such, was largely absent from Neorealism would seem to confirm this view.

In the mid 1960s, the left-wing literary critic Alberto Asor Rosa launched an indiscriminate attack on the anti-Fascist culture of the immediate postwar years and laid the blame for its generic engagement at the door of the PCI.[30] It alone could have created the conditions for a greater sense of definition in culture by clearly proposing a class discourse that would have avoided much of the confusion surrounding the vague notions of nation and people, he argued. Yet such a charge was surely the result of an extraordinary example of bad faith. For it was not the PCI but the Resistance that acted as midwife for the ideology of unitary, cross-class participation that marked Italian culture after the war. Furthermore, if Italian society expressed itself culturally at this time in terms of populism, rather than in purely class terms, it was not due to the strategy of the PCI, but because of the stage of development in which the country found itself: only partially penetrated by industrial development, with a very limited urban working class, an extensive peasant population and heterogeneous middle classes.

It would be equally misplaced to blame the PCI for the extreme politicisation of the arts and intellectual life in the 1940s, even though the Party emphasised engagement as a key to cultural regeneration. Political involvement was a widely felt need, an almost existential requirement for many intellectuals after the fall of Fascism and for this reason it remained one of the major themes in postwar Italian culture. The PCI simply offered an outlet for this phenomenon; it constituted a rock, a clear and coherent presence and a source of valued guide-lines at a moment of great intellectual and moral ferment. For this reason it was a powerful and authoritative presence that even non-left-wing artists had to reckon with and could not ignore. The Party, moreover, was not sectarian; its sphere of activity embraced and referred to the whole of culture. For much of the time it was also relatively open and undogmatic, perhaps more so than any Communist Party had ever been on cultural questions.

This is not to say that there were not serious problems with the cultural policy of the PCI. Even from a strictly internal viewpoint these were relatively numerous. At times, *Rinascita* seemed to be the only vehicle through which the Party intervened in a coherent and systematic fashion on culture. The internal structures that were supposedly charged with organising initiatives in this field functioned sporadically, with the result that Communist intellectuals were often left to their own devices and were rarely drawn into collective work or into real debate over major themes. There was also a failure to define precise policies geared to key cultural institutions: before the 1950s, little attention was paid to the educational system and much the same may be said for the theatre, the film industry and commercial publishing enterprises. But, perhaps most seriously of all, major problems were experienced in formulating an approach to popular culture. Within the Communist sphere of influence, this was conceived purely in pedagogical terms, with no significant attempt being made to mediate the real desires and cultural pursuits of ordinary people. Instead, there was an educational fervour, a desire to widen Italy's very small reading public and spread the fruits of learning more generally in a society that, for all its noble intentions, failed to look at the issue from the point of view of the common people. Pavese stood out as a solitary example of someone more alert to the problems involved in operations of this type. Intellectuals and writers, he said, should not 'go towards the people', as this meant 'dressing them up, making them an object of our tastes and our desires'. Rather, they should seek to become *of the people* and begin to try and think from the point of view of the common man.[31]

The causes of these problems were often contingent and could be found in the lack of resources and expertise, the unfamiliarity of even high-level Communists with certain fields of work, and confusion about the appropriate methods of intervention. But larger issues were also involved that were bound up with the whole mode in which Togliatti formulated and prosecuted the cultural activity of the PCI after the war. This had as its primary objective the permanent implantation of the Party and its philosophy in the life of the country. To this end, Communism was inserted into the national tradition and Marxism presented as the highest and most developed moment of a broadly uninterrupted continuum. The tasks of regeneration were thus set within tradition and future hopes grounded in past glories, in a way that left little space for genuine innovations. The benefits which accrued to the PCI as a result of this policy were considerable. It successfully sank roots in Italian culture and became a fully national force. Marxism, moreover, was introduced in a way that did not jar or polarise, but rather enhanced the prestige of the Party as a whole. But it may be said that this line of action also impoverished the PCI as an innovative force and undermined its potentially disruptive effect on a range of cultural relations that, nominally, it wished to overturn. The Party held a very traditional view of culture as the result of privilege, acquired knowledge and academic study that conserved within it the conventional emphasis on the arts and the humanities at the expense of science and technique, and on established rather than novel forms of creative expression.

How was it that the PCI, to all intents and purposes a revolutionary party, came to to be so imprisoned within the conventional framework of Italian culture? To a significant degree it was the weight of the Crocean heritage which conditioned a range of options unconsciously. Many left-wing intellectuals, including Marxists and several Communist leaders, had received their intellectual training in an environment steeped in Crocean Idealism. The Party's own policies, however, did little to reduce this influence or break free of it, and this unconfessed continuity would have a range of consequences.

The deep immersion in tradition, which in the character and make-up of individuals like Togliatti preceded its adoption as a theme, was an important factor in the PCI's reactions to the attempt to introduce recent and contemporary European and American culture into Italy. Certainly, there were political objections to this project that, not by chance, would come to a head in the early stages of the Cold War. But in this respect, Zhdanovism merely reinforced certain characteristics, hardened up existing judgements and set the scene for pronouncements and interventions of an authoritarian nature. The preference for the national bourgeois tradition over cultural internationalism was already well-established in the PCI. But although the Party unquestionably showed the worst of itself over the *Il Politecnico* case, can it be said actually to have played a role in impeding the cross-fertilisation of Italian and Western culture and therefore to have confirmed parochial trends within national life? From one point of view this question cannot but be answered in the affirmative. The intimidation of *Il Politecnico* made it clear to left-wing intellectuals that certain foreign and heterodox reference points were unacceptable and this served to restrict the horizons of progressive culture in Italy for many years. But it should not be overlooked that, whatever its obvious appeal, *Il Politecnico* failed to find a real base in the cultural life of postwar Italy. The magazine attracted scant support from artists and writers and did not succeed in reaching a mass readership. In this sense, Togliatti's approach, for all its conservatism and limited horizons, was perhaps more consonant with the cultural context as well as the political one. The concern to embrace and to redefine the national tradition served not only the needs of the Party, but also the requirements of society. It provided a more authentic framework for the rediscovery of self that characterised Italian culture after 1945 and was thus more readily accepted, or tolerated, by a majority of the nation's intellectuals and artists.

Notes

1. Rossana Rossanda, 'Unità politica e scelte culturali: Togliatti e gli intellettuali italiani', *Rinascita*, 22:34 (28 August, 1965) pp. 19–23.
2. See, in particular, Renato Guttuso, 'Una azione culturale communista', *Rinascita*, 23:4 (22 January 1966) pp. 35–7. A survey of the reactions of prominent intellectuals to Rossanda's article is contained in Gian Franco Venè, 'Per chi suona il piffero', *L'Europeo*, 21:37 (12 September 1965) pp. 12–13. For a retrospective commentary on Communist cultural policy in the 1960s, see Rossana Rossanda, 'Sulla politica culturale e gli intellettuali', interview with Carla Pasquinelli, in *Problemi del socialismo*, n.s., no. 6 (September–December 1985) pp. 159–77.
3. In the elections to the Constituent Assembly in 1946, the PCI won 19 per cent of the vote. In 1948, Socialists and Communists presented a joint list of candidates under the banner of the Fronte democratico popolare, which took 31 per cent of the votes. In 1953, 22.7 per cent of electors voted for the PCI. See Marcello Fedele, 'La dinamica elettorale del PCI 1946/1979', in Massimo Ilardi and Aris Accornero (eds), *Il Partito comunista italiano: struttura e storia dell'organizzazione 1921/1979* (Milan: Feltrinelli, 1982) pp. 293–312.
4. See Nello Ajello, *Intellettuali e PCI 1944/1958* (Bari: Laterza, 1979), ch. 1.
5. See Romano Luperini, *Gli intellettuali di sinistra e l'ideologia della ricostruzione* (Rome: Edizioni di 'Ideologie', 1971).

6. Romano Luperini, *Il Novecento: apparati ideologici, ceto intellettuale, sistemi formali nella letteratura italiana contemporanea*, vol. II (Turin: Loescher, 1981) p. 380.

7. The official membership figures of the PCI were: 1,770,896 for 1945, 2,068,272 for 1946 and 2,252,446 in 1947. Party membership would remain over the two million mark until 1957. See Celso Ghini, 'Gli iscritti al partito e alla FGCI', in Ilardi and Accornero (eds), *Il Partito comunista italiano*, pp. 227–92.

8. 'Programma', *La Rinascita*, 1:1 (June 1944); now reproduced in Palmiro Togliatti, *La politica culturale*, ed. Luciano Gruppi (Rome: Editori Riuniti, 1974) p. 64.

9. For an acute portrait of Togliatti and his peculiar style, see Paolo Spriano, *Le passioni di un decennio 1946–1956* (Milan: Garzanti, 1986) pp. 50–5. The classic account, however, remains Vittorio Gorresio, *I carissimi nemici* (Milan: Longanesi, 1949).

10. Togliatti, *La politica culturale*, p. 65.

11. Ibid. p. 66.

12. See Palmiro Togliatti, 'Antonio Gramsci e don Benedetto' and 'La colpa è dell'Anticristo', in Togliatti, *La politica culturale*, pp. 82–4 and pp. 85–7, respectively.

13. See Luciano Gruppi, 'Note sulla politica culturale del partito nel dopoguerra', *Critica marxista*, quaderno no. 5, supplement to issue no. 1 (1972) pp. 126–69.

14. Cited in Spriano, *Le passioni di un decennio*, p. 59.

15. Ajello, *Intellettuali e PCI*, p. 51.

16. *Il Politecnico*, 4 (20 October 1945) p. 1.

17. *Il Politecnico*, 1 (29 September 1945) p. 3.

18. Ajello, *Intellettuali e PCI*, p. 127.

19. *Il Politecnico*, 28 (6 April 1946) p. 1.

20. Franco Fortini, 'Che cosa è stato "Il Politecnico"', in *Dieci inverni (1947–1957)* (Milan: Feltrinelli, 1957) pp. 54–5.

21. 'Una lettera di Palmiro Togliatti', *Il Politecnico*, 33–4 (September–December 1946) pp. 3–4. Vittorini's reply, 'Lettera a Togliatti', appeared in *Il Politecnico*, 35 (January–March 1947) pp. 2–5 and 105–6. An English translation of this may be found in David Overby (ed.), *Springtime in Italy: A Reader in Neorealism* (London: Talisman, 1978) pp. 41–66.

22. Mario Alicata, 'La corrente "*Politecnico*"', *Rinascita*, 3:5–6 (May–June 1946) p. 116.

23. 'Una lettera di Palmiro Togliatti', p. 4.

24. See Alicata, 'La corrente "*Politecnico*"', p. 116.

25. 'Intervento di Mario Alicata,' in *Atti dattiloscitti del V Congresso del Partito communista italiano*, pp. 1218–23.

26. Sereni also wrote a glowing obituary following Zhdanov's death, 'Andrei Zhdanov: modello di combattente per il trionfo del comunismo', which appeared in *Rinascita*, 5:9–10 (September–October 1948) pp. 333–4.

27. See Gruppi, 'Note sulla politica culturale', p. 146.

28. See Alberto Asor Rosa, 'Lo Stato democratico e i partiti politici', in

Alberto Asor Rosa (ed.), *Il letterato e le instituzioni*, vol. I of *Letteratura italiana* (Turin: Einaudi, 1982) pp. 549–643; and Nicoletta Misler, *La via italiana al realismo: la politica culturale artistica del PCI dal 1944 al 1956* (Milan: Mazzotta, 1973).

29.   Emilio Sereni, 'Per la cultura italiana', in *Scienza marxismo cultura* (Rome: Edizioni Sociali, 1949) p. 220. Cited and discussed in Luperini, *Il Novecento*, pp. 395–6.

30.   See Alberto Asor Rosa, *Scrittori e popolo* (Rome: Samona e Savelli, 1965).

31.   Cesare Pavese, 'Il comunismo e gli intellettuali' (1946), in Cesare Pavese, *La letteratura americana e altri saggi* (Turin: Einaudi, 1962) pp. 223–32.

2

Writing and the Real World: Italian Narrative in the Period of Reconstruction

MICHAEL CAESAR

It must have been hard to be a writer in 1945, and even worse in 1946. Not quite so bad perhaps for the younger ones, those who had not yet taken the fatal step of committing ink to page, but for the older ones, yes, the already established writers who were faced with the problem not of what to do, but what to do *next*, and some of whom had some explaining to do about what they had done *before*. It is fair to say that in the immediate postwar period, writers found themselves caught in the embrace of a powerful consensus: a consensus about the need to write, and, later, to some extent, about what to write. Such a position is not usually a comfortable one, and if there is an underlying theme, it is that of the pressure of various sorts to which writing is subject and of the spaces in which it actually takes place. For it has to be said that in speaking about the writing of this period, one has continually to acknowledge all that is not writing; it is not satisfactory to reduce literary history to a series of individual biographies and case-studies (which is the constant temptation, especially when one is dealing with a large body of material): one cannot not respect the dominant role of ideology, programmes, the social call. But it also has to be said that the cultural history of this period – as regards Italy at any rate – is *always* traced from the point of view of the programme, the project, that which the writer intends to do or ought to do, never what he or she actually does. It would be nice for once to descend into the magma of literary practice.

Let me begin with three pressure-points. First: to establish credibility with the postwar public, the writer must show himself (or herself) to be concerned with social and political reality. The statement is crude enough to subsume the blanket exclusion that it is also meant to convey, which is that the writing of liberated Italy

37

must be different from that of the black years which had gone before. Fascism had put its political stamp on a fiction that was programmatically unpolitical, by and large ignorant of social affairs, and generally indifferent to ethical questions. The world which that fiction depicted was, almost without exception, materially cosy and not given to sudden change, though it might also be riven by spiritual anguish. Above all, it was constrained, limited to a narrow compass, unwilling or unable to look out of the window. It was the literature of a time when the middle class was minding its own business and when the outside world, meaning the experience and preoccupations of other social classes and other regions of the country, otherness in general, perhaps, with the possible exception of the other sex, did not so much not exist as did not pose a problem.

All of that changed, of course, with the war, the fall of Fascism, the Resistance, the Liberation, Reconstruction. How much did it change? The case of Italy's best-known novelist at the time, Alberto Moravia, was exemplary, though not exactly typical. Moravia was precisely one of those close observers of the bourgeois interior, whose work went down well with readers of the 1930s even if it did not meet with the approval of the regime. From 1945, and for the next ten or twelve years, his fictional work extends into new dimensions. In the long short-story *Agostino* (1945), the thirteen-year-old's reliving of Oedipus's problem with his mother is played out to the accompaniment of a chorus: the working-class adolescents on the beach whose unabashed sexuality draws Agostino to a fuller awareness of himself. Moravia has discovered the other, the social other, which is both a challenge to, and a possible release from, the destiny of gyrating in ever-diminishing circles to which his incompetent middle-class male heroes are ever prone. This other is antagonist in the novelist's best work of the immediate postwar years, *La romana* (*The Woman of Rome*, 1947), the story of the relationship between the prostitute Adriana and the intellectual hero Giacomo who, unlike her, is incapable of loving without observing and commenting on himself doing it. Much later, a similarly positive, female, working-class hero will be at the centre of the novel *La ciociara* (*Two Women*, 1957). But the question is this: does the injection of the people, *il popolo*, into Moravia's imaginative universe simply translate into other, additional or complementary, terms the critique of bourgeois society which, with varying techniques, including the satirical and the grotesque, he had been conducting since *Gli indifferenti* (*Time of Indifference*) appeared in 1929? Or does the centre of his fiction continue to be that same rotten bourgeoisie, and the presence of the people merely a homage to the times, an updating of the content of the existential hero's anguished search for selfhood and purpose? Does the appearance of the *popolo* represent another literary technique, or another theme, or does it point to some sort of radical realignment of Moravia's prose?

The Moravia case is exemplary because it is actually rather difficult, looking at the writing of the late 1940s, to make up one's mind whether one is witnessing something like a rebirth or 'reconstruction' of the Italian novel on the ruins of the old, or a continuation of the same with different costumes and different props. The question arises as to whether there are the same changes within the novel as there manifestly are around it. Indeed, there is an implicit gap between what is demanded and what is done: a gap which might represent an inability of writers to meet the demands, or a form of self-defence. To come to the second of our pressure-points: the transformation of the political status and the political perception of the writer. The end of Fascism entailed a widespread and visible conversion of intellectuals to the political left wing. In many cases, the open declaration of political faith was the culmination of an anti-Fascism that over the preceding years had been latent and private, or militant and combative (many intellectuals had taken part in the Resistance), or had passed from one to the other. In other cases, the left-wing parties, especially the Communist Party, seemed to offer the only organic and organised solutions to the social and economic problems whose urgency was not in doubt. In a few others, one orthodoxy proved to be as good as another, and the authoritarian spirit (of critics, it must be said, more than writers) could be indulged as happily under the banner of Socialist Realism as it could under that of Fascist autarchy. But while the whole climate of postwar writing was affected by the global spread of the political, and this politicisation differentiated it sharply from the writing of the previous two decades, it would be as misleading to characterise the writing of the period in terms of the political *task* which many writers felt to be incumbent upon them, the 'commitment' which they undertook, as it would be to read the finished texts in terms only of their political or social *content*.

Pressure-point number three: 'Il presente vince sempre', asserts the first-person narrator of one of Vasco Pratolini's novels at the beginning of his narrative – the present always wins. The novel is *Allegoria e derisione* (*Allegory and Derision*), published in 1966, the third of the trilogy *Una storia italiana* (*An Italian Story*, or *An Italian History*), the first volume of which, *Metello,* had been interpreted in 1955 as portending the exhaustion of Neorealism. *Allegoria e derisione* is a historical novel in which subjective, psychological, time plays an important narrative role. The present always wins, according to the literary hero Valerio Marsili, 'weak on logic, strong on analogy' according to his girlfriend Ebe, in the sense that history is directed entirely to the present and cannot enable anyone to read the future towards which, on the other hand, time is projected.[1] The question of where we are in time, and in history, was fundamental to the writing of the postwar years. The strongest, and commonest, answer was 'Now', 'we are here', and the contemporary crowded in on the writer with the same insistence and the same urgency as the need to see the broader social reality and the pressure to do something politically. This response said something about what writers saw as the richness and fecundity of their present: there was so much to write about, it was of such pressing importance, that it almost imposed itself on the writing hand which had to do no more than transcribe. But perhaps it also said something else, almost the opposite; perhaps it was also an acknowledgement of the instability of the present and the rapidity of change. Mapping out the future was, implicitly, the principal task of reconstruction, but the overwhelming demand of the present is not only, as Pratolini suggests, a barrier to the future. It is also, in practice, an invitation to the past, because, very simply, the contemporary which is written is not only, or even principally, the immediate present, but, much more frequently, the immediate past. The narrative of postwar Italy is pre-eminently an excursion into recent history, a revisiting of just a while ago, nearer or further away as the case may be in chronological time (the war, Fascism, pre-Fascism). The present meets the barrier of the future and turns back upon itself; the question 'where are we?' becomes inevitably 'how did we get here?'. Documentation merges imperceptibly into reflection, and it is here that space opens up for the intrusion of the lyrical and the introspective. The narrative of the present is simultaneously a narrative of memory; if more than one sense of the term 'reconstruction' is allowed, I would suggest that for many writers its strongly contemporary sense of starting anew, building the 'new culture' for which *Il Politecnico* and others called, was in practice inseparable from its other, less often acknowledged, sense of recapturing and piecing together a reality that was scattered and volatile, or on the point of becoming so. Neorealism, too, might well be seen in this light, retrospective as well as prospective: 'every act of survival, every effort to think, every attempt to reconstruct a human order over the disorder of objects was an act of Neorealism: more precisely an act whose purpose was the mastering of new and unexpected aspects of the real' – one of the protagonists, Sergio Antonielli, who wrote an interesting account of life in a British POW camp in India, commenting after the event.[2]

In the vicinity of postwar fiction, assumptions of quasi-axiomatic force proliferate, even while within the writing itself, nothing is quite so certain. I have touched on three of these propositions – concerning the primacy of political and social themes, the politicisation of the writer, and the claims of the present – and would like to pass on to what I suppose could be regarded as a fourth pressure-point, one that directly concerns the writer as writer and not only the writer as citizen. Here narrative itself is at issue, and I should make the preliminary, empirical, observation that postwar writing, and particularly the writing that came to be identified as Neorealist, took a predominantly narrative form (two-thirds of all 'literature' titles published in 1947, for example, and that included philosophy and literary criticism as well as poetry, were accounted for by *narrativa*). Under this broad heading, it should be added, there was to be found a diversity of genres, as well as a steady progression over time from the short story to the novel as the preferred medium of fiction.[3]

In 1964, Italo Calvino republished his first novel, *Il sentiero dei nidi di ragno* (*The Path to the Spider's Nest*), set in the backstreets of his native San Remo and the mountains behind the city during the Resistance, a novel which had first appeared in 1947. He introduced it to a new public with a long preface which, together with the 1955 essay 'Il midollo del leone' ('The Lion's Marrow'),[4] probably tells you most of what you need to know about the Italian novel between 1945 and 1960. The preface describes, among other things, the difficulty of getting the novel started, of finding the right theme for it, the right characters, the right narrator, the right plot-devices, the right tone. The preface itself is a series of false starts, doublings-back, re-runs, and might put the bookish reader in mind of the series of beginnings which go to make up the much later novel *Se una notte d'inverno un viaggiatore* (*If on a Winter's Night a Traveller*, 1979). It is, in other words, a characteristically Calvinian exercise, but like all Calvino's exercises it has a point, for this reiterated attempt to explain helps to evoke, far better than mere argument could, a moment of extraordinary communicativeness in Italian life:

> The return of free speech was experienced by people to start with as an urgent desire to tell each other stories: in the trains which began to run again, packed with people and sacks of flour and cans of oil, every traveller told strangers about the things that had happened to him, and so did every customer who ate at the 'people's canteens' and every woman queuing at the shops; the greyness of daily lives seemed to belong to another era; we circulated in a multi-coloured universe of stories.[5]

Such a diffusion of narrative is a common experience to all survivors of dramatic or tragic events, relatively small ones such as a snowstorm or a road accident as well as great ones such as war. It does not last long. But what does it mean to the writer? The moment Calvino describes endured a few months, perhaps only a few weeks. Indeed, its transience is of the essence. Liberation was like a moment suspended in time, a huge party, a carnival, which was bound to end, but not yet. The stories swapped in café, tram and office were a way perhaps of prolonging the moment, and in order to do that they had to retain the freshness, spontaneity and immediacy of stories told as if for the first time – they must reject any suggestion of being recorded and made permanent. The stories of the Liberation were a genuinely oral repertoire which resisted writing – and the writer – however rich a pool of tales and however eager an audience they seemed to promise. Then, later, with the euphoria passed and people picking up the threads of their lives again, the writer could begin to draw on that material, but it was as something to which he or she, as a writer, was extraneous and subsequent.

Then there was at the same time a kind of writing which, rather than drawing on the oral repertoire, was its written equivalent. Already in the closing months of the war, the anti-Fascist underground press was publishing brief accounts of incidents of partisan life and pen-portraits (or obituaries) of comrades-in-arms. At the end of hostilities, numerous small publishing-houses came into being and survived on the publication of diaries, memoirs and re-evocations of life in the Resistance movement. Larger publishers and the cultural pages of newspapers continued to print such documents throughout 1945 and 1946, and after a time the flood of Resistance stories was swollen further by the memories of war veterans and survivors of the camps. These memoirs included a masterpiece like Primo Levi's *Se questo è un uomo* (*If this is a Man*), published by a small house (De Silva of Turin) in 1947 and little noticed at the time (Einaudi in fact turned it down), but surely the first attempt to confront at all, and even more to confront without rhetoric, the experience of Auschwitz. We are talking here about documentary writing based on factual experience, and it should be noted that the purpose of such writing was diametrically opposed to that of the oral narrative discussed above. People wrote down their experiences precisely in order to remember, to draw to the attention of others, and very often to point a moral or political lesson. But I regard this as a written equivalent to the oral repertoire for the simple reason that it presented itself as a direct representation of lived experience and had no doubts about the immediacy and directness of its contact with its audience. Writing as a means of preserving what might otherwise quickly be forgotten was also, in the eyes of the veterans who practised it, a means of carrying on the struggle in which hitherto they had been engaged militarily or politically, and it was very definitely not 'literature'. It was, if anything, a kind of anti-literature: events followed on paratactically one from another, there was minimal characterisation, moral choices were posed in black-and-white terms, the mimetic capability of language was unquestioned, language itself was made to approximate as closely as possible to the spoken norm.

I agree with those who see in these attitudes and aptitudes the immediate antecedents of Neorealism, in terms both of its ideological programme and some of its formal resources.[6] But that is not my concern here. What interests me is the break rather than the continuity between the two sets of phenomena. For the postwar writer of fiction, faced with the ineluctable demand to take 'reality' as one's subject-matter, meaning the political and social reality of the immediate past, it seemed as if not only was there a superabundance of reality to write about, but a superabundance of narrative too, from the oral anecdote to the written document. And it seemed also that this reality and this narrative had a privileged relation to each other in a closed circle that excluded the professional writer, the serious writer, and particularly perhaps the writer of fiction. Initially at least, the writer was more blocked than liberated by the end of dictatorship and foreign occupation. He found himself in the situation of the young intellectual locked in a cell measuring three metres by one-and-a-half with four other prisoners, in the SS headquarters in Via Tasso in Rome, described by Guglielmo Petroni in his memoir published in 1949, with the title *Il mondo è una prigione* (*The World is a Prison*):

> Then I began to undergo a new torment. I found peace, sometimes an infinite serenity, lazy and unthinking, in silence. But it was different for the other four. Silence was their worst enemy. It could make them aggressive and violent, it could streak their faces with tears and make them curse and cry out in terror and impotent rebellion. For that reason they talked, and for that reason they reacted when silence crept in and spread around the cell. 'Someone say something!' went up the cry, and then someone would talk. Often the voices would become sad and monotonous, sometimes what they said became complicated, abstract, speech without aim or purpose; but the words flowed on like an uninterrupted stream of water. They talked, yet I could find nothing to say except a few sentences. In fact, I realised that when *I* said something, it was like writing a page of a book, I had the same feeling, and for them what I managed to put together were not images but arguments, which sometimes made then nervous, and sometimes attentive and worried. *They* talked; every word was an image, every speech a world swarming with characters, emotions, children, mothers and lovers.[7]

This passage, and the context of psychological and ethical discomfort in which it is placed ('You never say anything!' Petroni's cell-mates accuse him), does not conceal the fact that the unease experienced by the writer in the presence of the uninterrupted flow of words is part of a wider sense of social and moral inadequacy: that of the 'aesthete' confronted by the 'working man', that of intellectuality confronted by the world of experience. With this, the problem posed to the writer by the superabundance of speech is linked to the sense of guilt which lacerates some postwar intellectuals. Another accusation: 'You know so many things Corrado, and yet you do nothing to help us.' The speaker: Cate, anti-Fascist activist, working mother, ex-lover of the school-teacher-protagonist who does not defend himself against the accusation. The book: Cesare Pavese's *La casa in colina* (*The House in the Hills*), also published in 1949. The 'house in the hills' is Corrado's family home, where he will escape all active responsi-bility in the remaining months of the war.[8] The theme: failure and betrayal, one of the reiterated themes of the fiction of the late 1940s and early 1950s, and a variant of the larger social theme of the disappointed revolution. Near the centre of the nexus writer–people–politics–present stands the anxiety-figure of the intellec-tual who let the side down, or could not rise to the occasion, or who remained, whether through his own fault or not, marginal to the situation which demanded by every means and at every opportunity his active participation. This dramatic, even tragic theme is grist to the mill of guilt, and represents an extreme and depressive solution to a problem which lies at the heart of postwar narrative. To examine this problem, I should like to remain within the space opened up by the writer's relation to narrative.

It is clear that in the period of reconstruction, the question of how writing stood in relation to the real appeared paramount in importance. Whether reality was conceived of as the product of direct experience, unmediated, so to speak, or as the product of some higher level of elaboration, interpreted, that is, through ideology, or reason, or, in the specifically literary context, through a 'realist' conception of the world, there was no doubt that writing had to define itself in relation to 'it'. Put in such broad terms, this relationship, and the problems to which it gave rise, is quite unmanageable. I should like, therefore, to explore this area by touching on some aspects of the treatment in writing of that corner of reality represented in Italian postwar culture by the war and the Resistance, and in particular the stance adopted by the narrator in narratives centred on these themes.

The narrative of the war and the Resistance begins, as I have already indicated, in the closing stages of the war itself with the publication of real-life stories, eye-witness accounts and some fictional stories in the pages of the underground press, and continues after the war with a large and increasing quantity of diaries, memoirs, reports and stories. The emphasis is always on the notion that what the readers have before them is a true account of what actually happened, that it is the facts that matter, that the job of the writer – who in this case is the person who went through the experience – is simply to put down in words the events through which he lived or which he witnessed. Very often this kind of writing, which was frequently produced by people who had never set pen to paper in their lives, was posited as a kind of anti-novel, meaning that it was not invented and it was not written *up*: 'this is not a novel, and it is not an exaltation of the partisan war', affirms one typical preface.[9] Once this factual content is established, however, different options as to *how* to relate the story become available. The stress might fall on the autobiographical nature of the account, which seems to guarantee its authenticity; this is a path which in its turn forks in two: along the first, the collective subject is brought into focus by the author stressing his ordinariness, his typicality, while along the second, it is the individual that is brought into focus by the author emphasising his own spiritual and personal development. Other narratives make less play of their autobiographical origin, while still keeping it in view, and stress instead the factual nature of the account and deliberately present a succession of events recorded with the chronological order, restraint of style and lack of literary pretensions of a report.[10] Others again have much more of an eye to literary effect (even in a purely factual, autobiographical, account) and exploit the dramatic possibilities inherent in the Resistance story, especially the element of suspense associated with the adventures of escape, chase, unexpected confrontation, trying to cross the lines, the frontier, the river, the open space without any cover, whatever, to get from A to B. But even one of the most effective, precisely, of such adventure-narratives, Pietro Chiodi's *Banditi* (*Bandits*, 1946), begins with the ritual recital 'This book is not a novel'.[11] The prime purpose of these accounts of wartime experience is to convey information, information that was hitherto unavailable and which the public (or a certain public) demands in order to answer the question 'What really happened?' and to complete its picture of the recent past.

Alongside this memorialistic writing, and to some extent growing out of it, there are those books which look back on the war and the Resistance commemoratively, even nostalgically, as a moment of national tragedy or achievement and pride, that was lived and should be remembered collectively. Although such feelings are sometimes expressed in the more factual, memorialistic kind of writing, their tendency towards a choral form and epic dimensions is more easily realised in the novel. One of the better examples, in terms of narrative quality, is Renata Viganò's *L'Agnese va a morire* (*Agnese goes to her Death*), which won the Viareggio Prize in 1949. Viganò was herself a partisan and part of her narrative at least, one presumes (or is told in the blurb), was based on personal experience. But in the figure of Agnese the peasant woman (or should we say in English 'the farmer's wife'?) who devotes herself body and soul to the Resistance when her husband is killed by the Nazis, the author sought to create an outstanding, exemplary, figure, a positive hero with whom, because of her own simplicity and natural goodness, ordinary people could identify. I do not want to enter at all on to the treacherous terrain of actual reader-response (it is interesting that the novel was republished and a film made of it in the 1970s), but it is hardly Viganò's fault if the sophisticated reader tires of a narrative that seems to consist entirely of the succession of events and of holding back, in expectation of Agnese's sacrifice and apotheosis, the kind of prolonged sob which passes for emotional involvement with the book.

In both these kinds of narrative, the memorialistic and the epic-celebrative, one (generally) fictional and the other not, the relation of the narrator to her material is one of humility: here is the story, my writing is the medium through which events speak for themselves, the story tells its own tale. Quite the opposite effect is achieved in what was, chronologically, the very first novel of the Resistance, Elio Vittorini's *Uomini e no* (*Men and Not-Men*), written during the author's involvement in the Milanese underground movement and published in June 1945. While the hero is an intellectual who succeeds, to a certain extent, in combining theory and practice at the level of his militancy in the Resistance, the novel (at least in its original edition) is predicated on a split between this intellectual activist and a shadowy figure who appears from time to time, in italicised sections of the text, to give voice to another reality, essentially that of memory, nature, the imagination, which is not realised in what we must call the main parts of the novel.[12] This figure is identified with the writer, and what Vittorini is doing with this metafictional device borrowed from Faulkner and, further back, Gide, is to establish that separate identity for the writer or, more exactly, the act of writing, away from the flow of reality for which other authors of his generation felt a particular need: Anna

Banti, for example, who in the marvellous novel *Artemisia* (1947) takes advantage of the biographical accident of the loss of her original manuscript about the sixteenth-century painter Artemisia Gentileschi to interweave the rewritten version with reflections on the novel and on the battle for Florence in 1944; or Elsa Morante, in *Menzogna e sortilegio* (*Lies and Magic*, 1948), with her juxtaposition of the writer Elisa and the family history which she relates on separate planes of narration.

If I may take, momentarily, Viganò and Vittorini as emblematic of two different sorts of postwar writing, and specifically writing about the Resistance, we can see that the relation between writing and the real is conceived in radically different ways. The subordination of the narrator in Viganò, who limits her active intervention at most to the celebration of qualities already inherent in the object of her narration and brought out by her, gives way in Vittorini to a separation between the narrated and the narrator which is potentially destructive: though not quite the same thing, it puts us in mind of the alienated intellectual anti-heroes created by Moravia and Pavese, two writers who like Vittorini, Banti and Morante had begun their writing careers in the 1930s. The spirit of division persists in writers of a younger generation, those whose earliest work begins to appear after the war, and in this they are closer to Vittorini than they are to Viganò. But the division takes a different, less dramatic, configuration. A writer like Calvino, for example, is not interested in exposing his consciousness to the public gaze, even if in oblique or symbolic form. Perhaps what *he* has learnt from the war writers is a certain modesty, even a certain shyness, about writing. But the problem of relating writing to reality remains urgent; while for Viganò and the memorialists, the world presents itself as rich and full, though perhaps morally simple (good and evil are easily identified and distinguished by political, even national traits), for Calvino the world presents itself as rich and confusing, and morally complex. His narration must allow the reader to see both what is and what is not, the other-than-the-narrated, and this without drawing attention to the author. The child's-eye-view adopted in *Il sentiero dei nidi di ragno* is perfect for his purposes, the view of a knowing child who sees the world as a series of adventures, who is both attracted and repelled by the adult world, and through whom the adult reader also perceives a reality which has few of the charms it possesses for the boy Pin.

Thanks to this variation of narrative perspective, Calvino also puts himself in a position to be able to reinterpret the Resistance 'from below': it reveals itself as the scene of heroism but also of cowardice, purposeful but also muddled, hopeful but also a lost cause for some, and so on, in what might seem like an act of fine balancing now, but which required insight and courage in 1947, in the midst of hagiography and myth-making. And I would like to mention one other, final, name in this connection, of a writer who devoted almost the whole of his short writing career (he died in 1963) to an exploration without sensationalism of the Resistance from underneath: Beppe Fenoglio. His is the world of the partisans of whom, in the opening words of the title-story of his collection *I ventitre giorni della città di Alba* (*The Twenty-three Days of the City of Alba*, 1952), 'two thousand captured Alba on the tenth of October and two hundred lost it on the second of November 1944'.[13] What happened to the other eighteen hundred and how the Resistance managed to snatch defeat from the jaws of victory as well as vice versa are valid starting-points for Fenoglio's revision of certain myths. A fascinating writer, who has been widely studied in recent years, Fenoglio adopts a narrative voice which has just that edge of self-mocking understatement typical of the popular narrator which a recent study of oral memories has found to be conspicuously lacking in the tradition of Italian populist literature (and particularly in the novels of Pratolini).[14]

What Calvino and Fenoglio have in common, and what marks them off from Viganò on the one hand and Vittorini on the other, is an ironic sense that both reality and writing are flawed and ambiguous, and a refusal to conceive the relation between writer and society in dramatic terms, whether of identification (Viganò) or dissent (Vittorini). In drawing attention to this development, I have not attempted to do justice to the wide range of postwar writing. I have not discussed, for example, the stream of writing about the regions, and especially about the South, of a semi-documentary nature as well as fiction, that flowed from Carlo Levi's *Cristo si è fermato ad Eboli* (*Christ stopped at Eboli*, 1945). But I hope I have made a first step towards answering the question raised in connection with Moravia: did postwar narrative represent a break with or a continuation of the pre-war novel? My conclusion is that there was a significant break, that it can be illustrated by looking at literary treatments of great historical events, such as the war and the Resistance, but that it was of a generational rather than a strictly chronological nature, that its origins are to be sought more in the cultural formation of the writers concerned than in the immediate impact of the events through which they lived and about which they wrote.

Notes

1. V. Pratolini, *Allegoria e derisione* (Milan: Club degli editori, 1966) p. 13.
2. Sergio Antonielli, 'Sul neorealismo, venti anni dopo', in *Saggi di letteratura italiana in onore di Gaetano Trombatore* (Milan: Istituto editoriale Cisalpino-La goliardica, 1973) p. 6.
3. See Alberto Cadioli, *L'industria del romanzo: L'editoria letteraria in Italia dal 1945 agli anni Ottanta* (Rome: Riuniti, 1981) p. 17.
4. Italo Calvino, *Una pietra sopra* (Turin: Einaudi, 1980) pp. 3–18.
5. Italo Calvino, *Il sentiero dei nidi di ragno: Con una prefazione dell'autore* (Turin: Einaudi, 1978) pp. 7–8.
6. In particular Maria Corti, 'Neorealismo', in her *Il viaggio testuale* (Turin: Einaudi, 1978).
7. Guglielmo Petroni, *Il mondo è una prigione*, in *Botteghe Oscure*, I (1949) pp. 52–3.
8. Cesare Pavese, *La Casa in collina*, published with *Il carcere* in the double volume *Prima che il gallo canti* [*Before the cock crows*] (Milan: Mondadori, 1972) p. 215.
9. Pierro Carmagnola, *Vecchi partigiani miei* [*My old partisans*], quoted in Giovanni Falaschi, *La resistenza armata nella narrativa italiana* (Turin: Falaschi, 1976) p. 28.
10. A good example is Roberto Battaglia's *Un uomo un partigiano* [*A man a partisan*] (Rome, Florence, Milan: Ed. U, 1945).
11. See, for example, the extract included in G. Falaschi (ed.), *La Letteratura partigiana in Italia, 1943–1945* (Rome: Riuniti, 1984) pp. 74–84, which described Chiodi's escape from a camp at Innsbruck and his picaresque journey across Northern Italy to Piedmont.
12. The italicised sections were deleted by Vittorini from the third edition of 1949; all but two were restored for the sixth edition, in 1965. See Anna Panicali, *Il romanzo del lavoro: Saggio su Elio Vittorini* (Lecce: Milella, 1976); and Joy Hambuechen Potter, *Elio Vittorini* (Boston: Twayne, 1979).
13. Beppe Fenoglio, *I ventitre giorni della città di Alba* (Milan: Mondadori, 1976) p. 3. See also, Roberto Bigazzi, *Fenoglio: personaggi e narratori* (Rome: Salerno, 1983) especially the first chapter: 'Personaggi e narratori'.
14. 'After listening to many working-class people talking about themselves, we can recognise their sentimentality as it appears in literature but not the laughter which follows it, the false bravado but not the self-irony, the high-minded tone but not its deflation' (Luisa Passerini, *Fascism in Popular Memory: The Cultural Experience of the Turin Working Class* (Cambridge: Cambridge University Press, 1987) p. 25; translated from *Torino operaia e fascismo* (Bari: Laterza, 1984).

3

The Making and Unmaking of Neorealism in Postwar Italy

DAVID FORGACS

There are two senses in which one might speak of Neorealism as
having been made and unmade in Italy. In the first, Neorealism
means a set of cultural practices and products – films, writings –
which have certain common characteristics. Neorealism in this
sense can be said to have been 'made' in the immediate postwar
conjuncture and 'unmade' in the period of reconstruction. As a
movement or a set of products, Neorealism is probably effectively
finished at least by the mid 1950s, if not earlier. In the second
sense, which is less obvious but is the one I am interested in here,
Neorealism is to be understood not as a set of works or as a
movement but as a critical concept, a way of defining and grouping
particular cultural products. This second sense is not, as one might
perhaps think, a mere critical shadow or trace of the first. I would
suggest that Neorealism was and is, first and foremost, a descriptive category which was produced and developed in criticism. It
did not derive from or reflect any underlying 'Neorealist essence'
in actual films or writings. Rather, those films and writings which
were originally designated 'Neorealist' were, in themselves, heter-
ogenous and capable of being described in a number of different
ways: capable of being grouped together, certainly, but also
capable of being ungrouped. Let me forestall accusations of
nominalism by making explicit that I am not saying that neorealist
works, or even a neorealist 'movement', did not exist. I am saying
that, where they did exist, it was always because of someone's
critical definition of them as neorealist. Critical definitions are
subject to challenge and to change. My interest here is in the
process whereby, in the criticism of the Left, the concept of
Neorealism was first promoted and defended, then challenged and
undermined.

By way of a rough periodisation, I would say that from the early

51

1940s to the late 1950s one has an ascending phase in which an aesthetic of realism emerges and becomes dominant in the area of what one might call progressive culture. This aesthetic, within which the concept of Neorealism is produced and given a strongly positive value, is linked to the political project of anti-Fascism and the popular front. From around 1960 to the present there is a descending phase in which this aesthetic, together with the concept of Neorealism and the political project which had sustained it, come increasingly under attack.

As this periodisation suggests, the unmaking of the Neorealism concept at the level of critical discourse is not synchronised with its unmaking as a set of cultural products and practices. Rather, it is precisely at the time when Neorealist film-makers are struggling to get their pictures made in a hostile political and economic climate and when the main wave of Neorealist creativity in both film and literature is over, in other words in the early 1950s, that the concept is most strongly consolidated and validated within criticism. I shall return to the significance of this at the end. Before doing so, I need to illustrate the rise and fall of a realist aesthetic in more detail.

The rise to prominence of a realist aesthetic in Italy begins in the period immediately following the Liberation. I do not mean by this that there were no prewar antecedents. It is, by now, well established that tendencies existed in both film criticism and literary criticism from the early 1930s which favoured realism: by the late 1930s and early 1940s these tendencies had become particularly prominent in so-called 'Left-Fascist' circles, from where many of the postwar Neorealist film-makers and writers sprang.[1] Yet until the post-Liberation period the promotion of realism was a fringe tendency, occupying a subordinate and limited place in relation to the critical mainstream. It is only in 1944–5 that it starts to undergo a quite new diffusion through the many publications produced by the anti-Fascist groups. Realism becomes a slogan dense with connotations, one in which many new meanings and oppositions are condensed.

If one looks, for instance, at the cultural arguments being put forward in Communist Party publications as they start to emerge out of clandestinity, one finds 'realism' being associated with engagement as against detachment, with the involvement of intellectuals in the working-class movement as opposed to ivory-tower intellectualism, with philosophical materialism as against idealism, with the concrete versus the abstract, with clarity of expression and the need for divulgation as against stylistic preciosity and difficulty.[2] A realist art or literature or cinema is opposed to one that is decadent or formalist. The truth and sincerity of realism is opposed to the falsity of purely commercial entertainment typified by the Hollywood film. The social dimension of realist art, its essentially mass, popular nature and its human warmth are opposed to the minoritarian appeal and intellectualism of the avant-gardes.[3]

Four points in particular seem to be worth noting about this early critical discourse of Realism on the Left. The first is the way it produces a powerful antipathy to Modernism. Modernist works are only valued positively when they can be interpreted in a realist or a socially committed key: the work of avant-garde artists belonging to or aligned with the Left, for instance Aragon or Picasso, is interpreted and defended in this way. Otherwise Modernist works are consigned to cultural waste-paper baskets variously labelled 'formalist', 'decadent', 'abstract', 'irrational', 'sterile', 'snobbish' and 'bourgeois'. The second point is that the discourse of realism does not just interpret and evaluate the art of the present. It also produces a reordering and redefinition of the art of the past in terms of affirmations and interruptions of a realist tradition. Realism is seen as the aesthetic of periods of an extension of democracy and progressive social advance – the mid to late nineteenth century, the period after 1945 – whereas anti-realism (decadence, formalism, avant-gardism) is seen as the aesthetic of periods of conservative involution and reaction – the turn of the century, the period between the two World Wars. In Italy this leads to important re-readings of the past literary tradition. The late-nineteenth-century writer Giovanni Verga, for instance, starts to be read in a Neorealist light, as a precursor – quite differently from the way he was read and evaluated in the 1920s or 1930s.[4] The third point is that this aesthetic strongly favours an art that is social, public and political, as opposed to one that deals with the personal, with private or inner life. This too produces, during the time the realist aesthetic is dominant, a reordering of artistic traditions, a downgrading of forms of writing or film-making which are not turned outwards in a social sense. The fourth point concerns the anti-Americanism in this aesthetic. Although there is a positive critical evaluation of some aspects of American culture – for instance, the films of Chaplin or the novels of Howard Fast – and although the social fiction of Steinbeck, Cain, Dos Passos and others was, as is well known, influential on Italian Neorealism as a creative practice, it is the strong deprecation in postwar criticism of what America represents in terms of mass culture and cultural imperialism that seems more significant. This anti-Americanism will later become an important part both of the Neorealism concept and the general cultural outlook of much of the Italian Left in the 1950s.

What were the conditions in which this new realist aesthetic rose to prominence at the end of the war? In the first place, there was, in liberated Italy in 1944–5, a strong subjective sense of break with the past, a sudden lifting of the cultural restrictions imposed by Fascism, a sense of a liberation of languages and a mingling of fictional and non-fictional genres. Natalia Ginzburg's testimony of this subjectivity is revealing in this respect:

> In the Fascist period, poets found themselves expressing only the arid, closed and sybilline world of dreams. Now there were many new words in circulation and reality once again seemed accessible. There came about a confusion between poetic and political discourse which had appeared mixed together.[5]

In the second place, there was, as a result of the war and the Occupation, a situation of objective disruption and dislocation of the normal functioning of cultural production and distribution. This created a temporary vacuum and made possible a brief flowering of new initiatives: low-budget pictures with non-professional actors, a plethora of small publishing houses; even, in what was to be a very short post-Liberation honeymoon, the running by elected councils of employees (*consigli di gestione*) of a number of cultural organisations, from the radio stations of the newly renamed state network, the RAI (Radio Audizioni Italia), in liberated cities like Naples and Florence to a large publishing firm like Mondadori in Milan.[6]

This exceptional situation did not last long, but it did at least produce, as a long-term effect, the occupancy by the parties of the Left of a cultural and discursive territory that had not existed under Fascism, a territory that came to be dominated precisely by an aesthetic of realism. The central role played by the Communist Party in staking out and holding this territory seems beyond question. Already in 1945–6, I think one can speak about the PCI as having a hegemonic project, in that it puts forward and seeks to

win support for a model of reconstruction led by the working-class movement and its anti-monopoly allies, an alternative to the model of reconstruction being promoted by the British and the Americans, by liberal economists and by the parties of the Centre-Right.[7] After 1947, the Left is expelled from the government and the trade union movement is gravely weakened by a split orchestrated by the Americans and the Christian Democrats. The Left is thus deprived, virtually at a stroke, of any real control over the economy, which proceeds unhindered along the high road of capitalist reconstruction. Yet even through the Cold War, despite a certain polemical hardening of attitudes, this hegemonic project, this concept of an alternative democratic reconstruction, continues. It continues, in other words, on the terrain of culture and criticism even after it has become strictly unrealisable at the level of the state and the economy.

The central phase in the making of the critical concept of Neorealism comes precisely at this time, at the height of the Cold War, in the period from about 1950 to 1954. It is at this time that the word 'Neorealism' enjoys its maximum circulation as a description of a movement, of a cultural phase that is retrospectively identified as having opened after the war. In 1950–1 a series of interviews on Neorealism with writers and critics is broadcast by the RAI and many books and articles appear which deal directly or indirectly with the Neorealist phenomenon.[8] It is also at this time that the Left begins to defend Neorealism more or less as a whole against the forces of capitalist reconstruction.

This defence of Neorealism is in some respects a continuation of the same realist aesthetic that had begun with the Liberation. It is conducted in the same terms of a championing of a tradition of social, public, critical values in opposition to private values, entertainment values, the cultural values associated with the Fascist period: escapism, rhetoric, decadentism, formalism. Nevertheless, the critical discourse is now also modified in a number of ways, particularly in relation to cinema. Firstly, the anti-Americanism becomes more intense as an effect of the Cold War, as a response to the government's promotion of a free market in film distribution which makes Neorealist films uncompetitive on the home market and deters producers from financing them, and as part of a promotion and defence of an Italian national tradition. The Neorealist tradition – Rossellini, De Sica, Zavattini, Visconti, Lizzani, etc. – becomes the national tradition, or at least the very best of the national tradition.[9] Secondly, the discourse of realism is modified by a retaliation against Catholic censorship, against the accusations of immorality and the complaint that Neorealist films export a bad image of Italy as a society of poverty, unemployment and delinquency.[10] One consequently finds critics on the Left championing alternative definitions of what is moral, defending the 'exceptional chastity' of the Neorealist film and ridiculing the propagandist images of reconstruction Italy shown in the Christian-Democrat-funded newsreels of the *Settimana Incom*.[11] Thirdly, the Cold War climate gives renewed sustenance to the idea of an essentially decadent and moribund bourgeois culture, and one witnesses a spate of attacks on the decadence of writers such as Carlo Levi who have turned their back on realism, as well as on Catholic artists and the avant-gardes.[12]

In a sense, the Cold War 'makes' the Neorealist concept in this form, that of the idea of an authentic national tradition that is promoted by the Left. For what is at stake, ideologically, in Italy in the Cold War is not primarily the struggle over whether the Soviet Union is the evil empire or the land of peace and plenty, or whether the United States represents freedom and opportunity or social inequality and reaction, but the struggle to occupy the crucial territory of democracy and the national tradition within Italy itself. The Christian Democrats in the early 1950s identify the nation with the corporate collectivity, the family unit, the rural hinterlands, the Catholic tradition, the economic reconstruction. They consequently push Neorealism beyond the pale of this national space – with some exceptions: Rossellini, the De Sica of *Ladri di biciclette* (*Bicycle Thieves*)[13] – because of its representations of social division, urban and rural poverty and sexual licence. The Left defines the national and the democratic in terms of its own model of reconstruction, that of the anti-Fascist tradition of progressive democratisation, advanced social legislation, anti-monopoly alliance. Taking a term from Gramsci, the Communist Party describes this as a 'national-popular' strategy. Neorealism in this discourse of the Left is the national-popular movement, the anti-Fascist cultural movement *par excellence*. The Left, therefore, comes increasingly to defend Neo-realism as a whole – by which I do not mean that Left critics suggest there are no differences between individual Neorealist works or that Neorealism is ideologically all of a piece, but that they present Neorealism as constituting a progressive national tradition, *the* national tradition that must be defined and constantly reasserted.

Let me now move forward to the 1960s and show how the concept of Neorealism with all these distinctive positive connotations comes to be unmade. I date this process from the early 1960s, despite the fact that already in the mid-1950s there are some very well-publicised discussions on the Left of a 'crisis of Neorealism', in particular over Visconti's film *Senso* and Vasco Pratolini's novel *Metello*.[14] In my opinion, these discussions, which involve arguments over whether Neorealism was exhausted around 1950, or whether it continued after 1950, and over whether the works in question should be defined as 'Neorealist' or 'realist', do indeed register a sense of crisis of Neorealism as a movement, but at no point do they call into question the validity of Neorealism as a descriptive category. More important, they do not challenge, but rather confirm, realism as the dominant aesthetic discourse.

The 1960s constitute a turning-point because it is then that this realist aesthetic, and the hegemonic project that goes with it, begins to be questioned on the Left. I think that three main factors converge to bring this about. The first is the rise of the new Left, which constitutes for the first time a major radical cultural force outside the orbit of the Communist Party. New Left intellectuals begin in the early 1960s increasingly to challenge the PCI's concepts of anti-monopoly alliance and progressive democratisation, and with them the strategy of a gradual transformation of society and the state from within. These concepts of the PCI were inextricably bound up with that outlook which had promoted realism for the past twenty years: the concept of a radical break with the Fascist past; a political project which sought to continue and develop the anti-Fascist, popular-front tradition; the notion of a democratic reconstruction led by the working class. Consequently, challenging the political line of the PCI also meant challenging the outlook that had sustained the Neorealism concept in the critical discourse of the Left.[15]

The second factor is the emergence of an avant-garde literary practice and of a Left criticism that speaks up for a Modernist aesthetic. The writers and critics of the Gruppo 63, for instance, were concerned not with mimesis but with exploring the formal resources of language. The more Left-orientated among them saw realist writing as reproducing a reified, mystified reality. They privileged non-realist language and difficulty for their ability to expose and question 'common-sense' reality.[16] After this there are many ramifications of a non-realist or anti-realist criticism, for instance the development in film criticism, from the late 1960s, of methods of analysis of film narrative drawing on semiotics and psychoanalysis. In all cases, not only was Neorealism as a creative movement called into question, seen as a superseded project; Neorealism was also undermined as a descriptive category. It became not only possible but also obvious and inevitable to see all Neorealist film-making and writing as having an oblique rather than a direct relationship to the things it represented, to be encoded in particular narrative conventions, to construct particular versions or models of reality. By the same token, non-realist or non-Neorealist writing of the 1930s, 40s and 50s came again to be valued rather than downgraded, the organisation of the cultural past in terms of affirmations and interruptions of realism was abandoned and replaced with an organisation in terms of different formal languages. It became possible once again to value forms of art that were not turned outwards in a social, public sense, to value fantasy, fictionality and representations of the personal.

The third factor is the development of a new, critical historio-graphy which no longer accepts either the traditional periodisation of a distinct break between Fascism and the Republic or the image of Fascism and Fascist culture that had been dominant since the Resistance. As I indicated, the realist aesthetic and the concept of Neorealism that emerged after the end of the war were premised on a rejection of Fascist culture *en bloc*, and on a strong subjective sense of 1945 as constituting a watershed, a turning-point. What starts to emerge out of this new historiography is first, a more dispassionate and more detailed account of the culture of the Fascist period, which shows it to have contained several contra-dictory strands and several lines of continuity with postwar cul-ture, and second, the thesis of 1945 as not so much a decisive watershed but as an interregnum, a hiatus in the political represen-tation of capital, a reorganisation of bourgeois hegemony between the collapse of Fascism and the construction of a new ruling bloc of the Republic. New historiographical periodisations, and new cul-tural periodisations, follow from this, inserting decisive breaks not at 1945 but in the late 1920s and early 1930s or in the late 1950s and early 1960s. These periodisations effectively erase the concept of Neorealism as a new and distinct phase as it had emerged in the late 1940s and had been sustained throughout the 1950s.[17]

When I talk about the concept of Neorealism in its earlier sense as having been unmade as a result of these processes, I am not suggesting that the word disappeared altogether, that critics no longer used the term. I mean simply that, when the terms realism and Neorealism were used after the 1960s, they did not carry the same range of positive meanings they had carried when they were used by critics of the Left in the late 1940s and 1950s. Realism and Neorealism were no longer slogans with the positive connotations of progressivism, anti-fascism, anti-formalism, a new relation between intellectuals and masses, a project of democratic reconstruction. Rather they either took on negative connotations of 'populism' or 'velleity', or else they became essentially descriptive terms, genre and period categories, and very unstable ones at that, given the uncertainty that now set in about when Neorealism began and when it ended, how far it broke with the past and how far it continued it.

Why did a Left project of cultural reconstruction centred on realism and Neorealism fail? There would seem to be three competing explanations. The first explanation is the one put forward by several critics to the left of the PCI in the 1960s and 1970s. They argued that the failure of the project was inherent in the nature of the project itself, that to talk the language of reconstruction at all in 1945–50 was to play the bourgeoisie's game. The Left should have been organising instead a revolutionary challenge to the new state rather than accommodating to it by developing a long-term cultural strategy. I do not have much to say about this argument, except that you either believe it or you don't. I don't. It seems to me inadequate and reductive.

A second explanation is that the Left's cultural project was liquidated by irresistible pressures from outside – Catholic censorship, political harassment, the drying up of funds and markets. There is certainly some truth in this explanation, as regards cinema at any rate, but it suggests that the sorts of cultural policies being advocated by the Left under the banner of realism and Neorealism could have continued and been successful had it not been for this outside interference. I do not find this suggestion convincing, since it seems likely to me that these policies were already becoming exhausted from within, but in any case it is strictly untestable since we have no way of knowing what would have happened if this interference had not taken place.

A third explanation suggests that the Left's project in the 1940s and early 1950s was overtaken and rendered obsolete in the late 1950s and 1960s by the sudden propulsion of Italian culture into late-twentieth-century conditions: an effect of the rapid rise in living standards, the spread of consumer culture, increasingly centralised ownership and control of the cultural industries. This view seems to me a lot nearer to the truth, but there is still a problem with it. Although I think it correctly identifies a failure of the Left, and not just of the PCI, to understand and respond strategically to the full extent of the cultural changes taking place in the 1950s and 60s, particularly in the area of mass culture and taste, it tends to suggest that the development of a modern consumer culture was an inexorable, ubiquitous and levelling process which overcame any alternative cultural project. I feel one needs to be very careful to avoid all such explanations which suggest an *inexorable* process of capitalist modernisation. One also needs to get away from seeing industrialised culture, as the Left has seen it for so long, as simply inauthentic culture, culture sullied by being dragged through the market-place. Modern culture needs to be seen as necessarily organised in a set of industries involving the distribution and consumption of particular products. Where I believe the promotion of a concept of realism fell down, along with the policy of building a mass national-popular culture through the mediations of intellectuals, was precisely that it was not thought out in terms of strategic interventions into the cultural industries, but as a molecular operation conducted outside or alongside them in civil society, by the development of voluntary initiatives, through party organisations or flanking organisations, through popular recreations and festivals, through clubs and circles – in other words in traditional terms that were in no way adequate to the new conditions and forms of cultural distribution and consumption.

Giuseppe De Santis has recalled, in relation to this, that he proposed soon after the war that the Communist Party set up its own film production company and distribution network, but that his proposals were rejected. He believes, I think with some justification, that:

If, in 1948, there had already been centres of production and concentration in the hands of the parties of the Left, there would have been some system for defending them at the moment when the Communists were thrown out of the government and the harassment, boycotting and what I call the state assassination of Italian Neorealism began.[18]

This seems to me to be the nub of the question, and it brings me back to my starting-point, that problem of why the Left continued to promote the idea of Neorealism and a realist aesthetic even when Neorealism as a practice, as a set of products, was in eclipse. The Left continued to promote its model of democratic national reconstruction based on a traditional conception of molecular cultural activity at a time when the capitalist reconstruction of culture was taking quite different forms. The Left concentrated almost exclusively on making and promoting cultural products and on influencing people, either by educating them, raising them up, or by disseminating progressive culture out to them. The Centre-Right parties, particularly the Christian Democrats, concentrated on getting control of the channels of distribution of popular and mass culture. The Left's strategy was to occupy whole areas of civil society by building its own organisations and extending its influence into spheres like the education system. The strategy of the Christian Democrats was to occupy posts in the state and the para-state, in other words to build a bureaucracy of political and cultural operators, to occupy the radio and television, to extend their influence into private cultural organisations by offering economic concessions and facilitations. It is easy to see which of these strategies was the more successful.

Notes

1. On the early circulation (from about 1930) of the concept of 'Neorealism' and the development of a realist aesthetic in both literary and film criticism, see Gian Piero Brunetta, 'Neorealismo: alle fonti di un mito', in *Intellettuali, cinema e propaganda tra le due guerre* (Bologna: Patron, 1972); and 'Il cammino della critica verso il neorealismo', in *Storia del cinema italiano 1895–1945* (Rome: Riuniti, 1979). On Left Fascism and the younger generation intellectuals in the 1930s and early 1940s, see Alberto Asor Rosa, 'La cultura', in Ruggero Romano and Corrado Vivanti (eds), *Storia d'Italia*, vol. II, pt 4: *Dall'Unità a oggi* (Turin: Einaudi, 1975) pp. 1567–83; and Vito Zagarrio, 'Primato degli intellettuali e neorealismo', in Lino Micciche (ed.), *Il neorealismo cinematografico italiano: Atti del convegno della X Mostra Internazionale del Nuovo Cinema* (Venice: Marsilio, 1975). On the 1930s antecedents of Neorealism, see (for cinema) Francesco Casetti, Alberto Farassino, Aldo Grasso and Tatti Sanguinetti, 'Neorealismo e cinema italiano degli anni "30"', ibid., and (for literature) Mario De Michelis, *Alle origini del neorealismo:*

Aspetti del romanzo italiano negli anni '30' (Cosenza: Edizioni Lerici, 1980).

2.   On the need for a new relationship between intellectuals and the working class and the opposition to intellectualism, see the editorial in the first issue of *Società* in 1945, nos 1–2, pp. 6–7:

> In this work [of reconstruction], which is common wealth, the work of the intellectuals constitutes an essential and vital element. They are the salt of the earth. However, they do not constitute a class apart and it is to their disadvantage and to that of their vocation if they try to constitute a caste or separate category. That general and ideal service to truth and humanity is inextricably linked to those forces which effectively operate in the particular concrete situation.

Compare L. Lombardo Radice, 'Alla scuola della classe operaia', in *L'Unità*, 30 November 1944: 'The process of the proletarianisation of the intellectuals, their complete assimilation, that is, into the vanguard class, is a long and laborious process.' For criticism of Idealist philosophy (in particular that of Giovanni Gentile and Benedetto Croce), see: Fabrizio Onofri, 'Irresponsabilità dell'arte sotto il fascismo', *La Rinascita*, 1:4 (1944) pp. 31–5, and Palmiro Togliatti's articles, 'Croce' (1944) and 'Gramsci e Croce' (1947), in *I corsivi di Roderigo* (Bari: De Donato, 1976). On clarity of language, see, for example, R. Bianchi Bandinelli, 'Cultura e popolo', *Rinascita*, 2:2 (1945) p. 48:

> We categorically reject all preciosity, all arcane aspects, all obscurantism, the extreme forces of the decadence of Romanticism, and we ask of intellectuals not meagre and banal communication, but the effort implied in reducing their complex thought into a kind of expression which is clearer, simpler, more elementary, permeable, without losing anything of the actual substance and, indeed, concentrating it.

3.   On the formalism/realism opposition, see G. Trombadori, 'Artisti e critici dopo la liberazione', *Rinascita*, 2:1 (1945) pp. 27–9. On the avant-gardism/abstraction correlation, see, for example, Massimo Caprera on Paul Valéry:

> The undeniable seriousness of Valéry does not redeem the limitations of the abstract nature of his bourgeois intelligence. Indeed, it seems to us that it reduces still further the possibility of contacts with reality and renders impossible any solidarity with those who struggle and fight for work and bread, for progress and for the liberty of all.

4.   See Mario Pomilio, *Le fortune del Verga* (Naples: Liguori, 1963) pt I, Ch. 1.

5. Natalia Ginzburg, *Lessico famigliare* (Turin: Einaudi, 1963) pp. 171–2.
6. On the experience of *consigli di gestione* in the RAI, see Franco Monteleone, *Storia della RAI dagli alleati alla DC, 1944–1954* (Rome, Bari: Laterza, 1979) pp. 79–81. Monteleone points out that although control of radio was rapidly normalised, 'for a brief period and in an unrepeatable situation, the radio message was democratic and progressive' (p. 81). On the *consigli di gestione* at Mondadori, see Claudia Patuzzi, *Mondadori* (Naples: Liguori, 1978) pp. 65–6. The workers who had occupied the Mondadori offices in Milan and the printing works at Verona refused to let Arnoldo Mondadori back into the firm after the Liberation. In May 1945, a number of intellectuals, including Elio Vittorini, Alfonso Gatto and Francesco Flora, signed a petition in favour of his return. On 24 July an agreement was reached between Mondadori and the *consigli di gestione* by which Mondadori was allowed to return to his post after making a number of concessions, including a profit-sharing deal and representation of workers and management in equal numbers on the board.
7. Togliatti, for instance, wrote in 1945 of the need for financial sacrifices for the moment by workers in order to: 'realise a national plan of Reconstruction which tears the key economic positions from the hands of private enterprise and places them in the hands of the State for the good of the collectivity'.
8. Edited versions of the radio interviews were published in Carlo Bo (ed.), *Inchiesta sul neorealismo* (Turin: Edizioni Radio Italiana, 1951).
9. See, for instance, Carlo Lizzani, *Il cinema italiano* (Florence; Parenti, 1953) p. 52: 'The intolerance of a few people for the typically transatlantic cinema has become a state of mind diffused throughout the population, whilst on the other hand, the high quality of Italian art films has led to the greater appreciation of our films everywhere in the world.' In 1955 an unsigned article in the liberal weekly *Il Mondo* asserts that a manifesto in defence of the freedom of the Italian cinema launched by the Communist Party begins with: 'the amazing reduction of all postwar Italian cinema, the "national cinema", to so-called "Neorealism", and with a protest against the obstacles and persecutions that this cinema subsequently has found in its path'.

  Mario Alicata replied ('Gli intellettuali e la loro libertà', *L'Unità*, 20 May 1955, p. 3):

  It is evident in fact to everyone that the manifesto . . . condemns the fact that . . . the principal purpose of the attack conducted by the Americans and by our own present leaders against the Italian national cinema . . . is precisely that (for economic and political reasons) of destroying that 'type' of art film known under the name of Neorealism which has given to Italian cinema fame and success throughout the world.

10. See the notorious criticism levelled in 1952 by Giulio Andreotti (the

Undersecretary with responsibility for the cinema) against *Umberto D:*

> And if it is true that evil can be combatted by harshly laying bare its cruellest aspects, it is also true that if people are led to believe – wrongly – that Umberto D's is the Italy of the mid-twentieth-century, De Sica will have rendered a very bad service to his country, which is also the land of Don Bosco, of Forlanini and of a progressive social legislation. (Giulio Andreotti, in an open letter to Vittorio De Sica, in the Christian Democrat weekly, *Libertas*, 24 February 1952; quoted in Guido Aristarco, *Neorealismo e nuova critica cinematografica* (Florence: Nuova Guaraldi, 1980) p. 9)

11.   See Tommaso Chiaretti, 'Dietro lo schermo', *L'Unità*, 23 January 1954, p. 3:

> The main current of Italian cinema was one of exceptional 'chastity', of an extreme purity of feelings and problems. Look at the films of De Sica from *Sciuscià* to *Miracolo a Milano*, from *Ladri di biciclette* to *Umberto D*. Look at the purity of the servant-girl in *Umberto D*. And if that girl, that gentle little servant, that young actress full of poetic sensitivity, has *then* acquired various attributes, those of *sex*, those attributes have been given to her after *Umberto D* and as part of a polemic against De Sica.

On propaganda films, see Tommaso Chiaretti, 'Cinema di ventura', *L'Unità*, 17 February 1953, p. 3.

12.   See, for instance, Mario Alicata's essay of 1950 on Carlo Levi's *L'orologio*: 'The realistic commitment is at every moment elbowed out of the way by Symbolist contrivances' (p. 263); Levi's book uses: 'all the commonplaces ... all the junk of contemporary cultural decadence' (p. 264). On the decadence–Catholic link, see for instance, Luigi Cavallo, 'Decadenza di Mauriac', *L'Unità*, 17 September 1949; Mauriac is 'the Catholic writer who has the greatest awareness of the decadence of the culture and the divisions at the heart of the Catholic world'.

13.   For a Catholic defence of *Ladri di biciclette*, see Carlo Trabucco, 'Chiediamo disco verde per *Ladri di biciclette* (e suggeriamo un po' di prudenza ai nostri comunisti', *Il Popolo*, 7 March 1950, p. 3. Trabucco criticises the decision by the Motion Picture Association of America to ban the film, ostensibly because of the sequences depicting a brothel and a child urinating, but in reality – Trabucco suspects – because of the film's supposed Communism, an assumption which PCI spokespersons have helped foster by claiming the film as their own. However, Trabucco claims:

> the film is not Communist and neither is the director ... the film simply presents a slice of social life in which a poor unemployed

man does not know where to turn to find work, and merely because this happens to occur in Italy, there is no reason to blame Communism if De Sica has presented an extract of our wretched life, which would be very much more wretched, certainly, if America had not given us a hand and were not still helping us.

See also Franco Fortini's review of 1949 (reproduced in F. Fortini (ed.), *Dieci inverni* (Bari: De Donato, 1973) pp. 152–6), which mentions how 'the critic of the *Corriere della Sera* wishes to inform his readers that the film does not contain any social or class polemic. Young people of sixteen are informed that they can enter the Odeon without fear.' Fortini records that the film was appropriated in two different directions by Catholics who saw in the ending a message of pity and hope and by Communists who saw in the film a denunciation of a government which repressed political meetings, allowed the black market to thrive and the unemployed to starve.

14. See Carlo Salinari's review of *Metello* in *Il Contemporaneo* (12 February 1955) and his article 'Discussioni e conclusioni su *Metello* e il neorealismo', *Società*, XII (1956) pp. 604–6. See also Carlo Muscetta, '*Metello* e la crisi del neorealismo', *Società*, XII, 2 (1955) (reproduced in C. Muscetta, *Realismo, neorealismo, controrealismo* (Milan: Garzanti, 1976) pp. 107–41).

15. Among the fundamental documents of this critique of the 'popular front' cultural project promoted by the PCI, see Franco Fortini, 'Mandato degli scrittori e fine dell'antifascismo', in his *Verifica dei poteri* (Milan: Il Saggiatore, 1965), translated in *Screen*, 15, 1 (Spring 1974) pp. 33–70; and Alberto Asor Rosa, *Scrittori e popolo: il populismo nella letteratura italiana contemporanea* (Rome: Samonà e Savelli, 1965) pt I. In film criticism, see Goffredo Fofi, *Il cinema italiano: servi e padroni*, 5th edn (Milan: Feltinelli, 1977) pp. 67–76, and Guido Aristarco, *Neorealismo e nuova critica cinematografica* (Florence: Nuova Guaraldi, 1980).

16. See Gruppo 63, *Il romanzo sperimentale* (Milan: Feltrinelli, 1980); Edoardo Sanguineti, *Ideologia e linguaggio* (Milan: Feltrinelli, 1965).

17. For examples and discussions of this reperiodisation, see Alberto Caracciolo, 'Un 'ipotesi di periodizzazione', in *Quaderni Storici*, XII (1977) 1: *Letteratura ideologia società negli anni trenta*, pp. 54–7; Mario Isnenghi, 'Trenta-Quaranta: l'ipotesi della continuità', ibid., pp. 103–7; Romano Luperini, *Il Novecento* (Turin: Loescher, 1981). Luperini reperiodises twentieth-century Italian literary history into three slices which correspond not to political phases (liberalism, Fascism, republic), which would produce a break after each world war, but to economic phases (imperialism, 1903–25; birth and reconstruction of neocapitalism, 1926–56; apogee and crisis of neocapitalism 1956–79). This reperiodisation, it might be observed, would be well motivated if it corresponded to an analysis of culture in industrial terms, i.e. in terms of markets, relations between state and cultural industries, development of the mass media, dependency on American cultural exports, etc. But Luperini simply imposes this

periodisation on what is in many ways a conventional literary-historical narrative organised around high culture, canonical authors, the history of intellectuals and of literary movements.

18.　De Santis's statement is in Franca Faldini and Goffredo Fofi (eds), *L'avventurosa storia del cinema italiano raccontata dai suoi protagonisti, 1935–1959* (Milan: Feltrinelli, 1979) p. 218.

4

The Place of Neorealism in Italian Cinema from 1945 to 1954

CHRISTOPHER WAGSTAFF

To discuss the place of Neorealism in postwar Italian cinema is to raise a number of issues concerning approaches to history, approaches to cinema history, and notions of popular culture and art. Italian historians have a tradition of casting their analyses in an idealist light, seeing historical events as betrayals of what might have been: Gramsci dubs the *Risorgimento* a 'failed revolution', and this perspective is transferred to the reconstruction of Italy at the end of the Second World War with the notion of a 'restoration'. It is therefore asserted that as Italian film-makers began making films that in their style and content opposed the escapism and repetitive formalism of both the Fascist cinema and Hollywood, the combined forces of Hollywood's industrial monopoly, reactionary forces in Church, State and among the Allies, and the weakness and amateurism of Italian cinema industrialists contrived to deprive these films of their exhibition market and of the funds necessary for their production. The Italian cinema revealed the possibility of a mass popular culture which was not purely entertainment, but reactionary forces reinstalled the mechanisms that had controlled the cinema during the Fascist regime, forcing it back into entertainment.[1] This view in turn relies on certain assumptions about art and popular culture: that an art form that takes the people and their lives and experiences for its subject matter is more authentically 'popular' (in the ideological sense) than one which relies on the narrative formulae which the largest number of viewers have regularly consumed; that an artistically valid cinema should prevail commercially over the stereotyped formulae of Hollywood; that the best way to market commercial commodities with exchange value is to produce them as cultural products with a use value. It is very understandable that people should make these assumptions, but the extent to which they enable us to understand the cinema industry of the late 1940s can be questioned.

There is little agreement over what Neorealist cinema is, and this adds to the debate over the history of Neorealism. The more tightly you draw the boundaries around the phenomenon, the more travailed and short-lived becomes its story. In other words, to say that *Riso amaro, Non c'è pace tra gli ulivi* (De Santis), *In nome della legge, Il cammino della speranza* (Germi), *Vivere in pace, Anni difficili* (Zampa), *Stromboli* (Rossellini), *I vitelloni, La strada* (Fellini) are not truly Neorealist films, is to strike off the list those films that achieved commercial success, and to assert either that the films belong to genres that pander to an existing, non-realist, cinema taste, or that their success was due to artistic compromises forced on the film-makers by commercial pressures. As an example of the first case, both of Germi's films are frequently described as owing a great deal to the American western. As an example of the second case, that of Giuseppe De Santis' *Riso amaro,* Michael Silverman asserts that since the artist could not find funding except through a global release scheme (which means in the USA) based on American investment arranged by De Laurentiis through the Italian production and distribution company Lux, the film itself could no longer address a discourse to Italians about the labour disputes and working conditions of the rice-harvesting industry, but had to construct a more conventionally cinematic discourse about the beauty of women's bodies:

> Mangano in *Riso amaro* walks left of frame through a rice paddy perpendicular to an undifferentiated mass of less strikingly attractive women, all of whom are bent over their work. As she moves to the middle distance she raises her skirt out of the water to just below her buttocks. Our eyes no longer watch the right side of the frame, the mass of working women, but take in the movement of the skirt, the revelation once again of the body. Not only voyeurism and the gaze, not only the Bazinian middle distance, but the documentable trace of American capital investment is marked by the movement of that skirt.[2]

I think it would neatly fit the scheme of artistic and political integrity defeated by commerce if what Silverman says were true, but I wonder whether it really is. De Santis himself, according to Silverman, 'argued that the project had meaning only within the terms of a specific struggle, that to make it an "international" film would be to rob it of any social context'. That is one point. But the implications that De Santis was under commercial pressure to use Mangano, that an American release would require a less political content, and that Lux would be antagonistic to De Santis' aims bear further scrutiny. I shall let De Santis speak:

It was no mere chance that so many Italian directors, like myself, Germi, Lattuada, Zampa and others gathered around Lux. You see Lux represented the ideal as a production company, it was the model of an industry in the sense of being systematic and organised. Headed by Gualino – a Turinese financier – it had as director general Gatti – an intellectual, a scholar of musical history in particular. So it was also a company represented by men of a notable intellectual level. Moreover, it could guarantee total seriousness thanks to the northern industrial groups that it had behind it, for whom the cinema was, certainly, an activity secondary and collateral to their main businesses, but nonetheless not to be taken lightly . . . .

The character played by Mangano, around whom the story unfolds and who serves to explain the film ideologically, is an extremely subtle character who, inside the story, continually develops with her good aspects and her bad ones . . . .

The eroticism in my films is attributable, I think, to my nature, with its particular sensibility. . . . Over *Riso amaro* I had a very lively polemic with trade unionists in the very columns of *L'Unità*. They maintained, among other things, that it was inconceivable that a rice-picker should dance the boogie woogie in one of our farmyards where, according to them, only traditional dancing took place . . . You see, for some party figures the Italian woman shouldn't break the mould, certain things shouldn't appeal to her. Naturally, not all of them. Togliatti understood them perfectly well, and he congratulated me.[3]

De Santis chose Mangano for her beauty and her physical appearance. The producers were aghast; De Laurentiis thought she would be a disaster (but he married her none the less). One word from Elio Petri:

According to me, in the creation of his own particular cinematic eroticism De Santis had to repress himself. This is another of the things that can be held against the moralism of the communists and the moralism of critics of both left and right. Because De Santis is someone who, in his system of archetypes and myths, placed woman at the centre. Women were the centre of this whole system, and around the woman pivoted all the rest, even society. In a certain sense, even politics, if one looks closely at his films. And even the growth of class consciousness. And this eroticism of his was castrated, they made him pay for it.[4]

I have pursued this one detail in order to illustrate the dangers that lie in store for the historian who sets up an idealist notion of a Neorealism betrayed by Mammon.

Nevertheless, the ideological debates over Neorealism more than warrant a study, which I have no time to supply here. An example would be the debate between, on the one hand, Aristarco,[5] holding a Lukácsian position, praising Visconti for rising from the *cronaca* and naturalism of De Sica's films to the *storia* and realism of *Senso*; and, on the other hand, Chiarini, for whom Neorealism was a style expressing a moral position:

> They had in common a new spirit, born of the Resistance, which was revealed in the display of a new form, the fruit of a study, almost a conquest of cinematic language. . . . The characters of previous conventional narrative were replaced by men rooted in their reality; the prefabricated plots of novels and plays were replaced by first-hand accounts of daily existence, whether it be exceptional or banal.[6]

The history of Neorealism as a style is complex. During the Fascist regime the cinema industry had become centralised, partly nationalised, and funded with state subsidies.[7] The Fascist administrator in charge of cinema, Luigi Freddi, strove to create a vigorous, high quality, commercially successful Italian cinema, and promoted the establishment of institutions to bring this about, in particular, the studios of Cinecittà and the state film school, the Centro Sperimentale di Cinematografia. The latter became a hive of anti-Fascist theorising, and in particular the source of many ideas about how a truly indigenous, realist cinema could develop in Italy. In the periodicals *Cinema* and *Bianco e Nero*, critics examined closely all the Italian films that were made, and in the words of Franco Venturini in 1950:

The endeavour of this critical activity, notwithstanding the complexity of its various positions, seems dominated by a common purpose: the grafting of an indigenous tradition, going back to Giotto and Dante, through Verga, Fogazzaro, Manzoni, Goldoni, Caravaggio, Masaccio, in the illusion of discovering in it, ready-made, the quintessence of the genius of the race, to be injected intravenously into the Italian cinema.[8]

Verga, in particular, was seen as a source for an Italian approach to reality that could be applied to the cinema. What Micciché calls a red thread of realism was sought in Italian cinema, and was found beginning with the Neapolitan realist silent film made in 1914 by Nino Martoglio, *Sperduti nel buio*, as well as in the films of Blasetti (*1860* and *Vecchia guardia*) and Camerini (*Gli uomini che mascalzoni* and *Darò un milione*), the major directors of the 1930s. There were calls to create a fusion of the feature film with the documentary. France was looked upon as an example of a cinema that had found its own realist cinematic style, particularly in the work of Renoir. Since the characteristics of cinema as an art form were seen to be those of photography, the ability to reproduce reality, the word '*paesaggio*' became important in critical theorising. Critics spoke in code in those days, and *paesaggio* was a word that expressed a desire for a respect for the importance of the regions, their customs and dialects, in the cinema, while the Fascist regime was doing all it could to homogenise the nation, which it did through the cinema by making all films in Rome studios. The cinema could show people in their environment, in the environment that determined them, and in the environment that they had created with their labour.[9] Towards the end of the period in which these ideas were being expressed, 1939–43, a series of films were coming out that were hailed by these critics and by other film-makers as examples of serious realist film-making: Franciolini's *Fari nella nebbia*, De Sica's *I bambini ci guardano*, Blasetti's *Quattro passi tra le nuvole*, De Robertis' fictionalised documentary *Uomini sul fondo*, and the film that struck people most of all, Visconti's *Ossessione*.

So there is a school of thought that locates the sources of Neorealism in the theorising and the film-making of the period 1941–3, and sees the postwar movement as picking up that thread. There are others, however, who question whether the abrupt break with previous cinematic styles and methods that we find with Rossellini and De Sica in films like *Paisà* and *Sciuscià* are really in any kind of line of continuity with the pre-Liberation films. In other words, a break with the past, an interruption in continuity, would *only* be asserted for a very few rigorously Neorealist films. The bulk of postwar films were produced, directed, written, acted, photographed and distributed by exactly the same people who had made exactly the same kind of film before the war. I do not intend to delve into the controversy over continuity, but for the purpose of illustrating the historiographical issues I must point out that much hinges on how widely or how loosely you define Neorealist cinema. A tight definition would include Rossellini's *Roma città aperta, Paisà*, De Sica's *Sciuscià, Ladri di biciclette, Umberto D*, Visconti's *La terra trema*. I put *Roma città aperta* in the list because tradition would not allow me to omit it, though if I were to use the criteria that critics use to measure the Neorealist purity of films, I might have to exclude *Roma città aperta* for its use of stars, its traditional melodramatic structure, its reliance on comedy and stereotypes, and its facile populism. The tighter definitions look for stylistic purity, the absence of rhetoric, a resistance to the temptation to let narrative dominate, the use of non-professional actors, location shooting, concentration on the '*popolo*' as protagonists, and their accurate placing in a social and economic context, a political commitment to social reform, and above all a film-making that makes no compromises with the conventions of cinematic entertainment. The tighter you go, the fewer the films, until you are just left with *Umberto D*.

I would favour a loose definition of Neorealism, because I think the more purist perspective has little to offer the cinema historian. If one is to try and define the position of Neorealism in postwar Italian cinema for the ten years between 1945 (considered the date of the first Neorealist film, *Roma città aperta*) and 1954 (rather less unanimously considered the moment when Neorealism definitively ended), the exercise seems pointless if one is only talking about ten films out of the total of around nine hundred Italian films produced in that period; it becomes more interesting if we can define a category containing about four dozen films. Certainly, the question of the death of the movement hinges rather on how you define it. There are those who say that the movement contained the seeds of its own demise right from the start, in that it was not a truly popular cinema, but was rather a bourgeois avant-garde artistic movement. [10] Others are more inclined to look at the forces ranged against the movement, and to explain some of the movement's compromises and its demise in the light of those forces.[11] There is no doubt that the latter position obliges us to look closely at the place of Neorealism in the Italian cinema industry of the time, rather than cordoning off a group of films and examining them as though they could have existed independently of the bulk of the nine hundred Italian films, and the many thousands of foreign (mostly American) films that were being shown in Italian cinemas during the ten-year period.

It is in this light that I shall side-step the hotly debated question of how popular – in the commercial sense – Neorealist films were with the public. In terms of box-office takings, they did, as a group, about as well as any other homogeneous group of Italian films: some very well, some average, some badly;[12] but among the total flops there were films that were universally acknowledged to be masterpieces of world cinema. For want of the time to go into the question, I shall have to allow my account of Neorealism's place in the industry to suggest, by implication, how complex and possibly insoluble the question is. The place of Neorealism in the context of the cinema industry is, I think, particularly relevant for this discussion, because between 1945 and 1954 the Italian cinema industry was 'reconstructed'. Or let us be more precise, and say that the production sector of the industry was reconstructed, for the other two sectors, namely distribution and exhibition (the latter by far the largest sector of any nation's cinema industry), never suffered the damage that the war and its aftermath inflicted on film production.

The production sector produces films, the distribution section hires them to cinemas in the exhibition sector, who show them to the public in exchange for the price of an admission ticket. One indication of the state of the production sector is the number of films produced per annum: about a dozen in 1930, gradually rising, and accelerating noticeably when generous state subsidies coincide with the Hollywood majors' withdrawal from the Italian market in protest at a government monopoly of the distribution of foreign films in 1938, reaching a peak of over 100 in 1942, a trough of around 20 in 1944, and steadily regaining ground to reach over 160 in 1954 (the number continued to rise until Italy was second only to the United States in film production in the First World, reaching nearly 300 in 1967–8, and gradually falling off from that point onwards).[13] Quantity is not the only measure of the production sector: another is quality. Neorealist films were regarded very highly abroad, winning prizes and critics' polls, and earning good box-office receipts (of the films voted best of the year in Belgium in 1950, Italian Neorealist films take three of the top five places).[14] Other Italian films were by no means of that quality – the trade papers regularly categorised them as *mediocri* or *pessimi* (mediocre or dreadful). The Italian production sector was so very weak because it had almost no structure providing continuity of investment. Production companies were improvised, one-film affairs. In a three-year period, around this time, 217 Italian production companies made 371 films. 189 companies made less than one film per year; twenty-one companies made one or two; three companies made two or three; four companies made more than three films. Taking a neither tight nor loose definition of Neorealism, one can say that the number of Neorealist films to come out, compared with total Italian production, each year were in 1945 – two out of thirty (6.6 per cent), in 1946 – three out of sixty (5 per cent), in 1947 – three out of sixty (5 per cent), in 1948 – eight out of fifty (16 per cent), in 1949 – five out of seventy-six (6.5 per cent), in 1950 – six out of ninety (6.5 per cent), in 1951 – three or four out of 110 (3.5 per cent), in 1952 – seven out of 140 (5 per cent), in 1953 – five out of 165 (3 per cent), in 1954 – three out of 170 (1.7 per cent). From a critical point of view, quality is measured by quality; from an industrial point of view, quality is measured by quantity – box-office receipts: good films make money. Hollywood films made money in Italy in this period, Neorealist films often did not. Does this mean that Hollywood movies were better than Neorealist films?

From 1938 to 1945, much of the output of the eight Hollywood major companies had been excluded from the Italian market, and during the war itself, from a large part of the European market. When the Allies liberated Italy, the Americans brought their movies with them – a backlog of some 2000 films to unleash on a market whose own production sector was in tatters. They wanted to dismantle the panoply of protective laws that the Fascist Government had set up to protect its own production sector. In 1945 the Allied Film Board was set up, and the Chairman was the American Admiral Stone, who rose at the end of the Board's first meeting to say that the Italian cinema had to be destroyed, and that all the legislation created by the Fascist regime was to be abrogated. He added that the Italian cinema was a fascist invention and should be suppressed together with its instruments, including

Cinecittà, and that its industrialists were merely speculators, and that in any case Italy was an agricultural country and had no need of a cinema industry.[15] (Cinecittà was used as a refugee camp, and only got back into production in 1948; the Pisorno studios were requisitioned for Allied military warehousing, and were not derequisitioned until 1949.)[16] Alfredo Guarini was present at that meeting of the Film Board:

> I recall – when I was called to represent Italian cinéastes on the first Film Board set up by the Allies after the liberation of Rome – the attitude of the late deputy Proia who was representing the producers on the same committee. In response to a Philippic from Admiral Stone – who was chairing the Film Board – against the cinema industry, which was accused of Fascism, the good Proia could only reply by 'assuring the Admiral of the willingness of Italian cinema industrialists to make themselves available to their Allied colleagues in order to work out a new cinema policy'. This showed that Proia, and with him nearly all Italian producers – after the catastrophe of the war – were groping in the dark, and did not even remotely conceive the enormous possibilities that were opening up for our cinema by virtue of the simple fact that we had finally got our freedom back.
>
> I wanted to recall Proia and the Film Board not to pursue an easy target, but to clarify an incontrovertible fact: neorealism, and therefore the new Italian cinema, was born without the help of the industry.
>
> Rossellini, in order to make *Roma città aperta*, had to make do with an irregular financial backing from a noblewoman, and then had to have recourse to his tailor to finish the film. Two executive producers, who were counted among the best before the war, abandoned the film during production, appalled by the style of shooting of their 'madman' of a director. Vittorio De Sica, having completed *Sciuscià* in the midst of a multitude of problems, had his film turned down by the major Italian distributors.
>
> It is clear, therefore, that only the artists showed themselves to be aware of the situation, and only through their activity was the Italian cinema saved.[17]

This is not a critic speaking: Guarini was a director, producer and distributor, and yet he analyses the situation in terms of artists creating in the teeth of commercial crassness and incompetence. What he feels Proia is ignoring is the American desire to gain a total monopoly of the Italian cinema. This is not a conspiracy theory; firstly there is documentary evidence for this assertion,[18] and secondly the entire operation of the American cinema industry was based on monopolistic practices, which, it was openly argued, were indispensable for the viable functioning of the industry.[19] The monopoly worked through vertical integration. The keystone was the ownership of the large cinemas in the major urban centres. Distribution companies fed their best products at set rates into those cinemas, and only allowed films to go to other cinemas after they had been fully exploited at high ticket prices in those first run cinemas. A similar system was operated in Italy through the agencies and affiliates of the Hollywood majors in the main Italian cities. Films had to have a first run opening, or they would not get reviewed and brought to potential viewers' and exhibitor's attention. Thus, a small number of distribution companies controlled what the public could see and how much they had to pay to see it. But the circle is not complete, for this system also controlled production. Someone wanting to make a film would have to raise finance. If a distributor liked the project, it would generally offer contracts to its local agencies, based on a minimum guaranteed box-office yield. The local agency would issue promissory notes (called *cambiali* in Italian) to the national distributor, who would issue notes to the executive producer of the film. The producer would go to the bank, and on the basis of these *cambiali*, would apply for credit. Films were made in a cloud of *cambiali*, and there are famous cases of shooting grinding to a halt when the cloud suddenly evaporated – as we have just seen, Guarini recalls the case of *Roma città aperta*, Visconti's *La terra trema* was another famous case, as was, much later, Antonioni's *L'avventura*. If a distributor refused to offer a contract to distribute the film once made, then there was little point in making it, and it was extremely difficult, if not impossible, to find anyone to lend the money with which to make it. Distributors judged the viability of a project most of all on the basis of the stars performing in the film. Vittorio De Sica could get no distributor to undertake to distribute his projected *Ladri di biciclette* – though David O. Selznick, of RKO, offered not only to distribute but also to pay for the film if Cary Grant could play the lead. De Sica eventually, after months of searching, got finance from a consortium of Italian businessmen, and the state-owned distribution company, ENIC, undertook to distribute it. But his problems were not over, and it is Alfredo Guarini, who was at the time heading ENIC, who explains:

> Once the film was completed, the moment arrived to release it, and I had set up various private showings which it was my intention would serve first of all to acquaint those who worked in our business with the film, and to create around *Ladri di biciclette* an atmosphere of interest which would lay the basis for a new type of publicity launch. Unexpectedly – in my absence – and flouting the good faith of De Sica, the offices of ENIC decided to release the film in a few Italian cities. It was a huge flop, because a normal public could not guess from the simple posters of a film like *Ladri di biciclette* that they were being offered the masterpiece that De Sica's film in fact was.
>
> As soon as I heard the outcome I hastened to Rome, suspended the showings of the film, and agreed with De Sica a new system of release. Starting from Milan, the director personally introduced the film and explained it to the public in all the major Italian cities. So much interest was born from this that it brought about a considerable increase in box-office receipts, and today – at least as far as *Ladri di biciclette* is concerned – we have no reason to complain, as we do for so many other Neorealist films, about the lack of public response and thus of poor Italian receipts.... A new cinema requires a correspondingly new system of diffusion.[20]

This is a synchronic description of how the system worked, and how it functioned as a suffocating monopoly. It was the system operating in the United States, but in 1945 it was no longer operating fully in Italy, because the Fascist Government had in 1938 cut American distributors out of the market, and had taken over that monopoly for itself, operating it along ideological lines, but also on commercial lines (Luigi Freddi, the *gerarca* in charge of the cinema, had wanted above all a commercially viable cinema). Those same Fascist laws had decreed that Italian cinemas had to show a certain minumum number of Italian films per three-month period (*programmazione obbligatoria*), and that distributors had to pay a tax to the government on all foreign films dubbed into Italian, the proceeds of which went into the Sezione Autonoma per il Credito Cinematografico (SACC) of the Banca Nazionale del Lavoro (BNL), a state-owned bank.

The desire of the Americans to abrogate the Fascist laws is understandable. The way they set about reasserting a monopoly position in Italy was an example of masterly long-term planning. To begin with, during the Occupation, film distribution was in the hands of the Psychological Warfare Branch of the Allied forces, which acted as the emissary of the Hollywood majors, and flooded the country with subtitled or atrociously dubbed American films. In October 1945, a new law removed the Fascist restrictions, the dubbing taxes and the *programmazione obbligatoria*. Producers were offered a government subsidy equal to 10 per cent of the box-office takings of the film, plus an extra 4 per cent to films of particular artistic merit. The American distributors were, up to this point, operating through the PWB to unleash their backlog of films on the Italian market by selling distribution rights for cash to the highest bidder. With the passage of the 1945 law, they moved back into Italy, setting up agencies and affiliates in the major towns. Their policy was a straightforward one of dumping, and had the desired effect of crowding Italian domestic production out of cinemas. The United States made it a condition of signing the peace treaty that Italy did not impose import quotas on films. But in time the situation changed, laws were passed, as we shall see, re-establishing dubbing taxes and *programmazione obbligatoria*, and drastically limiting the ability of American companies to export the profits made in Italy, so that it became more profitable to enter the distribution and exhibition sector in Italy in order to control the enormous takings that were available there, and to consolidate further their hold over the market by investing their blocked assets in all three sectors of the Italian industry. The kind of position that can be achieved is best illustrated by the following statistics relating generally to the cinema industry of the period: 5 per cent of the films in circulation constituted 50 per cent of all film shows; 10 per cent of films shown received 80 per cent of total box-office takings.

There was an enormous growth in the exhibition sector. The number of cinemas rose 27 per cent between 1940 and 1946, only about 300 cinemas remained destroyed or not yet reopened by August 1945, and in the fifteen years between 1940 and 1954 cinemas doubled in number, from around 5000 to around 10 000. The number of cinema attendances (tickets sold) doubled from around 400 million in 1945 to 800 million in 1954 – though I could point out that in the United Kingdom, with the same population as

Italy, attendances were over 1500 million in 1948. Italians in large urban centres in the northern and central regions were responsible for the bulk of ticket sales, though the highest ratio of tickets sold per capita was, interestingly, quite definitely in the medium-sized towns; the numbers dropped for the South, and were very low for the less urban areas of the South and the islands, where many communities had no cinemas at all. Box-office takings rose enormously, even though ticket prices were rising at a little below the rate of inflation. Distributors and exhibitors were, therefore, at first unwilling for this trend to be threatened by protectionist legislation which would take the form of restrictions on the circulation of foreign films. Distributors and exhibitors looked for guaranteed earnings, and US films were a guaranteed success. But Italian producers – and most of all the creative personnel of the industry: directors, writers, actors and technicians – saw the situation differently. In 1946, only 13 per cent of those box-office takings related to Italian films.

In 1947 the Italian Government passed the next law to aid the Italian production sector. It imposed *programmazione obbligatoria* on Italian cinemas to show Italian films for eighty days per annum (France and England at the time had quotas of 140 and 162 days respectively), but protests from exhibitors led to a ministerial directive that more or less exonerated everyone from obeying the law. Some state subsidies were made available for production. Meanwhile, in the exhibition sector, the proliferation of cinemas and the enormous number of films circulating, meant that takings *per show* were dropping. Even exhibitors were complaining that there were too many very low quality American films being dumped on the Italian market (in 1948, 864 foreign films were imported, 90 per cent of them American). In this situation, Italian films were particularly badly hit, on average getting shorter stays at cinemas than American films. The Americans had by now used up their backlog of unreleased films, and because of drastically falling attendances in the USA and the Paramount anti-trust case loosening their domestic monopoly, they were producing fewer films. So the Motion Picture Export Association of America wisely signed a voluntary agreement with the Associazione Nazionale Industrie Cinematografiche e Affini (ANICA – the professional organisation of the producers and distributors) which, on close inspection, can be seen to limit American imports into Italy to about the entire output of the Hollywood majors. ANICA and the government trumpeted this as a huge victory over the Americans.

There were debates in parliament over a situation where Italian films were running away with all the international prizes, and yet could hardly get a showing in Italy. A rally in defence of Italian cinema was held in 1949 in the Piazza del Popolo in Rome. It is interesting to read the response of AGIS, the trade association of the exhibitors, to this rally:

> The rally will be remembered above all for the pathetic invocation of a notable actress to whom public rumour attributes a salary of Hollywood proportions.... Actually the situation is difficult. AGIS makes known a long list of receipts of Italian films; among them are films of notable directors, films of artistic merit, which have not met with the public's favour. A situation not to be passively accepted, but which certainly cannot be remedied merely by extending for one, two or five days the runs of the films in empty cinemas which have fixed overheads that cannot be reduced.[21]

The situation culminated with the passing, during 1949, of two laws. A 'small law' (*leggina*) imposed a sort of dubbing tax, requiring importers to make a *prestito forzoso*, a compulsory loan, to the Italian Government of two and a half million lire for each film in exchange for a coupon that was redeemable after ten years and transferable – I cannot even begin to go into the forms of speculation this opened up. The law was probably the best that Andreotti thought he could get out of the Americans. The 'main law' of December 1949 is called, after Giulio Andreotti, the cabinet under-secretary in charge of the cinema, the Legge Andreotti. Government subsidy remained at 10 per cent basic, but with an additional 8 per cent for artistic merit. The Legge Andreotti more or less reinstated the legislation contained in the Fascist Legge Alfieri passed in 1938, including the possibilities for censorship, as we shall see. The effects were swift: in 1949 Italian films had received 17.3 per cent of the nation's box-office takings; in 1950 they received 29.2 per cent, rising to 39 per cent in 1954. Film production doubled in the same period, from around eighty films a year in 1949 to over 160 in 1954. But the number of Neorealist films did not follow the same trend.

There are two kinds of explanations for the failure of Neorealism to thrive in Italy. One is to look for the reasons in the film-makers themselves: Rossellini's and Fellini's interest in spiritual themes; Antonioni's interest in the bourgeoisie; Visconti's theatricality; the move into comedy – all of which can be seen as the gradual development of a group of artists towards new styles and genres, and a wearing away of the barrier between Neorealist films and other, particularly popular, genres. The other explanation looks for causes in commercial, industrial and political pressures. I should like to continue the pursuit of the latter for a while.

Exhibitors and distributors were unhappy with Neorealist films because they did not make much use of well-known film stars. The star system was how films were marketed, and Neorealist films offered exhibitors little to publicise, and no guarantee whatsoever of ticket sales. Not only that, the popularity of Italian films grew as a new, post-Fascist crop of stars built up. These stars generally grew from comedy or melodrama, and as Neorealist directors became established, they built films around the genres that went with the actors. So you could say that once the crushing weight of American films had been lifted off Neorealism's chest, it found itself absorbed into a growing commercial indigenous trend – and in fact the comedies of Castellani, Emmer and Comencini (such as *Pane, amore e fantasia*, 1953, which grossed 1414 million lire) are seen as the inheritors of the remains of Neorealism. Nevertheless, this process of absorption of Neorealism took place over the corpses of an enormous number of socially and politically committed films which never got beyond the script stage.

The Legge Andreotti offered good subsidies. But in order to get the extra 8 per cent for artistic quality on top of the standard 10 per cent, the film's script, details of proposed financing, and of all the technical and artistic personnel involved had to be vetted by Andreotti's office. This was an extremely effective system of pre-emptive censorship. Suggestions for cuts and changes would be made. Andreotti's office had control over whether a film got subsidies, over whether it was to be deemed '*nazionale*', i.e. Italian, and admitted to the *programmazione obbligatoria*, and this control was used in a blatantly ideological way against Neorealist films that denounced social or political injustices. Once made, the film had to pass the censor (whose laws were those created in 1923 under the Fascist Government). If a distributor even sniffed the possibility of trouble at any of those stages, he took fright. One of the most common shackles a film might have to bear is a censor's certificate forbidding its showing to young people under 16, so cutting out a huge portion of the potential market. Films were held up by the censor, or denied export permits, and required press campaigns to get out. Projects that were rejected when a Communist was director were accepted when the producer changed personnel. I don't propose to go into details of censorship, but it was universally acknowledged to be crippling. To this picture must be added the element constituted by the Catholic Church. The Church had largely brought about the setting up of the infamous Hays Office, which had swept all socially committed and realist film-making out of Hollywood in the 1930s. In Italy it had a similar effect. The Centro Cattolico Cinematografico certified films according to the categories of *Parrocchiale* (for showing in parish cinemas), *Tutti* (suitable for all), *Tutti con riserve* (All, with reservations), *Adulti* (Adults only), *Adulti con riserve* (Adults, with reservations), *Esclusi* (forbidden). Scanning their lists I found that most Neorealist films received either E, or Ar, or A. Distributors, eager to be sure of a wide distribution, would ask for advice on ways in which films could be altered to make them more acceptable. The Church had one more weapon in its armoury against the Communist menace that Neorealism was seen as part of: its circuit of parish cinemas. The Church opened 4500 between 1945 and 1955. In a period in which the government had made legislation to curb the excessive and damaging growth of new cinema openings, the Church found no difficulty in getting the permits it needed from Andreotti, who spoke this way about the *sale parrocchiali*:

It was not enough to direct spectators towards some films and away from others. It was necessary to find ways of intervening *positively* in the various sectors of the national cinema.

A leading role fell to the ecclesiastical authorities, to whose work the State must guarantee that *freedom* that is not and has not always been accorded Catholics. There were no doubts or hesitations about identifying the necessary 'method' for giving a greater concrete efficacy to the activities of such organisations. The importance was immediately perceived of a circuit of cinemas, solid and respected, with which to influence the moral orientation of film production. And in the postwar period parish cinemas truly multiplied, to become a conditioning element in the market. . . . The weight of the one thousand, two thousand, four thousand parish cinemas gradually began to influence in a determining way the profits of distributors, and consequently of producers.

The purpose of the parish cinemas is thus affirmed through the effects of their presence.[22]

Hence, the forces ranged against Neorealism were those of the government, which wanted to suppress the films' denunciation and exposure of social ills, and to cover up the political divisions deriving from 20 years of Fascist rule; those of the Church, which were in many ways similar; those of the Hollywood majors who wanted to maintain a monopoly over the Italian cinema; distributors who refused to take risks; exhibitors who maintained that Neorealist films were not popular; a certain indifference from the Left who were intolerant of the less than Zhdanovian correctness of the Neorealists' art. Nevertheless, the films attracted attention and earned money abroad (this is partly due to the development, particularly in the United States, of the 'art house' cinema circuit, which was brought about, among other things, by the Supreme Court's Paramount anti-trust decision in 1948, and its reading cinema into the First Amendment, and the universal weariness of audiences with Hays code films – foreign films had controversial subject matter, exoticism, and a franker attitude to sex). Not only that, they were part of a movement that greatly improved the quality of Italian film-making, which then drew Italian audiences away from American films, thus enabling the Italian industry in due course to break the worst of the American monopoly. Once there were enough good Italian films in circulation, exhibitors could negotiate better hiring rates from the American companies for their films. Neorealist films played, in this sense, a crucial role in the reconstruction of Italian cinema, and this, in its turn, was an enormous source of pride for Italians who were reconstructing a sense of national worth: now their films were highly prized in the land of their conquerors, and in the Olympus of the cinema world. Neorealism can also be seen, however, as standing in opposition to establishment and reactionary political and commercial forces, and in opposition to the needs that the cinema met: for fantasy, for stars and heroes, for sentiment, for laughter. It has been argued that the large mass of the cinema-going public in Italy was not ready to embrace this new cultural function of the cinema. The successful Italian genres during the period under discussion were comic films, ironic tales of everyday life called *la commedia*

all'italiana, and the *strappalacrime*, sentimental tearjerkers of inno-
cence wronged, typified by Raffaele Matarazzo's trilogy *Catene,
Tormento, I figli di nessuno*.[23] When De Sica's *Umberto D* was
released in February 1952, Andreotti published an open letter in
the organ of the Christian Democrat Party addressed to De Sica. It
was a long letter, and I can only give a taste:

> And if it is true that evil can be combatted by harshly laying bare
> its cruellest aspects, it is also true that if people are led to
> believe – wrongly – that Umberto D's is the Italy of the
> mid-twentieth-century, De Sica will have rendered a very bad
> service to his country, which is also the land of Don Bosco, of
> Forlanini and of a progressive social legislation.
>
> It has been said in this postwar period that the cinema must
> realistically conform itself to reality, by not representing an
> unreal, false and sugar-coated society. A principle in itself
> acceptable for a certain kind of production, but always within the
> limits of balance, of objectivity and of proportion, without which
> one gets lost in the destructive paths of scepticism and of
> despair. . . .
>
> Let it not displease De Sica if we ask him never to forget this
> minimum commitment to a healthy and constructive optimism
> which might truly help humanity to advance and to hope. It
> seems to us that the international role that our director has justly
> acquired gives us the right to ask it of him, and lays upon him
> the duty of pursuing it.[24]

1954 sees the first of the really successful Italian mythological films,
Ulisse, an American co-production starring Kirk Douglas and
Anthony Quinn, directed by Mario Camerini, the man who had
directed the great satirical comedies of the 1930s, such as *Darò un
milione*, often cited as a precursor of Neorealism, with Zavattini as
scriptwriter, rooting for the poor and burlesquing the rich, and
Vittorio De Sica as the young lead star. In the same year, the
cinemas were showing De Sica's and Zavattini's first Hollywood-
style film, starring Jennifer Jones and Montgomery Clift, *Stazione
Termini*.

Notes

1. Such positions are taken by the two major historians in the field: Lorenzo Quaglietti, *Storia economico-politica del cinema italiano, 1945–1980* (Rome: Editori Riuniti, 1980); and Gian Piero Brunetta, *Storia del cinema italiano, 1945–1982* (Rome: Editori Riuniti, 1982).
2. Michael Silverman, 'Italian Film and American Capital, 1947–1951', in Patricia Mellencamp and Philip Rosen (eds), *Cinema Histories, Cinema Practices* (Los Angeles, Calif.: American Film Institute/ University Publications of America, 1984) pp. 35–46.
3. Quoted in Franca Faldini and Goffredo Fofi (eds), *L'avventurosa storia del cinema italiano raccontata dai suoi protagonisti, 1935–1959* (Milan: Feltrinelli, 1979) pp. 182–3, 153–5.
4. Ibid., p. 156.
5. See Guido Aristarco, 'È realismo', *Cinema Nuovo*, 55 (25 March 1955); and *Neorealismo e nuova critica cinematografica* (Florence: Nuova Guaraldi, 1980).
6. Luigi Chiarini, 'Tradisce il neorealismo', *Cinema Nuovo*, 55 (25 March 1955).
7. See G. P. Brunetta, *Storia del cinema italiano, 1895–1945* (Rome: Editori Riuniti, 1979); and the introductory chapter and appendices of Quaglietti, *Storia economico-politica del cinema italiano*. For an account in English, see Christopher Wagstaff, 'The Italian Cinema Industry during the Fascist Regime', *The Italianist*, 4 (1984).
8. Franco Venturini, 'Origini del neorealismo', *Bianco e Nero*, XI: 2 (February 1950).
9. See Michelangelo Antonioni, 'Per un film sul fiume Po', *Cinema*, 68 (25 April 1939); Giuseppe De Santis, 'Per un paesaggio italiano', *Cinema*, 116 (25 April 1941); Mario Alicata and Giuseppe De Santis, 'Verità e poesia: Verga e il cinema italiano', *Cinema*, 127 (10 October 1941); Alberto Lattuada, 'Prefazione', in *Occhio Quadrato* (Milan: Corrente Edizioni, 1941); Luchino Visconti, 'Cinema antropomorfico', *Cinema*, 173–4 (25 September–25 October 1943).
10. See Carlo Asti, 'Popolarità e impopolarità del cinema italiano', *Cinema Nuovo*, V, 93 (1 November 1956); Lino Micciché, 'Verifica del neorealismo', in L. Micciché (ed.), *Il neorealismo cinematografico italiano* (Venice: Marsilio, 1975).
11. See Brunetta, *Storia del cinema italiano*; Quaglietti, *Storia economico-politica del cinema italiano*; Mino Argentieri, *La censura nel cinema italiano* (Rome: Editori Riuniti, 1974).
12. Films that did very well: *Roma città aperta, Paisà, Il bandito, Anni difficili, In nome della legge, Riso amaro, Il cammino della speranza, Non c'è pace tra gli ulivi, Due soldi di speranza, I vitelloni, Senso, La strada.* Films that had a certain success: *Il sole sorge ancora, Vivere in pace, Senza pietà, Sotto il sole di Roma, Ladri di biciclette, Cielo sulla palude, Il mulino del Po, Achtung Banditi, Europa 51, Le Ragazze di Piazza di Spagna, Anni facili.* Films that did very badly: *Giorni di gloria, Sciuscià, Amore, Caccia tragica, Germania anno zero, Francesco giullare*

di Dio, La terra trema, Bellissima, Miracolo a Milano, Luci del varietà, Lo sceicco bianco, Umberto D., Amore in città, Siamo donne, I vinti, La paura.

13.   In the text I give rough figures for the numbers of Italian films produced in a given year. I give below four sets of figures for the period 1945–54, with their sources as follows:

(A) *Venti Anni della'ANICA per il Cinema Italiano, 1944–1964* (Rome: ANICA, n.d.).

(B) *Annuario del cinema italiano, 1979–1980,* ed. Centro Studi di cultura, promozione e diffusione del cinema.

(C) *Lo spettacolo in Italia* (Rome: Societa Italiana degli Autori e Editori (SIAE), annual).

(D) *Catalogo Bolaffi del cinema italiano.*

Quaglietti, *Storia economico-politica del cinema italiano,* p. 246, notes to tables, gives B and C, and favours B.

Year	A	B	C	D
1945	–	48	27	17
1946	51	62	65	43
1947	54	60	69	45
1948	57	54	49	54
1949	76	71	95	40
1950	104	92	74	93
1951	107	104	115	109
1952	148	132	141	127
1953	163	146	170	145
1954	172	190	145	164

This should illustrate the problems relating to statistics. I shall not, henceforth, give sources for all statistics, which are generally taken from the bulletins of the trade associations (ANICA, AGIS, SIAE), and sometimes at second hand from trade papers, such as *Intermezzo, L'Eco del cinema e dello Spettacolo, Cinemundus* (who quote the trade association communiqués).

14.   1st: *Cielo sulla palude* (Genina); 3rd: *Riso amaro* (De Santis); 5th: *Ladri di biciclette* (De Sica).

15.   Quaglietti, *Storia economico-politica del cinema italiano,* p. 37.

16.   Brunetta, *Storia del cinema italiano,* pp. 20–1.

17.   Alfredo Guarini, 'Il neorealismo e l'industria', *Cinema,* 123 (15 December 1953) – his address to the *Convegno di Parma sul neorealismo cinematografico.*

18.   See Brunetta, *Storia del cinema italiano.*

19.   See Tino Balio, *The American Film Industry* (Madison: Wisconsin University Press, 1976).

20.   Guarini, 'Il neorealismo e l'industria'.

21.   AGIS, *25° 1945–1970* (Rome: AGIS, 1970) p. 25.

22. Giulio Andreotti, in an article published in *Rivista del cinematografo*, quoted in Argentieri, *La censura nel cinema italiano*, pp. 87–8.
23. See Adriano Aprà and Claudio Carabba, *Neorealismo d'appendice. Per un dibattito sul cinema popolare: il caso Matarazzo* (Florence: Guaraldi, 1976). Recently, there has been a revaluation of these films, with a season on television.
24. Giulio Andreotti, an open letter to Vittorio De Sica, in the Christian Democrat weekly, *Libertas*, 24 February 1952.

5

Tradition and Social Change in the French and Italian Cinemas of the Reconstruction

PIERRE SORLIN

Cultural history is faced with a specific difficulty: the artistic forms of a given period and their relationship with the context can be described, but we are ignorant, most of the time, of what the actual practices were, to what extent contemporaries enjoyed the works we analyse and were influenced by them. The problem is even more crucial when we have to deal with short periods, such as the Reconstruction of Europe: these years witnessed a total upheaval in some sectors of the economy, a rejection of old values, a significant shift in political institutions, new trends in philosophy, literature and painting, but it would be hard to tell whether Europeans as a whole were affected by this eruption of ideas and controversies.

It is only with the development of mass entertainment that historians can find some evidence of the attitude of large audiences towards cultural objects: mass products require huge investments and their sponsors want to know if they are profit-earning. In this respect, cinema is central to any study of the Reconstruction era: we are no position to evaluate the impact (that is to say, not the literary influence but the effects on the average citizen) of Karl Mannheim's or Sartre's books, but we can say who saw (and liked?) such and such a film. Where films are concerned, we are given a chance to scrutinise, at one and the same time, changes in audience behaviour as well as in aesthetic forms.

Before the war, France and Italy, unlike Britain and Germany, had no big, American-type film companies: they produced annually as many pictures as the other countries, but these films were made by small, independent firms and the war did not change the system. Contrary to economic logic, this structural weakness served the Latin countries well: the big companies were unable to maintain a reasonable level of production and declined after 1950, whilst scores of small French or Italian firms succeeded in developing production and even topping the prewar figures. Not only was the cinema extremely popular in the two countries, but it became as well, for the first time, an object of political dispute. Rome and Paris had for a long time taken an interest in the defence and control of the studios, but merely for economic motives. In the late 1940s, however, newspapers, political parties and deputies expressed great concern for 'their' films: meetings were held, demonstrations took place in the streets. In France and Italy, the cinema had become a national problem.

What did people pay for when they went to the cinema? We shall attempt to answer this question first and this will help us to delimit the background against which film evolved after the war. It is generally admitted that important experiments were undertaken during these years: Neorealism is as much a symbol of Reconstruction as the blockade of Berlin or the beginning of the Cold War. Therefore, difficult though it is, we have to evaluate the stylistic changes which occurred in Italy, as well as the reasons why France did not develop in the same way. Despite noticeable artistic differences, the films of the two countries picture the contemporary world. We shall see how the film-makers conceived the society that surrounded them and what image they provided their spectators with.

Film exhibitors – even those born after 1950 – view the mid-century, the years that run from 1946 to 1955, as the Golden Age of their profession: from an average of 250 million a year before the war, the number of film-goers rose to unexpected heights during the Reconstruction era. An acceleration can be observed in both countries, although the trends are not strictly comparable: the growth begins earlier in Italy, goes higher and last much longer; France reaches its peak in 1947, with 430 million spectators and then stabilises for a few years slightly under 400 million. Italy tops 500 million in 1947 and attains her peak in 1955, above 800 million. We shall account for this difference later; suffice to say now that films were more popular after the war than at any other time. Yet these figures are not sufficient: they must be contrasted with those of other countries. With a comparable population (France was slightly less populated, but the gap was not very significant), the cinemas of Great Britain entertained more than 900 million spectators before the war, a figure which rose to 1600 million in 1946. The very notion of 'popularity' must therefore be questioned: before the television era, which modified the situation, films were never as popular in France or Italy as they were in Britain.

It still remains that 'something' happened in the Latin countries during the period of Reconstruction and that the nature of this change must be analysed. It is often claimed that, after going through a terrible ordeal, people wanted to enjoy life and have as much fun as possible, but there is no way of measuring such a supposed desire and the contrary argument could be advanced, rather, that people having spent years under shelter, no longer wanted to be closed in darkened rooms. Let us rely on more concrete factors: how much money was available for entertainment? Owing to the extent of physical destruction there was no scarcity of work and workers were more reasonably paid: between 1946 and 1949, wages increased more than two-fold in France and by about 50 per cent in Italy. It is hard to compare the figures, since the statistics were established on somewhat different bases in each country, but there is no doubt that more people had a job and that they earned more money than before the war. At the same time, governments, anxious to prevent inflation, did their best to freeze prices: increases in the cost of food, housing and essential articles were severely controlled; the cost of living rose from 100 to 115 in Italy, from 100 to 180 in France. But there were also very few commodities available: there was a shortage of linen, furniture, and especially individual means of transport (in 1950, there were 10 per cent fewer cars than in 1939). Theoretically, people had more liquid assets and fewer opportunities to spend them: hence their rush towards the cinemas. Unfortunately, we lack important evidence: the level and rise of prices on the Black Market; and it is difficult to tell whether the members of cinema audiences were those who had some 'excess' over what they could actually spend for their daily life, or whether they visited cinemas from other motives. Cinema and entertainment expenditures are known and we can tell how much spectators paid every year. Nevertheless, the comparison between France and Italy is likely to remain perplexing. The price increase was exactly the same in both countries – in 1950, a cinema seat cost three times as much as in 1946 – but the general advance in prices and wages was much faster in France, and the increases in the price of box-office tickets could not have the same meaning for the two societies. No direct correlation can be found between prices and attendance, and the contradictory behaviour of two nations living in relatively similar conditions demands closer examination.

The French National Centre for Cinematography, instituted in 1946 to co-ordinate activities connected with film and film-production, undertook a series of surveys to determine the habits and expectations of cinema-goers. We can thus notice that irregular attendance decreased progressively from 1947 onwards: in other words, in 1947, the public consisted of a stable nucleus of spectators who saw films as often as once a month, and of an unstable set of casual film-goers. The classic distinction between regular spectators and others was particularly relevant in this case: the latter, instead of reinforcing the former, dropped out little by little after 1947. Although the samples were not very extensive (statistics were then in their childhood), other conclusions can be inferred from the available data. Decline in cinema-going was especially marked among workers, possibly for political reasons: the Communist Party took a great interest in cinema immediately after the Liberation; it published an excellent film-weekly and showed films; with the Cold War, however, it moved to the margins of French society and began fighting the 'American invasion', the one on the screens. Another important factor is that the spectators became younger and younger: middle-aged people who used to go to the cinema in the mid 1940s stopped around 1950. Yet the percentage allocated to entertainment in household budgets increased regularly during the period of Reconstruction and after. As far as money is concerned, apart from secondary motivations such as politics, the casual film-goers abandoned the cinemas and put their francs away for vacations or to buy cars, the two often being linked. An ideal type would be a clerk, twenty-two years of age in 1945, a fellow-traveller of the PCF, used to attending films, who got married in 1947, stopped frequenting the cinemas, had two children, and bought a car in 1953.

In 1950, Italians went to the cinema on average thirty times a year, the third highest rate in the world after the Americans and the British. All classes were involved, even the workers and the peasants, and the increase in money spent on films was perfectly consistent with the increasing expenditure of lire on entertainment. The strong influence of family life must be taken into account: married couples went to the cinema with their children, parents and other relatives, and no break occurred after the age of twenty-five as in France. Needless to say, this is insufficient by itself to account for the differences between France and Italy.

Films being goods, supply must not be forgotten. In both nations, new cinemas were opened every year. Italy counted one cinema for 11,000 inhabitants before the war, one for 6000 in 1950; at that time, France had one cinema for 9000 inhabitants. The French cinemas were mostly concentrated in big cities, whereas in Italy they were spread throughout the peninsular: even in remote provinces, the peasants had the opportunity to watch films, which was not the case in France. Another difference was more important. Before the war, many people felt concerned with the development of a cinematic culture; the Vatican encouraged priests to show 'good' films in parish halls, to guard their flock against evil influences. Firmly backed up by the Christian Democrats, who monopolised power after the war, the Italian Catholics established some 3000 parish cinemas during the period of Reconstruction: anxious to compete effectively with the Communists, they projected the most popular films – westerns and comedies, which were always successful. The French Catholics were also interested in film culture, but they had no support from the hierarchy, which was engaged in other battles, such as Catholic schools and worker-priests. Most so-called 'Christian' film-shows were managed by film-buffs, who insisted more on quality than on 'rightness' or fun. These screenings were valuable for the deepening of a more sophisticated taste among the viewers, but they attracted few spectators.

Against the Church, non-Catholics were tempted to use cinema as a weapon by sponsoring film-societies. Typically, these film-societies were called 'ciné-clubs' in France, with considerable snobbish connotations at the time, and 'circles' in Italy, the most common name for any sort of friendly organisation. Again, where-as the Italian circles presented as many films as possible, the French offered mostly 'quality' works. During these years, cinemas became the most important centres of social life in Italy – all the more popular in that there were no other places where both sexes and all ages were admitted. As Pasolini recalls:

The film-theatre was decorated with posters which gleamed in the sun. In front of it there was a bar and, around it, some twenty youths. The balcony was overcrowded, people had to stand, packed like sardines, in the smell of sweat. A small baby was crying while his father had fallen asleep, owing to the heat.[1]

A reminiscence confirmed by Sciascia:

> The show-room was an old theatre and we always went to the
> balcony. From there, we spent hours spitting at the stalls; the
> voices of the victims burst out. . . . At the beginning of the love-
> sequences we started breathing loudly, as though from desire;
> even the elders did it.[2]

It would not take long to find a great many other pieces testifying
to the fact that the cinemas were highly popular places of sociabil-
ity, whereas in France they were mere theatres.

Umberto Eco, who was then under twenty, says that he became
a film-addict because of *Stage-Coach*, which, the first time he saw it,
was the shock of his life, and he is not an exceptional case: after the
Liberation, the whole of Europe welcomed US-made films. The
distributors were keen on getting Hollywood hits, since there was
no other way to fill their lists and since American films, already
paid for thanks to the national market, were cheaper than any
others. Similarly, American companies wanted to sell their products and urged the State Department to back their efforts.
Anxious to please Washington, Rome gave way to the pressure of
Italian distributors and opened up the country to American films:
Italian films were only guaranteed one out of six days screening,
and even that rule was not respected before 1950. Paris, in
contrast, began by banishing all foreign films, but after long
negotiations other films were admitted, with at least two out of five
days reserved for national productions. Year after year, the number of American films shown decreased in France, whilst it
remained at the figure of over 350 in Italy until 1960.

This is confirmed by a comparison of the data for the year 1950:

	Number of national films produced	Percentage of national films shown	Percentage of American films shown	Number of spectators
France	117	42	49	370 million
Italy	104	23	65	662 million
UK	99	19	55	1400 million

The number of spectators correlates with the number of films
available, which in turn correlates with the number of American films
in distribution. A much larger choice was offered in Britain and Italy,

which does not totally account for the attendance figures (see the difference between the two countries), but helps us to understand the slow, constant decline in the number of French spectators.

We are now in a position to draw two models of cultural practice. Initially, the conditions in France and Italy were identical: a surplus of income with respect to available goods and a fear of inflation which prevented people from putting money away. Large-scale leisure consumption thus began in the two Latin countries. The Italian exhibitors were the winners, who went through ten very brilliant years until the 1950s: a concentration of political concerns, the spread of local activities and a calculated development of film-shows provided Italians with cheap entertainment; films were enthusiastically absorbed, as long as they were not challenged by television and as long as Italians could not afford to buy other, more expensive products. In the peninsular, the 'film years' were an extensive prelude to a direct entry into mass-consumption. The same conjuncture, however, did not take place in France: the film supply was not sufficient; few people were interested in spending money in cinemas; the political attitudes were purely negative. More importantly, Frenchmen began to cautiously invest in other sectors of leisure much earlier: whereas the French shop-assistant used his car to spend a Sunday afternoon at the sea-side, his Italian counterpart rode his motorbike and took his girlfriend to the nearest cinema.

Oddly enough, these contradictory behaviour patterns did not affect film production. In France, the Left and the unions did not stop protesting against American intrusion and complaining that the national industry was being killed by Hollywood. As a matter of fact, despite their different markets and attendances, France and Italy had been producing approximately the same number of films since 1948. France quickly restored her prewar position and Italy fared comparably, notwithstanding the American competition. In both countries, the number of spectators was sufficient to finance increasing production.

'Culture' is generally studied more in terms of 'works' than in terms of practice; yet, if there were no consumers, there would be few, if any, cultural objects. Thanks to the cinema, the period of Reconstruction witnessed an impressive social change: along diffe-rent paths, the French and Italian middle classes shifted from casual and irregular to systematic leisure-expenditure. Financial instability was a causal factor in this, but it may also be suggested that the shock of the war and the confusion of the postwar period helped to modify cultural behaviour.

It might be argued that an important element has been omitted. If both France and Italy made, from 1945 to 1950, some twenty or thirty valuable films, films which can still appeal to audiences,[3] Italy distinguished itself by producing two masterpieces, *Ladri di biciclette* and *La terra trema*, together with a third, less outstanding film, *Roma città aperta*, which is the perfect symbol of the Liberation era, and also because some of the best Italian films can be clustered under the label of Neorealism,[4] whereas French films of the same period belong to no school or dominant stream. Is this in itself not sufficient to explain why the Italians were more fond of films than the French?

Again, we must turn to the statistics. *Ladri di biciclette* was a success; *Roma città aperta* brought some profits; *La terra trema* was a financial disaster and has never been released since, except in film festivals or in arts cinemas. The Italian hits of the period were first and foremost epics, according to a half-century-old tradition of Italian cinema: the most striking successes were a new version of the evergreen *Last Days of Pompei*, *The Ten Commandments* (of 1945, and not to be confused with Cecil B. De Mille's film of 1955 with the same title) and *Fabiola*, the common feature being that the three deal with religion and pleased the Church, which promoted them actively. The other popular genres were comedies and melodramas. In France, the five hits of 1949 are typical of the dominant taste: two comedies of manners, adapted from literary texts, two melodramas and a fantasy.

Although they showed concern about American films, either through enthusiasm or fear of their attractiveness, film-makers learned little from Hollywood. Visual quotations of, or references to, famous American films are to be found in a few films: *In the Name of the Law* is a tentative western relocated in Sicily, and there is an obvious endeavour towards a prolonged suspense in *The Tragic Hunt* or *Bitter Rice*. Still, the plots and characters are Italian and the hints were lost to everyone but the film-addicts. The only obvious example of American influence is the burst of detective stories in France: there was no strong tradition of thrillers before the war and the rare detective stories pictured the classical phases of an enquiry. The films made during the period of Reconstruction, which amount to one fifth of French production, are orientated towards mystery, malaise and fear, and include extensive night-scenes. However, apart from the use of artificial lighting, these works have nothing in common with the thrillers of the Bogart–Hawks generation, the clearest definition being that they never showed any form of violence.

This leads us to a characteristic shared by the two cinemas: both avoid blood. They often depict extreme feelings, paroxysms of hatred in familial or social relationships, but injuries or crime fade out. *Germany Zero Year*, which pictures a crime and a suicide, was a total failure, and successful films dealing with conflicts, such as *In the Name of the Law* or *Tomorrow is too Late*, introduce elements of struggle but smooth them away quickly. A few famous pictures, *Roma città aperta*, *Paisà*, *La Bataille du rail* and *Les Portes de la nuit*, might lead one to believe that war and Resistance were common themes, but those were exceptional films. In each country only fifteen films evoked the underground war against the Germans, and their number decreased along with the passing of the years. The same happened in the aftermath of the conflict: the characters in *Sciuscià* or *The Tragic Hunt* have been unsettled by the war, but those of *Ladri di biciclette* or *Riso amaro* simply suffer misery or unemployment, which existed before, and after, the conflict.

Besides comedies, melodramas, epics and thrillers, little room was left for Neorealism, which was an exciting attempt to modify the rules of the cinematic art but nevertheless remained rather marginal. It was not a 'school', not even a grouping of friends. In the 1920, the adjective 'Neorealist' served to designate, very loosely, texts aiming to describe day-to-day life with no recourse to fictional heroes: it was a vacant signifier which found its significant when critics began imposing the term on a few novels and larger set of films, but the directors who were thus lumped together had little in common. Journalists got in on the act: their polemics, in fact, to a large extent helped to create the notion, made it exist as a label. Screenwriter Zavattini said in 1953: 'Neorealism has perceived that the most irreplaceable experience comes from things happening under our eyes, from natural necessity.'[5] This sounds good, but the reference to 'simple things' was understood, in the late 1940s, in totally different ways. In Italy, the Church strongly opposed Neorealism because it ridiculed Catholics (those pious wealthy who, in *Ladri di biciclette*, force beggars to attend a mass before granting them a piece of bread and some soup) and gave a 'depreciating vision' of Italy. On the contrary, the Left praised it: by staging ordinary people, by showing their problems in the precise manner of documentaries, Neorealism was meant to criticise capitalism and trigger class-consciousness. While the Italians equated Neorealism with an understanding of social reality, the French critics developed a different interpretation: mostly Catholics, they did not care for the presentation of the Church; controversies were then harsh between Existentialism and Personalism, the non-sense or the tragic sense of human existence; Neorealism provided Catholics with a metaphysical image of human-beings faced with loneliness – by refusing heroes, the new cinema was supposed to express the very essence of life.

These opinions do not call for debate: they are simply pieces of history. However, it is necessary to understand them in their context. The debate, which began early, was almost entirely concentrated upon De Sica's *Ladri di biciclette*, whose script had been written by Zavattini, because the Church hated the film and wanted it to be censored. Other Neorealist films and, more important, the rest of Italy's film production, were ignored. *Ladri di biciclette* was credited with three innovations which were, by inference, extended to Neorealism as a whole: the main character is not an actor, he is a worker, a 'real protagonist of everyday life'; the 'banal' story (a worker has found a job which requires the use of a bicycle; he has his bike stolen and hunts for it throughout Rome), transfigured by the film, becomes rich and complex; minute aspects of Rome are objectively described.

These arguments have been endlessly reprinted from book to book since 1950. We are not concerned here with the debates carried out during the period of Reconstruction itself and we are able to observe the problem from a distance. De Sica recruited non-professional actors, but most Neorealist film-makers preferred stars, such as Anna Magnani, Silvana Mangano, Vittorio Gassman, and other directors, like Bresson, whom nobody would ever label Neorealist, opted also, in, for example, *Journal d'un curé de campagne*, for non-professionals. The plot of the majority of neorealist films, including those of De Sica, is not different from the story told in average melodramas: the latter generally stage 'simple stories', whereas the former do not ignore the most trite devices of the traditional theatre (in *La terra trema*, for example, the Good Man, who is poor, is doomed to failure: his sister becomes a whore, his girlfriend betrays him for the Bad Man, who is evil and humiliates the loser). As for the documentary aspect, that was the only important cinematic inheritance of Fascism, which had sponsored the Luce Institut, a first-class school of short film-making. The documentary sequences in Neorealist films are more often than not directly borrowed from patterns established by the *Luce* before the war. The French and Italian social dramas, be they Neorealist or not, were highly interested in contemporary life. There were, of course, tremendous stylistic differences, but, as far as plots and locations were concerned, there were no consistent contrasts.

It is therefore appropriate to compare, from a cinematic point of view, sequences taken from two films. I have chosen *La Ferme du pendu*, of 1945, and *Il camino della speranza*, of 1950, because both show the life of a remote village and the arrival of the coach. In the latter, the village is seen in long shot, from outside, with no relation to any of the inhabitants: angles and framing change with every shot, but the spectator is never provided with those small clues which link every shot to the previous one and give the sequence its apparent necessity. When the coach enters the screen, we wonder whether it is only part of the setting or an element of the plot, and the camera follows it at length without answering the question. In *La Ferme du pendu*, the village is a mere background: every shot is centred on a character who meets another character and starts talking. Before entering the coach, we see, on the screen, a few men who tell us that a coach is expected and that its arrival is of importance for the fiction. To put it another way, 'classical' films give priority to the plot whose logic and continuity are involved in the minutest detail. *La Ferme du pendu* contains a twelve-minute sequence which is an excellent documentary on a rural wedding in 1945; yet even here, the characters do not stop to speak and behave in order to communicate to us more information about the narrative. 'Classical' films cannot unfold without constant references to causes and consequences, the most important motivations being of a psychological order and inducing the viewers to think that they 'understand' the personality of the characters.

Neorealism ignores psychology. When the bicycle is stolen in De Sica's film, we get no hints as to the worker's state of mind: we simply witness his immediate, erratic reactions. People's actions are reduced to their functional aspect and are never separated from the surroundings: the worker tracks his thief in the middle of the crowd; he disappears and reappears; we understand what he is doing without being able to follow him closely. The setting does not seem empty or uninteresting, as is often the case with 'classical' films; its density compensates for the otherwise excessive presence of the characters. Instead of being a rectangle which frames the actors, the screen is treated as a surface open to various uses. Hence, the above-mentioned screening of the village: people, objects, places irrelevant to the story are explored by the camera because they are part of the background. Space is exploited for its visual and plastic potentialities: sometimes, as in *Il camino della speranza*, the editing-process induces the variations; more often, people move and give the background its depth. In many respects, the Neorealist films are itineraries, journeys through a portion of land: *Ladri di biciclette* takes us from central Rome to the suburbs and back; *The Tragic Hunt* makes us visit the Po Valley; *Il camino della speranza* leads us from Sicily to Piedmont. Yet the important thing is not the accurate description of various landscapes, but the autonomy of these scenes in relation to the plot. Of course, the settings are not chosen at random; they correspond to the location of the story, but the representation of streets, fields and so on does not help to develop the fiction: it intervenes like a break in the continuity of the narrative. This introduces, in the spectator's mind, an unfamiliar impression, another feeling of passing time. The experience of a plot-empty time is never pushed as far as it is in *La terra trema*, where long shots of (generally beautiful) land-scapes are moments of filmic pleasure (there are still pictures and sounds) outside the leading strand of the story. It is no wonder that spectators used to uninterrupted flows of action did not welcome the Neorealist films: they could easily cope with the despair of a poor worker provided it was packaged in a non-stop succession of events. Neorealism was basically an experiment, an attempt to promote another rhythm and to exploit the shape as well as the perspective depth of the screen, instead of limiting it to the figuration of a narrative. It had no follow-up and died away at the beginning of the 1950s, at a time when new experiments were already in progress. During the following decades, many film-makers said they owed it a great deal: is there a link between it and the new Italian cinema of the late 1950s or the New Wave? Directly, none; but Neorealism obviously contributed to challenging the tradition of psychological, uninterrupted fiction which still pre-vailed in the mid 1950s.

Original though it was, Neorealism belonged to its period; it pictured mid-century Italy, which was also extensively represented in other films. For historians, fiction remains a valuable source of evidence which documents different visions of social life. The screened world is not the actual world, but it is not unreal either: it is made up of bits borrowed from reality and reorganised so as to provide the spectators with an interpretation of life. Lots of stories filmed during the period of Reconstruction take place in the capital cities, Rome and Paris. It is amazing, nowadays, to observe the car-free streets, to see that the worker in De Sica's film cycles so easily from his far-away block of flats to the centre; conviviality is not yet an empty word; friendly relationships exist between neighbours; social celebrations – mostly weddings and funerals – are attended by everybody. Still, the same vision had already been pictured before and during the war: until the late 1950s, cinema kept describing pre-megolopolistic towns. Now, if we list the possible locations, we perceive a specificity of the late 1940s: the country-side, which was previously less often represented than the cities, has its revenge. On the screen, Italy and France are half-urban, half-rural. Films give us excellent, documentary-like images of rural techniques: hoeing, ploughing, harvesting. The equipment is totally unsophisticated; farm-work is equated exclusively with manual labour; the farmers are obsessed with the necessity of finding workers and the latter, although exploited, nevertheless know how to resist their employers. This cinematic vision is obviously distorted: the emphasis on rural conflicts serve to dramatise the fictions, and the almost total silence about industry, seldom pictured, and limited to its most archaic sectors – mines and railways – show how biased the film-makers were. Are these films, then, valueless for historians? They must not be taken as sociological surveys, but as images based on factual observations. The cinematic vision is partial: it does not fit with the plans and political programmes orientated towards industrial reconstruction, but it does coincide with statistics revealing the shortage in rural manpower and the predominance of agricultural income. Films are not neutral: they reveal the likely unconscious beliefs of many people who did not conceive of Reconstruction except in terms of the cultivation of the land. They also illuminate two different conceptions of the countryside: the French farm, in *La Ferme du pendu*, is a smallholding run by the father, with the help of the mother, their children and a worker; the Italian farm is a large estate in the Po Valley, which attracts scores of temporary workers during the summer. In cinematographic terms, France ignores her big farms, and Italy forgets her huge majority of small rural exploitations. These representations must be referred to old models: the dream of a democracy of small-farm owners inherited from the Revolution, in France; the myth of independance linked to big estates that prevailed at the end of the Risorgimento in Italy. We must be careful to separate these records of history from the visual documents: we can gain useful information from the films, but it is framed in an interpretation of the present borrowed from the past. Film-makers look at the world in which they live with the glasses of their grandfathers.

Yet society changes, a fact that the cinema cannot ignore. Melodrama is the test of that transformation. Classically, it staged well-off characters momentarily reduced to misery and oppressed by other rich people. This contrast of wealth with poverty no longer worked in 1950: in France, melodrama declined; in Italy, it gave way to a renewed drama, inaugurated by a massive hit, second only to epics, *Chains*. In this film, the protagonists are middle-class people, a garage owner and his family. The man works alone; he would like to improve his business but, clearly, he does not even think to ask for a loan from a bank, so he has recourse to a private individual. Though he lacks capital, he is not hard up: he has a large, well-furnished flat, one child, lots of friends, a great deal of fun, an easy life. On the screen, princes, farm-workers and bicycle thieves are slowly fading out.

Film is an art, a way of mixing and matching expressive materials. As such, it did not change during the period of Reconstruction: Neorealism experimented with a new treatment of time and space and produced a small number of films highly appreciated by film-amateurs, but it did not modify the rules of classical narration. Film is also a form of popular entertainment: the period of Reconstruction did not witness a modification of dominant taste. Society had to evolve first; the cinematic images would follow; in terms of representation, the late 1940s stuck to traditional modes. But, because of films, the importance of leisure in private expenditure was transformed. Was this a limited change? The rush towards cinemas led the French and the Italians to modify, within an extremely restricted period, their relation to money; at the time, no other form of consumption was likely to produce the same evolution and, in this respect, cinema was of critical importance for the late 1940s.

Notes

1. Pier Paolo Pasolini, *Una vita violenta* (Turin: Einaudi, 1979) pp. 82–3.
2. Leonardo Sciascia, *Gli Zii di Sicilia* (Turin: Einaudi, 1964) p. 14.
3. The major films of the period in France and Italy were as follows:

	France	Italy
1945	*La Ferme du pendu*	*Roma città aperta*
	La Bataille du rail	
1946	*Le Diable au corps*	*Sciusià*
	Les Portes de la nuit	*Paisà*
	Panique	*Il Bandito*
	Martin Roumagnac	*Vivere in pace*
1947	*Dédé d'Anvers*	*Caccia tragica*
	Quai des Orfèvres	*Anni difficili*
	Jour de fête	
1948	*Entre onze heures et minuit*	*Germania anno zero*
	L'Armoire volante	*Nel nome della legge*
	Une si jolie petite plage	*Ladri di biciclette*
	Manon	*Il mulino del Po*
		Rizo amaro
		Senza Pietà
		La terra trema
1949	*Manèges*	*Una domenica di Agosto*
	La Beauté du diable	*Non c'è pace tra gli ulivi*
	Les Enfants terribles	*E primavera*
	Au Royaume des cieux	
1950	*Dieu a besoin des hommes*	*Catene*
	Justice est faite	*Miracolo a Milano*
	Journal d'un curé de campagne	*Il camino della speranza*
		Domani e troppo tardi

4. Much has been written on Neorealism, but more on the twenty or thirty films labelled as 'Neorealist' than on the relationship between Neorealism and other films or with Italian audiences. A list and analysis of the most important films is to be found in Roy Armes, *Patterns of Realism* (New York: A. S. Barnes, 1971; London: Tantivy Press, 1971).
5. Quoted in Christopher Williams, *Realism and the Cinema* (London: Routledge and Kegan Paul, 1980) p. 30.

6

Humanism and National Unity: the Ideological Reconstruction of France

MICHAEL KELLY

For fully fifteen years after the Second World War the dominant ideological tendency in France was Humanism, revolving around the central notion of man. For most of the Fourth Republic Humanism was so much taken for granted that it came to function as a touchstone of value, recognised by all competing ideologies, wholly uncontroversial, and scarcely even acknowledged as ideological until the theoretical onslaughts of the 1960s. I hope to show how this Humanist dominance of postwar France developed in the specific circumstances of the Liberation as an ideological framework within which to reconstruct the political unity of the French nation, and within which to conduct the struggle for control of its postwar destiny.

The nature of ideology has been the subject of intense debate in recent years, and many different accounts are available. The view with which I shall work is that ideology is a field of ideas and representations acting both cognitively, to form more or less coherent conceptual frameworks, and socially, to articulate the interests and objectives of more or less extensive groups. This view of ideology enables a link to be drawn between France's profuse, interpenetrating intellectual movements, and the complexities of postwar French history. The ideological reconstruction is to be seen both as a process of cultural and intellectual reconstruction and as an integral part of the process of political and social reconstruction of France as a whole.

Humanism, as a specific ideological framework, will therefore be approached in its historical development. The purpose will be to show how it arose, what kinds of discursive strategies it made possible and how these were connected with the rebuilding and reunification of the nation. Humanism did not, of course, spring suddenly from the air in 1944. The circumstances of the Liberation provided it with ideal conditions for growth, but the groundwork for this surge was laid during the prewar and Occupation periods.

Up to the late 1920s, Humanism in France meant largely the great rediscovery of classical learning that took place in Europe during the fifteenth and sixteenth centuries. However, during the early 1930s, tendencies emerged among Catholic educators to argue for a renewal of teaching in the Greek and Roman classics, to be accompanied by some modern Humanities taken from the literary canon, and given a distinctively Christian emphasis.[1] The idea was taken up by younger Catholic philosophers like Emmanuel Mounier and the *Esprit* group, who programmatically declared the need to 'Remake the Renaissance'.[2] Jacques Maritain, neo-thomist philosopher and inspiration of the nascent christian democratic movement, developed the notion further in his *Humanisme intégral* of 1936, which became the standard reference work for socially conscious Catholics, and has frequently been reprinted since that time.[3] Canon Masure expressed it succinctly: 'Humanism is the will to be man in all perfection'. And in Christian terms, perfection could only be aspired to by an opening to God and an imitation of Christ.[4]

A somewhat less assertive version of Humanism had long been present, at least intermittently, in the Socialist movement. Derived from Ludwig Feuerbach and the German Social Democrats, Humanism as a brand of ethical Socialism had been handed down through Jean Jaurès to leading Socialist Party intellectuals like Charles Andler and Léon Blum. Andler, a professor at the Collège de France, published a volume of essays in 1927 under the title *L'Humanisme travailliste*, calling for a new programme of popular education.[5] Léon Blum, the Popular Front Prime Minister, distilled his views into his wartime book *A l'échelle humaine*,[6] which exercised a great deal of influence in postwar France. This current of Socialism was given a considerable impetus in the late 1920s and early 1930s by the publication for the first time of Karl Marx's early writings, especially the Paris Manuscripts of 1844, which were heavily marked by Feuerbachian Humanism. Some young Communist intellectuals, such as Georges Friedmann, Henri Lefebvre and Norbert Guterman were drawn towards a Humanist Marxism as a result, and undertook a re-examination of classical culture, ancient and modern, in that light.[7]

In the two years before the election of the Popular Front Government of 1936, the French Communist Party (PCF) began to adopt Humanist themes. Inspired by the efforts of leading left-wing writers Romain Rolland and Henri Barbusse, the Communists began to see the value of a Humanist approach in building a national movement on a broad platform of anti-Fascism and social progress. Paul Vaillant-Couturier played a key role in promoting this vision of man and the nation, energetically supported by major figures like the former Surrealist Louis Aragon and novelist André Malraux.[8]

These two strands of Humanism undoubtedly contributed considerably to the ethos of the Popular Front movement, but their ideas were rarely echoed in conservative circles, and even in circles close to the Popular Front they were not unanimously welcomed. Roquentin's devastating attack on the various examples of Humanism in Sartre's *La Nausée* is a peremptory reminder of how little unanimity existed.[9] Paul Nizan, from a Marxist perspective, was at the same period denouncing the duplicity of existing forms of humanism.[10]

On an international scale there were other Pro-Humanist pressures. Stalin's slogan, 'man, the most precious capital', introduced Humanist notions into the Communist movement at the period of the Second Five-year Plan.[11] The flagging League of Nations attempted to develop a 'new Humanism' through its intellectual co-operation programme.[12] And the exigencies of a broadly based popular defence programme against Fascism gradually made Humanism a rhetorical rallying point of the anti-Fascist movement.

After the ambiguities of the 'phoney war' period, the fall of France in 1940 effectively muzzled most of the proponents of Humanism, at least at a public level. The National Revolution of Vichy and the New Europe of the pro-Nazis were programmes of exclusion. The cultural and ultimately physical eradication of whole sectors of the population could not sit easily with a broadly inclusive Humanist discourse, though some attempts were made to project Hitler's racialist conception of the 'new man' as a kind of Humanist ideal.

The one branch of Humanism which did retain a public voice was Catholic Humanism. This was to be a decisive point. Taking advantage of the régime's ambiguities, and expressing themselves with great caution, influential Humanist-inclined prewar reviews continued to appear, at least for a period, under Vichy. These included Emmanuel Mounier's *Esprit*, Stanislas Fumet's *Temps présent* (renamed *Temps nouveaux*) and the Jesuit fathers' *Études* (renamed *Construire*). A new review of Catholic social studies was founded in Marseille in early 1942 under the title *Economie et humanisme*, which continued virtually uninterrupted until 1959. Books were less available, but from early 1941, the Dominican Irénée Chevalier's short *vade mecum*, *Humanisme chrétien*[13] was in circulation and later Adrien Ferrière's *Libération de l'homme*[14] conveyed a similar spiritualist and personalist Humanism. A good deal of the Catholic activities in the Vichy youth movements were based on Humanist aspirations, and the influential Ecole des cadres at Uriage aimed explicitly at 'a complete Humanism'.[15]

In Resistance circles, Humanist ideas generated around the Popular Front provided not only a common discourse but also a powerfully motivating one. A battle waged on behalf of *l'homme* or *les hommes* was capable of inspiring extremes of dedication and heroism. It is perhaps no accident that the first coherent movement of Resistance was the one based in the Musée de l'homme, which provided the first Resistance martyrs. The Resistance poets developed the notion of *l'homme* into a rallying call, as in Louis Aragon's clandestine poem of 1943, 'Prélude à la Diane française', which begins:

> L'homme où est l'homme l'homme L'Homme
> Floué roué troué meurtri
> Avec le mépris pour patrie
> Marqué comme un bétail et comme
> Un bétail à la boucherie.[16]

An approximate translation is:

> Man where is man man Man
> Swindled beaten wounded bruised
> Contempt now his native land
> Branded like a steer and like
> A steer to the slaughter led.

The linking of *l'homme* and *la patrie* in this stanza is characteristic of the close interweaving of Humanist notions with the themes of national liberation and national unity. The poem ends by evoking the battle of Valmy, a much-repeated symbol of the victorious French nation.[17]

The elaboration of a common doctrine of man, leading to an agreed programme of action for the Liberation and beyond, was a constant preoccupation of the various clandestine movements, pursued through study groups, one of which took the name 'Humanisme et Action' (Humanism and Action), and eventually in association with Gaullist circles in London and Algiers.[18] Its fullest expression can be found in André Hauriou's book *Vers une doctrine de la Résistance: le socialisme humaniste* (Alger, 1944). Hauriou, an academic lawyer, was delegate of the metropolitan Resistance at the Provisional Consultative Assembly in Algiers. His argument was that the Resistance had two positive objectives – liberty and Socialism – which could be brought together in a Humanist Socialism: 'between historical materialism and absolute voluntarism, Humanist Socialism claims, not to choose between them, but to go beyond them'.[19] He went on to develop a detailed programme of government guided by this ideal, premissed on an independent France, standing between the capitalist West and the Communist East, and finding its own distinctive, creative synthesis. Hauriou claimed, with some reason, that his majestic vision represented a broad range of Resistance thinking, and certainly if his social and political programme was rapidly overtaken by events, his ideological framework proved surprisingly hardy.

The ideological conditions of the Liberation were beginning to emerge clearly in the summer of 1944. The Resistance, rallying round an agreed charter modelled on the Popular Front programme, was adopting a Humanism in which social democrats and Catholics could feel at home, and to which other forces, particularly Communists and nationalists, could more or less subscribe. On the other side of the divide, the *ultras* of collaboration were degenerating into an increasingly destructive and self-destructive rhetoric, amply reflected in the deeds of their military and paramilitary wings. Vichy, reduced to a rump, began to split into diehards and opportunists. The latter, easily a majority, fled for the most part under the copious skirts of Mother Church. Joining the *attentistes* and other 'workers of the eleventh hour', they found that Christian Humanism had kept a foot in both camps and offered a very convenient ideological lifeline. Hence, when the liberation of Paris marked symbolically, though not yet materially, the end of the Occupation, very little ideological adjustment took place. Certainly, the *ultras* and the more prominent *vichyssois* ideologists were constrained to a temporary silence, but the potential vacuum was soon filled by the blossoming discourse of Humanists of every ilk, eagerly seizing their opportunity.

Humanism did not become an immediate watchword. The first few weeks, in late August and early September of 1944, were dominated by the liberation of the nation, by the swift punishment of traitors, and by the possibilities of revolutionary change.[20] The latter possibilities, being quickly ruled out by the Provisional Government, were replaced by concerns for the unity of the nation.[21] In the first year after Liberation, the issue of punishment for traitors was a major area of political contention, posing as it did the issue of how far the unity of the nation could require the incorporation into the new social order of either former collaborators or the legal and social structures of Vichy. It was in relation to this thorny nexus of issues that the values of Humanism were mainly invoked in the early Liberation period.

Though the daily newspapers and the radio liberally used the buzz-words *l'homme*, *les hommes* and *l'humanisme*, it was in the reviews, and to a lesser extent in books that the terms were defined, refined and fought over. The Catholic Left played the leading role in establishing the ground. *Témoignage chrétien*, having come out of clandestinity in August, carried a homily in its fourth issue from Mgr Saliège, the only Catholic archbishop with a Resistance record. In a piece entitled 'Vocation de la France', Mgr Saliège declared: 'To increase man's responsibilities, to enable him to accept them for himself and master them, that is the true Humanism'.[22] This was, of course, a coded message that the Church would resist extensive State intervention, especially in the form of educational reforms which might take back too many of the benefits Vichy had bestowed on Catholic education. The point, though, is that the discourse of Humanism was being established as the language in which important issues were discussed, and in particular issues involving questions of continuity with Vichy.

Esprit, the first monthly review to reappear, had a foot in both the Social-Democratic and the Christian-Democratic movements. It saw an opportunity for its personalist Humanism to exercise decisive influence and from its first issue began a debate on the rewriting of the Declaration of Human Rights.[23] This was a Humanist gesture by any token, but also one which harked explicitly back to the founding document of the First Republic, and proposed the re-establishment of national unity on a new personalist conception of man.

Temps Présent, directed by Stanislas Fumet, had much in common with *Esprit* and *Témoignage chrétien*, but strong links with traditional nationalism – Charles de Gaulle was a paid-up 'Friend of *Temps Présent*' before the war.[24] Highly defensive about the Church's wartime activities, it argued for the inclusion in the nation of Vichy Loyalists,[25] and for the building of national unanimity,[26] a project which it tried to implement through the formation of a broad organisation, *L'Amitié française* in early 1945.[27] Humanist terminology percolated gradually into *Temps Présent*, and by November it could headline a series of feature articles 'We must rebuild with man in mind'.[28]

The autumn and winter of 1944 saw the widespread distribution of writings originally produced in clandestinity, and expressing the same concern for *l'homme* and *les hommes*. An entire collection, dominated by the socialists, took the title 'Défense de l'homme'. Jacques Maritain's works written in New York were made available, with titles like *Les Droits de l'homme et la loi naturelle* [The Rights of Man and the Natural Law], (Paris, 1945) and *Principes d'une politique humaniste* [Principles of Humanist Policy] (New York, 1944).

In early 1945 the Socialists began to identify their position explicitly as a Socialist Humanism. The MLN leader Philippe Viannay was an early proponent,[29] strongly supported by Jean Lacroix, the philosophy columnist of *Le Monde*.[30] The intention was to establish a broadly based movement subscribing to a sufficiently all-inclusive common doctrine. Lacroix argued that Socialism, rejuvenated by Humanism, could bring together such diverse strands as Christian Humanism, *travaillisme* (labourism), Liberal Socialism, and Humanist Marxism. While the Socialist component of this new synthesis was concerned with common action in the social and political fields, he saw the Humanist component as an aspiration for broad access to culture. 'Now, culture is what we receive, precisely, from the nation, which can also be defined as a cultural environment. If Socialism wants to be Humanist, it has to begin by demanding culture for everyone.'[31] The relationship between Humanism and national unity is presented in terms of participation in a national culture. The same general themes were taken up extensively in Léon Blum's *A l'échelle humaine* (Paris, 1945) which was largely written in a Vichy prison. Hence, it became clear by the spring of 1945 that Social Democrats and Christian Democrats were broadly at one in subscribing to a Humanist Socialism.[32]

The formula had benefits for both sides. Laying particular emphasis on the term Socialism, the SFIO Socialists were able to present it as the spirit of the Resistance, with themselves as the authentic voice of that spirit. They were able to claim the prestigious label 'issu de la Résistance' (born of the Resistance), at the same time as offering the same ideas and strategies as before the war. Robert Verdier, assistant general secretary of the party, writing in the spring of 1945, declared bluntly: 'Traditional Socialism is in our view sufficiently "Humanist" for it not to need any doctrinal revision.'[33] The inclination of the Socialists to serve up the old wine in new bottles was pointed out by, among others, the Catholic commentator Jean Emmenecker, who ironised:

> Then, of course, there is the *Humanism* of Léon Blum ('changed finally by eternity into Jean Jaurès!'). Humanism is now the current term; one might equally say Moralism or Realism. His book *L'Echelle humaine*, the speeches at Montrouge and Sceaux, the address to congress are all literally dripping with Humanism.[34]

Emmenecker spoke from a tradition which was well accustomed to moralistic and idealistic language, and was often striving to shake it off in favour of the more hard-nosed language of social transformation and struggle. If, as it appears, Socialist Humanism enabled the Socialists to steal the Catholics' intellectual clothes, it was a gesture the Catholics amply reciprocated.

As a formula, Socialist Humanism had enormous advantages on the Catholic side. Inevitably, the emphasis was on the humanist dimension, which enabled Catholic writers to argue that a *thoroughgoing* Humanism (*humanisme intégral*) necessarily involved a transcendental, spiritual dimension in order to be complete.[35] From this standpoint, humanism could be used as a virtual synonym for Catholicism. René d'Ouince, editor of the conservative Jesuit review, *Etudes*, declared: 'Truly, no doctrine is as ambitious for man as Catholic doctrine, which venerates in man the image of God.'[36] Clearly, this was a form of Humanism which did not necessarily require fundamental changes in Catholic thinking. So Paul Alpert's book *Economie humaniste* (Paris, 1945) was a reworking of Catholic social encyclicals. The Dominicans' review *Economie et humanisme* undertook similar research. Furthermore, if Catholicism were accepted as real Humanism, then it immediately became possible to attack other currents of thought for being insufficiently Humanist. This was done particularly in the cases of Marxism and Existentialism, where it was argued principally that an atheist Humanism was unsustainable. As Jean Daniélou put it: 'Atheist Humanism is self-destructive. There can be no real Humanism without a foundation in something beyond man.'[37]

From a practical point of view, the Humanist label provided an ideological umbrella for many Catholics of a more traditional stamp. Those whose wartime situation had been, like that of the Church itself, highly ambiguous, were given a moral language in which to express attitudes which could not be stated politically. Hence, without making a potentially dangerous political defence of Vichy and collaboration, it was possible to offer a defence on moral and human grounds. Even if such a defence did not exonerate past activities, it could at least abate the various forms of sanction they might incur. In this way, Humanism opened the door to allow people who had 'backed the wrong horse' under the occupation to be reintegrated into the nation. Part of the price was that Humanism was often a flag of convenience, cynically invoked.

More positively, however, the Humanist orientation also provided a point of contact between Catholics and the political and intellectual movements of the Left. Over time, it permitted many rapprochements which eventually bore fruit, not least in the rethinking of Catholic theology and social doctrines in the light of Marxism.[38] Humanism also provided a fertile soil for the innovative work of Teilhard de Chardin, attempting to synthesise the biological sciences with Christian cosmology. His major work *The Phenomenon of Man* was completed at this period, and though unpublished during his life, its contents were partially known in manuscript form and through speeches and articles.[39]

If the Catholics and the Socialists provided the core of the new dominant ideology, the other two main currents of thought emerging from the Resistance, Marxism and Existentialism, were gradually drawn into it.

Notwithstanding the spirited resistance to Humanism of Sartre's Roquentin, the Existentialists marked out their postwar positions on the basis of *l'homme*. The watchwords of *L'Etre et le néant* were assertions about man: from 'Man is the being through whom nothingness comes into the world'[40] to 'man is a futile passion'.[41] *Les Temps Modernes* continued the same language in its keynote articles. Francis Ponge contributed ringing declarations to the effect that 'Man is a god who does not know himself'[42] and 'Man is the future of man'.[43] Simone de Beauvoir described the humanising project of Existentialism as follows: 'To reconcile morality and politics is to reconcile man with himself; it is to declare that at every moment man can accept himself totally'.[44] The attempt to bring morality and politics together was thus confirmed as a central human (and humanist) aspiration. It might be remarked in passing that the founder of modern feminism was at this period speaking quite unselfconsciously about man and men, without raising the issue of how far these terms were marked by their gender. The male emphasis of Humanism was undoubtedly linked to the postwar drive to return women to the home and to occlude their key role in the war, notably in the Resistance. When the question of gender was broached by Humanist writers, it was usually dimissed with some coy comment to the effect that 'the masculine embraces the feminine', or otherwise treated as self-evidently irrelevant.

Attacked particularly by Catholics on the moral grounds of abasing man,[45] the Existentialists replied by strengthening their Humanist emphasis. Beauvoir replied that their philosophy was one which 'places its trust in men'.[46] Sartre replied with the celebrated lecture at the Club Maintenant, published under the unambiguously assertive title *L'Existentialisme est un humanisme* [Existentialism is a Humanism]. The English translation of the text carries the more non-committal title 'Existentialism *and* Humanism'. It is true that he later tried to disavow the text, but its thrust does reflect the intense ideological pressure which whipped Existentialism willy-nilly into the Humanist camp.

Similar pressures were at work among the Communists. The attempt to maintain unity among the Resistance forces drew heavily on the Humanist spirit of the Popular Front. However, there were many Marxists who had no time for what they regarded as dewy-eyed Humanist waffle. The rationalist inclined review *La Pensée* was of this persuasion, and tended to see Humanism as a mystifying tactic promoted by the Church for largely reactionary ends. Henri Lefebvre, the most prolific Marxist writer of his generation, was of an opposite view. His widely distributed text of 1939, *Le Matérialisme dialectique* became almost a standard primer of Marxist theory, presenting a very Hegelian Marxism which took its goal to be the attainment of *l'homme total*.[47] Somewhere between those opposed positions, Pierre Hervé found himself having reluctantly to accept the Humanist tag because it was beginning to be synonymous with admission into the nation. In a response to *Esprit*'s enquiry into Humanist Socialism he complained:

> They talk about Humanist Socialism. Fine, so long as it is understood that Marxism is a Humanism . . . But every time they talk of a liberal, French, or Humanist Socialism, you get the distinct impression that there is an unspoken polemic. The truth is, they have it in for Communism.[48]

This complaint, amplified in Hervé's polemical book *La Libération trahie* (Paris, 1945), reflects the marginalisation of the Communists, like the Existentialists, within the national Humanist consensus. Georges Cogniot implicitly acknowledged the same process in his address to the PCF's tenth congress. Calling for an intellectual renaissance, he described France as 'Humanism's own chosen country', and saw Humanism as a unifying movement centring on the values of human dignity, freedom and reason.[49] The unity of the nation, based in a common culture, was the explicit goal of both Cogniot and Hervé. In both cases, whether they liked it or not, their efforts had to be channelled through Humanism. For Communists, this was both a strategy of national unity and the price of their own acceptance into the nation, an acceptance which was beginning to be contested, as Blum's jibe about the PCF being a 'foreign nationalist party' was increasingly linked with criticism of the Marxist account of man.[50]

With the Existentialists' and Communists' submission to the Humanist frame of reference during the course of 1945, Humanism flourished virtually unchecked. Its rapid spread can be gauged from the plethora of books published in 1946 with some variant of *l'homme* or *l'humanisme* in their title: *L'Humanisme du XXe siècle* ['Humanism of the Twentieth Century', André Ulmann], *L'Humanisme agissant de Karl Marx* ['Karl Marx's Humanism in Action', Luc Somerhausen], *Du marxisme à l'humanisme* ['From Marxism to Humanism', Jacques Rennes], *L'Humanisme: essai de définition* ['Humanism: An Attempted Definition', Robert Fernand], *Machine et humanisme* ['Humanism and Mechanisation', Georges Friedmann], *L'Homme est révolutionnaire* [Man is a Revolutionary', Georges Izard], *Style d'homme* ['Man's style', Daniel Perrot], *L'Homme libre, ce prisonnier* ['The Free Man, this prisoner', André Lang], *Les Grands appels de l'homme* [Man's High Callings',

André George *et al.*], *Tous les hommes sont mortels* ['All Men are Mortal', Simone de Beauvoir], *Les jeunes devant l'humanisme intégral* ['Youth and complete humanism', Edward Montier], *Humanisme et prière* ['Humanism and Prayer', Louis de Lavareille SJ], *Humanisme et sainteté* ['Humanism and Sanctity', Charles Moeller], *Perspectives d'humanisme militaire* ['The Military Humanist Outlook', Lieut.-Col. Xavier de Virieu], and, of course, *L'Existentialisme est un humanisme* (Jean-Paul Sartre), which was followed within a few months by Jean Kanapa's *L'Existentialisme n'est pas un humanisme* (Paris, 1947).

As these last two titles remind us, there were from the end of 1945 many and bitter polemics between Existentialists, Communists, Socialists and Catholics of various political and theological colours. Divisions were fuelled by such issues as the new constitution, education, colonial policy, the treatment of collaborators, and other contentious matters. But the dissentions were almost entirely contained within, and expressed through, the common discursive framework of Humanism.

The existence of this common frame of reference was an expression of the successful reconstitution of a single French nation, where the wartime divisions might have hardened into more entrenched oppositions. Its first achievement was to draw the cadres and supporters of Vichy into the new post-Liberation order, throwing the veil of national reconciliation over a dubious past. Only a small minority of French people could have felt their wartime activities to be without ambiguity and above reproach. Among Catholics especially, there was a strong incentive to 'forgive those who have trespassed against us', in the hope of obtaining similar clemency themselves. But they were not the only ones to embrace the new Humanism for what it allowed to remain unspoken. The alacrity with which it was so widely embraced is a measure of Humanism's success as a holding operation at the level of ideas and values, in the relative absence of stable social and political structures. It acted as an ideological bond, helping to cement the nation together during the first year and a half after the Liberation. Thereafter, it slowly settled into a less obtrusive presence as the context of presuppositions for the developing struggles of the later 1940s and 1950s.

The ideological marriage of Catholic moral doctrine and ethical Socialism gave postwar French Humanism its distinctive characteristics, though other currents of thought also contributed something of their own. To a large extent this dominant ideological mix reflected and expressed the balance of political forces throughout the Fourth Republic. It helped successive administrations to maintain political stability within the Centrist coalition, and to hold the excluded forces, notably the Communists and Gaullists, in a posture of loyal opposition. Only after the collapse of the Fourth Republic and the consequent realignments did Humanism itself come under serious challenge. And when that challenge came, it arose in the *Université*, to use the more inclusive French notion, that is, in the institutions of education, which in 1944–5 had been entrusted with the mission of producing and reproducing the Humanistic culture in which the nation could recognise itself.

With the benefit of forty years of hindsight, it is not difficult to see that the Humanist consensus of 1945 was a provisional and defensive one. On the one hand, it successfully amputated the excrescence of Fascism and incorporated all other forces within the nation. But on the other hand it also damped down class divisions and blocked many far-reaching proposals for social reform. The uniting and conserving power of Humanism stems from its assertion of our common membership of the species. It provides a moral high ground from which to condemn the treatment of some fellow beings as less than human, or to protest against the threat of planetary extinction. On the other hand it also provides a global alibi with which to excuse a vast spectrum of misdeeds, or to forestall any but the most timorous of social advances. In Liberation France it was the language of restoration, recovery and reconciliation. It may not have been very adventurous or very heroic, but it enabled the nation to lick its wounds and get back on its feet again. It was a strategy of survival: that is the historical reality. The question of whether, in the circumstances, France could have done any better, must remain in the realms of historical speculation.

Notes

1. The Catholic fortnightly *Foi et vie* undertook a substantial enquiry, directed by Paul Arbousse-Bastid, and published under the title 'Pour un humanisme nouveau', in March–April 1930.
2. Emmanuel Mounier, 'Refaire la Renaissance', *Esprit*, 1 (October 1932) pp. 5–51.
3. Jacques Maritain, *Humanisme intégral* (Paris: Aubier, 1936). A new edition was published in 1947.

4. Chanoine Eugène Masure, *L'Humanisme chrétien* (Paris: G. Beauchesne, 1937) pp. 186–91, in particular p. 187.

5. Charles Andler, *L'Humanisme travailliste: Essais de pédagogie sociale* (Paris: Bibliothèque de la Civilisation française, 1927). The volume contained speeches and articles from 1919 to 1921.

6. Léon Blum, *A l'Echelle humaine* (Paris: Gallimard, 1945).

7. See Georges Friedmann, *La Crise du progrès: Esquisse d'histoire des idées, 1895–1935* (Paris: Gallimard, 1936) which went into many editions. Friedmann also directed a collection for the PCF publishing-house *Editions Sociales Internationales*, under the title 'Socialisme et culture', which included studies of major figures in European culture, aiming to identify 'their contribution to the great currents of Humanism and Socialism', as the blurbs put it. See, for example, the blurb on Paul Nizan's *Les Matérialistes de l'antiquité* (Paris: Editions Sociales Internationales, 1936).

8. This period is well documented by David Caute, *Communism and the French Intellectuals* (London: André Deutsch, 1964), and Nicole Racine, *Les Ecrivains communistes en France, 1920–1936* (Paris: Editions Sociales Internationales, 1973). I am indebted to Dr Margaret Atack for emphasising the PCF's role.

9. Jean-Paul Sartre, *La Nausée* (Paris: Gallimard, 1938). See the 'Folio' edition, pp. 165–7. Roquentin, in the process of deriding the different varieties of Humanism, recognises their capacity for integrating even antagonistic views and attitudes, and concludes: 'I don't want them to integrate me, I don't want my fine red blood to help fatten his lymphatic beast: I won't be so foolish as to call myself "anti-Humanist". I just *am not* a humanist, that's all' (p. 167).

10. Paul Nizan, 'Sur l'humanisme', in *Paul Nizan, intellectuel communiste 1926–1940*, vol. II (Paris: Maspéro, 1970), pp. 32–7. The essay was first published in *Europe* in 1935. Nizan wrote: 'Historically, Humanism has been essentially a mythology. It made promises to a universal man who was but a figment of the mind, promises which could not be kept: there was among the Humanists a duplicity which was less a matter of their intentions than a history's recalcitrance' (p. 32).

11. The Second Five-Year Plan began in 1933, after a period of preliminary discussion, during which Humanist notions were promulgated.

12. The International Institute for Intellectual Cooperation of the League of Nations held yearly conferences during the 1930s. The Budapest meeting, from 8 to 11 June 1936, addressed the promotion of a new Humanism. See the special number of *Bulletin de la Coopération Intellectuelle*, 75–6 (March–April 1937) pp. 95–129, entitled *Vers un nouvel humanisme*, with contributions from Thomas Mann, Paul Valéry, Georges Duhamel, J. Huizinga, Jean Piaget, among others.

13. Irénée Chevalier, OP, *Humanisme chrétien* (published by Castermann, dépôt légal, September 1941).

14. A. Ferrière, *Libération de l'homme*, 2nd edn (Geneva and Annemasse: Editions du Mont-Blanc, France, 1944). This book, like that of

Chevalier, who taught at the University of Fribourg, confirms the importance of neutral Switzerland in supporting the propagation of Catholic personalist and Humanist ideas. The Swiss section of the *Esprit* group, including Albert Béguin and Denis de Rougemont, played a significant role in this regard.

15. There are many studies of Uriage, the most useful of which are the special numbers of the *Revue d'histoire de la deuxième guerre mondiale*, in October 1964, on Vichy youth policies, and in January 1966 on Catholic movements under the Occupation. The school was a leadership training institute, aiming to form the next generation of the country's elite, and sponsored in the early stages by Vichy before being closed down. Many of the staff and students joined the Resistance and became prominent in postwar public life.

16. Louis Aragon, 'Prélude à la *Diane Française*', in Ian Higgins (ed.), *Anthology of Second World War Poetry* (London: Methuen, 1982) p. 59. The poem was first published clandestinely in *L'Honneur des poètes*, edited by Paul Eluard and published in July 1943 by Les Editions de Minuit.

17. At the Battle of Valmy, in September 1792, the French Revolutionary forces overcame Prussian and Austrian armies for the first time, to shouts of 'vive la nation!'.

18. See H. Michel and B. Mirkine-Guetzévitch, *Les Idées politiques et sociales de la Résistance* (Paris: P.U.F., 1954); and H. Michel, *Les Courants de pensée de la Résistance* (Paris: P.U.F., 1962).

19. André Hauriou, *Vers une doctrine de la Résistance: le socialisme humaniste* (Algiers: Editions Fontaine, 1944) p. 95. Historical materialism here refers to the Marxism of the Communists, while absolute voluntarism refers to the nationalism of De Gaulle.

20. Revolutionary expectations were widespread, even in moderate publications. *Combat* took the subtitle: 'De la Résistance à la Révolution'; *Temps Present* entitled an editorial: 'L'Heure révolutionnaire', in its edition of 15 September 1944; *Témoignage chrétien*, on 14 October 1944, had a feature entitled: 'Vers la révolution sociale'. *Action*, the Communist weekly, sponsored a vivid poster, placing 1944 in the continuity of 1789, 1848 and 1871, though it was banned by the Provisional Government.

21. See André Mandouze, 'Nous avons rompu, nous saurons unir', *Témoignage chrétien*, 9 September 1944, p. 1. The themes of national unity and revolution coexisted for a period, the former coming to predominate over the latter during late 1944 and early 1945.

22. Mgr Saliège, 'Vocation de la France', *Témoignage chrétien*, 30 September 1944, p. 1.

23. See Emmanuel Mounier, 'Faut-il refaire la Déclaration des droits de l'homme?', *Esprit*, December 1944, pp. 118–27. The discussion continued in the review until the May 1945 issue.

24. See Stanislas Fumet, 'Charles de Gaulle, ami de *Temps Présent*', *Temps Présent*, 26 August 1944, p. 2.

25. See Gabriel Marcel, 'Hiérarchie des fidélités', *Temps Présent* 8 September 1944, p. 6.

26. See Jean Lacroix, 'Socialisme et unanimité nationale', *Temps Présent*, 8 December 1944, p. 8.

27. From 9 March 1945, the magazine carried the subtitle: 'Organe de l'Amité française'.

28. 'Il faut reconstruire en pensant à l'homme', *Temps Présent*, 24 November 1944, pp. 4–5. The articles dealt with various aspects of rebuilding destroyed areas.

29. See Indomitus, *Nous sommes des rebelles* (Paris, 1945). Indomitus was Viannay's Resistance pseudonym, and the book was published in the 'Défense de l'homme' collection. The MLN (Mouvement de Libération Nationale) was a small Resistance movement.

30. See Jean Lacroix, 'Socialisme humaniste', *Esprit*, May 1945, pp. 857–64; and his *Socialisme?* (Paris: Editions du Livre français, 1945).

31. Jean Lacroix, *Socialisme?*, p. 66.

32. See the editorial, 'Humanisme socialiste', *Temps Présent*, 28 September 1945, p. 1. It argued in particular that the Socialist Party and the MRP were now virtually indistinguishable.

33. Robert Verdier and Pierre Stibbe, 'Socialisme humaniste', *Esprit*, April 1945, p. 691.

34. Jean Emmenecker, 'Socialisme et contre-révolution', *Temps Présent*, 31 August 1945, p. 4.

35. See Jean Mouroux, *Le Sens chrétien de l'homme* (Paris: Aubier, 1945).

36. Rene D'Ouince, 'A Nos lecteurs', *Etudes*, January 1944, pp. 8–9.

37. Jean Daniélou, 'H. de Lubac: Le Drame de l'humanisme athée', *Etudes*, May 1945, p. 275.

38. See R. P. Chenu, 'L'Homo oeconomicus et le chrétien: réflexions d'un théolgien à propos du marxisme', *Economie et humanisme*, May–June 1945; Jean Daniélou, 'La Vie intellectuelle en France: communisme, existentialisme, christianisme', *Etudes*, September 1945, pp. 241–4.

39. Pierre Teilhard de Chardin, *Le Phénomène humain* (Paris, 1955). It was not published during the author's lifetime owing to the opposition of the Jesuit order to which he belonged. Written between 1938 and 1940, it was reworked after the war, and the 'avertissement' is dated March 1947. See also his article 'Hérédité sociale et l'éducation', *Etudes*, April 1945, pp. 84–94, in which he argues: 'For the Christian Humanist – loyal therein to the most reliable theology of Incarnation – there is now no independence or disharmony, but rather a coherent subordination, between the genesis of mankind in the world and the genesis of Christ, through his Church, in mankind' (p. 92).

40. Jean-Paul Sartre, *L'Etre et le néant* (Paris: Gallimard, 1943) p. 60.

41. Ibid., p. 708. See also his: 'Présentation des *Temps Modernes*', in *Situations*, II (Paris: Gallimard, 1948) pp. 9–30, which opened the first issue of *Les Temps Modernes* in October 1945. Rejecting notions of human nature, he argued that 'man is only a situation', but one which is 'lived and transcended towards a particular goal' (p. 27), and declared pragmatically: 'our review will devote itself to defending the autonomy and the rights of the human person' (p. 28).

42. Francis Ponge, 'Notes premières sur l'homme', *Les Temps Modernes*, October 1945, p. 68.
43. Ibid., p. 75.
44. Simone de Beauvoir, 'Idéalisme moral et réalisme politique', *Les Temps Modernes*, November 1945, p. 266.
45. See, for example, Jeanne Mercier, 'Le Ver dans le fruit', *Etudes*, February 1945, pp. 232–9, which concludes: 'Ambiguity of the demonic and the divine. Derisoriness of this infra-human man. There is for the Christian something satanic in this blasphemy. There is for man something ignoble in this betrayal of the spirit' (p. 249).
46. Simone de Beauvoir, 'L'Existentialisme et la sagesse de la nation', *Les Temps Modernes*, December 1945, p. 404.
47. Henri Lefebvre, *Le Matérialisme dialectique* (Paris: P.U.F., 1940), especially pp. 145–65. See also his *Le Marxisme* (Paris: P.U.F, 1948) pp. 36–48, in the popular paperback 'Que sais-je?' series.
48. Pierre Hervé, 'Un "socialisme humaniste"?', *Esprit*, February 1945, p. 409. These discussions must also be read in the context of negotiations on the possible unity of the Socialist and Communist Parties which continued into late 1945.
49. Georges Cogniot and Roger Garaudy, *Les Intellectuels et la Renaissance française* (Paris: Editions du P.C.F., 1945).
50. See Gaston Fessard, S.J., *France, prends garde de perdre ta liberté* (Paris: Editions du Témoignag e Chrétien, 1945). The issue is discussed in Ronald Tiersky, *French Communism 1920–1972* (New York and London: Columbia University Press, 1974) and in Max Adereth, *The French Communist Party: A Critical History (1920–1984)* (Manchester: Manchester University Press, 1984).

7

Les Lettres Françaises and the Failure of the French Postwar 'Renaissance'

NICHOLAS HEWITT

It is a feature of the Occupation of France and the Resistance movements which it subsequently engendered that so much of the conflict was carried out in cultural and literary terms. With the French lacking, until the very end of the Occupation, very much in terms of concrete political or military power, the realm of ideas and expression achieved an almost disproportionate importance. For the German occupying forces, it was essential, as Pascal Ory demonstrates in *Les Collaborateurs*, to immediately convey to the French a sense of continuity and normality, and one key feature of this operation was the importance accorded to writers, journalists, dramatists, artists and film-makers as the guarantors of a certain continuity in French culture.[1] Hence the vital significance for the Germans in maintaining established publishing-houses and prestigious reviews, such as the *Nouvelle Revue Française*, albeit in its guise of Drieu la Rochelle's *Nouvelle Nouvelle Revue Française*, and of fostering overtly collaborationist literary and intellectual journals such as *Je suis partout* and *La Gerbe*. Within the diverse Resistance movements, it was no less important to assert the independence and resilience of French culture, through clandestine newspapers, such as Camus's *Combat* or D'Astier's *Libération*, or through more specialised, exclusively literary, publications, such as Pierre Séghers' *Poésie* series, produced in the Southern Zone, in Villeneuve-lès-Avignon. On both sides, however, the procedure was essentially the same: to lay claim to the continuity of the French cultural tradition and to look forward to a new vision of France and Europe. For the Resistance writers, as indeed for its politicians, this dual vision, depending upon recuperation of the past at the same time as speculation about the construction of the new civilisation, constituted a central ambiguity of the entire undertaking and in many ways led directly to a falling-short of its ideals.

Within the plethora of literary and intellectual publications which emerged from the obscurity of the Resistance to the open market of the Liberation, *Les Lettres Françaises* occupies a unique place. It was the major cultural and intellectual journal which came out of the Resistance, published immediately as an eight-page 'grand format' weekly newspaper, on the lines of the prewar *Marianne* or the Occupation *Je suis partout* or *La Gerbe*, and with an initial print-run of 235,000 copies,[2] which put in on a level with major daily newspapers, such as *L'Humanité*, *Le Figaro* and *France-Soir*.[3] It owed its initial success to its privileged position as the official mouthpiece of the Comité National des Ecrivains, the major grouping of Resistance writers and intellectuals, and, from 1944 to 1948, it served as the dominant forum for intellectual and artistic debate in France, with an unrivalled range, both in terms of contributors and subject-matter. Its first non-clandestine number of 9 September 1944, set out clearly its perception of its role, as a custodian of the memories of the Occupation years and as a pioneer in the construction of the new France:

This first number of *Les Lettres Françaises*, appearing in the full light of freedom, will attempt to present the record of our activities during the last four years.

Tomorrow, our weekly will be the reflection of a liberated France, of that new life for which we have fought.

All possible subjects (theatre, cinema, art, music, fashion, etc.) will be covered.[4]

As such, *Les Lettres Françaises* was conceived of as an authentic expression of a new French 'Renaissance', encompassing political life, urban redevelopment and a whole range of cultural activity, which was seen, in the early days of the Liberation, as the legitimate reward and goal of the Resistance. Yet, within just over three years, that vision, in which artist and society were inextricably involved, in which eclecticism and debate were central, had become soured and *Les Lettres Françaises* had become a sectarian Communist Party journal, one of the many weapons in the Party's arsenal for the battle of the Cold War, along with *La Pensée*, *Europe*, *Arts de France* and *Action*.[5]

What makes the case of *Les Lettres Françaises* so important is that its evolution from openness to sectarianism within the space of three years is indicative of what happened to the French 'Renaissance' in general in the years immediately following the Liberation, in which so much experimentation and debate were stifled. In the first place, the journal was the victim of general economic conditions in the first years of the Fourth Republic which helped to wipe out a large proportion of Resistance publications. Secondly, it was no less the victim of the effects of the Cold War, from 1946 onwards, which not only polarised political opinion and helped to freeze out the middle ground, but which drastically altered the internal policies and perceptions of the *Parti Communiste Français* itself. At the same time, whilst most historians pay attention to *Les Lettres Françaises* only insofar as it exemplifies Communist Party hegemony in the late 1940s, many of the journal's problems were of its own making and stemmed directly from its Resistance origins. The constant concern to claim legitimacy from the Resistance experience, to hark back to the years from 1940 to 1944, was by no means without intellectual or, particularly, aesthetic implications. Similarly, the function of the journal as the official organ of the CNE, concerned particularly with the *épuration* of writers and publishers, in its three *listes noires* of Autumn 1944 and in its acerbic comments and condemnations contained traditionally on its second page under the rubric 'Des Vérités nécessaires', began to operate against the editorial eclecticism: as Paulhan was to notice very rapidly, such procedures were hardly different from denunciations in the collaborationist press under the Occupation, and *épuration*, once begun, opened the doors to the later exclusion of any writer. Finally, *Les Lettres Françaises* fell victim to the Resistance, and collaborationist, habit of claiming legitimacy from a certain notion of French culture which often itself militated against innovation and experimentation: the journal was particularly keen to invoke in its defence a number of highly traditional French intellectual and literary figures and its very concept of the new 'Renaissance' was narrowly utilitarian and rationalist. In other words, an examination of the first four years of non-clandestine production of *Les Lettres Françaises* helps to explain, not merely the external forces militating against the initial openness of Resistance writing, but also the internal ambiguities which meant that it was often less innovative than many of its European counterparts.

The history of *Les Lettres Françaises* has been well-enough recorded in intellectual accounts of the period, although almost exclusively used to support the thesis of gradual PCF hegemony over cultural activity.[6] The journal stemmed from the Comité National des Ecrivains, set up in 1941 by Jean Paulhan and the Communist former editor of *Commune*, Jacques Decour, with Jacques Debû-Bridel, Charles Vildrac, Jean Guéhenno, Jean Blanzat and the R.P. Maydieu.[7] To help set up *Les Lettres Françaises*, Decour was joined by a former colleague on *Commune*, Claude Morgan, a fellow-Communist who had just returned from a prisoner-of-war camp in Germany, and whose father was the permanent secretary of the Académie Française, Charles Lecomte.[8] Preparations for the first number were disrupted in February 1942, with the arrest, and subsequent execution, of Decour, together with Georges Politzer and Jacques Solomon, and the texts had to be destroyed. Thereafter, Morgan found himself in a curious position: due to the clandestine organisation of the CNE, whilst he had worked closely with Decour, he had never met other members of the committee, particularly the co-founder of *Les Lettres Françaises*, Jean Paulhan. It was only in July 1942 that Pierre Mauchent, a permanent official in the PCF, who owned his own Roneo machine, placed Morgan in charge of the delayed first number, which eventually appeared on 20 September 1942. At the very beginning of the journal's history, therefore, its key editorial personnel were Communist, as was the control of its production, albeit in some ways as the result of circumstances, and this helps to explain why the PCF continued to regard *Les Lettres Françaises* as part of its cultural empire, even when, until the winter of 1947, it was officially independent.

It was the return of Edith Thomas to Paris in the Autumn of 1942 which put an end to Morgan's solitary task of producing *Les Lettres Françaises* single-handed and ushered in a new phase of the journal's existence. Knowing both Claude Morgan and Paulhan, she was able to bring them together for the first time and to set up a full editorial committee with Debû-Bridel, Guéhenno, Vildrac, Blanzat and Vaudal, which met regularly, from January 1943 onwards, in her apartment at 15, rue Pierre Nicole. Throughout 1943, the organisation was rapidly expanded to include figures such as Mauriac, Sartre, Camus, Eluard and Queneau, with the benevolent, if unofficial, help of Georges Duhamel, to the extent that Claude Morgan could later comment: 'It was only in February 1943 that *Les Lettres Françaises* began to really become the living mouthpiece of the Comité National des Ecrivains.'[9] At the same time as the committee's membership expanded, the technical quality of *Les Lettres Françaises* was greatly enhanced by the recruitment, in October 1943, of George Adam, a former journalist with the Communist evening paper *Ce Soir*, who had access to a professional printer. Thereafter, the review appeared as a printed large-format newspaper, with an initial print-run of 12,000 copies, broadening its scope in the last months of the Occupation by incorporating René Blech's two specialist reviews, *L'Ecran Français* and *La Scène Française*, two areas in which it was to be particularly strong after the war, and even producing a 100-page *Almenach des 'Lettres Françaises'*.[10]

When the review appeared for the first time in liberated Paris on 9 September 1944, it bore the inscription:

> Founded by Jacques Decour (shot by the Germans) and Jean Paulhan.
> Director: Claude Morgan.
> Editor: George Adam.

Thereafter, it ran through two phases, Adam's editorship, from 9 September 1944 to 25 October 1946, and that of the poet Loys Masson, from 15 November 1946 to 8 January 1948, before coming under direct PCF control with the editorship of Pierre Daix. From 15 January 1948 onwards, the review only bore the heading:

> Founder: Jacques Decour.
> Director: Claude Morgan.

Paulhan had become a non-person; Masson, the last independent editor, had been sacked; *Les Lettres Françaises* was no longer the eclectic, experimental journal of the immediate postwar period.

Undoubtedly, under the editorship of George Adam, *Les Lettres Françaises* benefited hugely from the experience of a professional journalist, both in its last year of clandestinity and in its first two years as a freely-available newspaper. Whilst on the staff of *Ce Soir* before the war, Adam had been a close friend of Nizan's and dedicated his novel of 1944, *L'Epée dans les reins*, 'To the memory of my friend Paul Nizan, killed by the enemy on the 23 May 1940 at Audruicq (Pas-de-Calais)',[11] an act which was not to endear him to the Communist Party after the Liberation. Claude Morgan records that it had always been Adam's ambition to edit a full-blown newspaper and it was towards this aim that he directed his energies as soon as he began collaborating with the clandestine *Les Lettres Françaises*. In peacetime, Adam oversaw the transition of the journal from a publication still marked by its polemical, clandestine experience, to a general arts review of a much broader appeal. Whilst editor, he managed to increase the paper's technical quality, expanding it in the course of 1946 from eight to ten pages, although this was later cut back in the following year, and making increased use of photographs and line-drawings. In short, by the time Adam left the editorship in October 1946, *Les Lettres Françaises* had acquired an immeasurably more modern layout than the ex-Resistance journal which first appeared in September 1944.

In terms of content, *Les Lettres Françaises* from 1944 to 1946 was remarkable for the number and variety of its contributors and for the range of its subject-matter. The journal retained throughout its early postwar period, and indeed throughout most of its career, a fixed format: the front page was devoted to major articles or serialisations, often continued inside, and to Claude Morgan's editorial; the second page was made up of 'Des vérités nécessaires', a collection of short news items or pieces of gossip, mainly drawing attention to the ineffectualness of the *épuration* and calling for punishment for former collaborators; the rest of the journal was then equally divided between fiction, either in the form of short-stories or serialised novels, and general arts news and reviews. The back page was devoted in part to the women's section, first called 'La Vie féminine', then 'Si belle en ce miroir' and finally 'Souvent femme varie'. In these pages appeared the dominant figures of the CNE: Claude Aveline, Georges Duhamel, Jean Guéhenno, Michel Leiris, Jean Paulhan, Raymond Queneau, Jean-Paul Sartre, Edith Thomas and Vercors. Most noticeable was the policy of serialisation: not only were French novels, such as Queneau's *Loin de Rueil* or Elsa Triolet's *Le Premier accroc coûte 200 francs*, published at length, but also works by foreign, mainly Anglo-Saxon authors: Hemingway, H. E. Bates, Steinbeck and Saroyan. Equally important was the role of the reviews section, particularly in the non-literary domain: the cinema was covered first by Roger Leenhardt and then by Georges Sadoul, fine art by André Lhôte and music by Georges Auric. In these reviews there was considerable openness to foreign production and to innovation: Leenhardt and Sadoul looked particularly towards the

American cinema as indicating a new direction in film-making; Georges Auric wrote sensitive and complex articles on Modernist composers such as Prokofiev and Hindemith. In the area of painting, there was more uncertainty: Henri Serouya provided a long article on Soutine, but with regard to Cubism both Louis Parrot and André Lhôte were considerably more circumspect. At the same time, whilst expressing certain reservations regarding Cubism in general, and Picasso in particular, Lhôte stressed strongly the independant and apolitical nature of art and defended it against those who tried to recuperate it for political purposes.[12]

This receptivity to Modernism, innovation and artistic independence, however, was considerably less marked in the field of literature, despite early publication of a fragment of Sartre's *Le Sursis* and the serialisation of *Loin de Rueil*. The dominant subject-matter for French short stories and serialised longer fiction was the immediate past and particularly the exploits and sufferings of the Resistance, and this tended to imply traditionalism in narrative form. At the same time, the book reviews, whether by Max-Pol Fouchet or Louis Parrot, concentrated on the celebration of the major literary figures emerging from the Resistance, in hagiographical rather than critical form. Similarly, in the realm of literature, there was little concern in *Les Lettres Françaises* under Adam's editorship with innovation: rather, the review was at pains to stress the continuity of French writing under the Occupation, in the form of reports on clandestine literary production and the work of French writers in exile and, most important of all, evocations of the great literary martyrs of the period 1940–4, Saint-Pol Roux, Max Jacob, Robert Desnos and Saint-Exupéry. Indeed, throughout the first months of the journal's career, great stress was laid on the return of writers to Paris, either from exile in the south or from further afield, particularly the Americas, who guaranteed, not a radical break and a new beginning, but a return to the forms of writing so rudely interrupted by the German invasion of May–June 1940. Similarly, when looking back at the past, *Les Lettres Françaises* chose to celebrate those figures who embodied the most accessible, most conventional and often the most rationalist aspects of the French cultural tradition: the Pantheon of French writers included Anatole France, Voltaire, the Alexandre Dumas of *Les Trois Mousquetaires* and Zola, but not Baudelaire, Flaubert, the Symbolist poets or Proust. In short, in the early *Les Lettres Françaises*, literature, particularly fiction, was viewed in a different way from film and painting and, to a lesser extent, theatre, and was expected to conform to more traditionalist and rationalist lines. At the very beginnings of the review, therefore, were the seeds of the dispute which was to break out in 1947 over the concept of Socialist Realism.

Nor was the review's status as a potential forum for innovation and experimentation aided by its obsession with the process of *épuration*, the exclusion, if not punishment, of those writers, journalists and publishers who were deemed to have collaborated with the Occupiers. This is not to deny that such a concern was entirely legitimate, not least in the months immediately following the Liberation. What made it problematic, however, was its own internal contradictions and its increasingly retrograde nature as France progressed into the Fourth Republic: two years after the Liberation, the repetition, in the 'Des vérités nécessaires' section, of the same complaints at official appointments of ex-collaborators, however justified, or the same lamentations in Claude Morgan's editorials that the *épuration* was not working, testified increasingly to an attempt to hang on to the past, to retain legitimacy in the experience of the Occupation and to refuse to enter a society which was rapidly changing. Nor could it be said that the policy of literary *épuration* was in any way consistantly applied, not least by the review itself. The three CNE 'listes noires', published in *Les Lettres Françaises* on 9 September, 16 September and 21 October 1944, were in fact remarkably indulgent as far as creative writers were concerned: only glaring and extreme offenders were cited, such as Céline, Brasillach, Rebatet, Drieu la Rochelle, Abel Hermant and Abel Bonnard, and in most cases these were figures who had occupied positions in the government or the media under the Occupation. Writers who regularly published their literary work in notorious collaborationist journals, such as Dorgelès, Mac Orlan, Marcel Aymé and Anouilh, appeared on none of the lists, even though they suffered some disapproving remarks in the Resistance press. Indeed, the case of Aymé, who published regularly in both *La Gerbe* and *Je suis partout* throughout the Occupation, illustrates how difficult it was to be included on the 'listes noires': after detailed debate at a meeting of the CNE, at which Claude Morgan himself reluctantly voted for Aymé's inclusion, the novelist nevertheless escaped mention on any of the three blacklists.[13] Similarly, if a writer were included on one of the 'listes noires', he could be rehabilitated, as was the case with Pierre Benoît, who appeared on the first list, against the advice of Morgan, but was 'rayé de la liste noire' in November 1946.[14]

At the same time, *Les Lettres Françaises*, in its effort to establish the continuity of French writing and to constitute as broad a church as possible, was remarkably lenient to many writers whose record in the period 1940–4 was highly dubious and, indeed, acted as a means by which those writers were able to re-establish their reputations. This process of 'dédouanement' was particularly true in the case of a writer like Dorgelès, who contributed regularly to *Gringoire* throughout the Occupation but returned to respectability with an article on the massacre at Marsoulas in *Les Lettres Françaises* in December 1944.[15] Gide attempted to rehabilitate himself in the same way, after a blameless if cosy war, with an article on 'La Délivrance de Tunis', but this backfired when Aragon, still bitterly hostile after the betrayal of *Retour de l'URSS*, complained publicly to the review.[16] The most conspicuous case of rehabilitation, albeit posthumous, was that of Giraudoux, who died in mysterious circumstances just before the Liberation and who, in spite of the notably authoritarian tenor of *Pleins pouvoirs* of 1940, was treated to a highly respectful article in September 1944 on his last writings which claimed him as yet another martyr of French literature and enrolled both him and *Pleins pouvoirs* into the Resistance camp.[17]

Finally, as Paulhan was to recognise very rapidly, along with Schlumberger and Duhamel, the constant concern with *épuration* militated against freedom of expression, had unpleasant overtones of the immediately previous regime and helped pave the way for the subsequent process of 'exclusions' within the ranks of Communist intellectuals and writers, one of the major victims of which was Adam's successor as editor of *Les Lettres Françaises*, the poet Loys Masson.

Adam's last number of the review was on 25 October 1946. There then followed a two-week interregnum until 15 November, when the editor was named as Masson. Of all the minor victims of the Cold War in France, Loys Masson was one of the saddest; as Claude Roy recalls: 'The most melancholy of all those whom I knew who had been banished from the Garden of Eden was certainly Loys Masson'.[18] He was, by any standards, an unusual figure in French literary circles: born and brought up on the British island of Mauritius, he had shown an early talent for poetry and, thanks to the generosity of his friends, was able to come to Paris. With characteristic bad timing, he arrived in the French capital just

before the Germans in 1940 and immediately moved south, joining
Pierre Séghers' *Poésie* group in Villeneuve-lès-Avignon, where
Claude Morgan met him in 1942. Under Morgan's patronage,
Masson, who had joined the PCF, moved back to Paris after the
Liberation and began contributing to *Les Lettres Françaises* during
George Adam's editorship.[19] During his own period as editor of
the journal, from November 1946 to December 1947, he showed
considerable flair, building upon Adam's professionalism and
creating a genuinely lively and pioneering newspaper. This
concept of left-wing journalism, however, by mid to late 1947, no
longer coincided with the intellectual policy of the PCF, and it was
Masson who was made the scapegoat for the financial difficulties
in which *Les Lettres Françaises* found itself. As his successor, Pierre
Daix, acknowledged later, the victimisation of Masson was quite
unjustified: 'It was unfair because, on the contrary, he did bring to
his newspaper a certain style, but a literary one, a humorous one.
Every week, he published an anthology, drawn throughout
Europe, of the best work of the great cartoonists'.[20] The loss of his
post as editor of *Les Lettres Françaises* was a blow from which he
never recovered, and he gradually parted company from the PCF:

> He had sung 'Mother Revolution' . . . But Mother Revolution had
> shown herself to be a hideous hag, and whilst the good Catholics
> cautiously let Loys pray by himself in a low and lonely chapel, he
> was forced, step by step to distance himself from the apron-
> strings of Mother Revolution, to draw away when Stalin attacked
> Yugoslavia and to leave for good when Rajk was hanged.[21]

As Claude Roy sums up his fate: 'He died of a broken heart, like so
many of our comrades',[22] although Claude Morgan is more specific: 'Loys felt alone . . . So he killed himself'.[23]

Under Masson's editorship of *Les Lettres Françaises*, however, the
journal became a genuinely international cultural review. Daix's
political condemnations: 'They produced a general interest magazine, in which only Morgan's editorial presented any Communist
element',[24] whilst accurate on one level, also points to an attempt
on the part of Masson to take *Les Lettres Françaises* in a new and less
overtly partisan direction. One form which this attempt took was a
breaking-away from the domination of the Occupation period and
the *épuration*: under Masson, the 'Des vérités nécessaires' section
became much shorter and concerned with more contemporary,

often Third World issues, although the issue of the *épuration* was never entirely absent, as evidenced by the debate on Paulhan's resignation from the CNE in March 1947. At the same time, Masson maintained the review's interest in the United States and American culture, although with increasing reservations as the Cold War began to bite. As Daix suggests, one of Masson's most important innovations was the creation of a whole page of cartoons, with no political content whatsoever, under the rubric: 'Rire!', at the end of the journal. Nor were these cartoons merely restricted to European artists: many were drawn from American publications, especially the *New Yorker*.

Quite clearly, in one sense, Masson was attempting to reduce the partisan polemical content of the newspaper and to turn it into what Daix dismissively refers to as: 'an inoffensive weekly, which added one or two drops of red to the fashions of the literary cafes'.[25] The real crime, in the eyes of the PCF, however, was not the apparent depoliticisation of *Les Lettres Françaises*, but the assertion of its political, ideological and literary independance within the Left. In this respect, the model was clearly Vittorini's *Il Politecnico*, which enjoyed the same fraught relationship with the Italian Communist Party as *Les Lettres Françaises* was begining to do with the PCF. One of the most significant publications under Masson's reign as editor, therefore, was the interview, on 27 June 1946, with Vittorini, undertaken by Edgar Morin and Dionys Mascolo, writing under the name of Jean Gratien.[26] In this interview, although Vittorini attacked common enemies, such as Sartre and Camus, his defense of cultural independance and his attack on 'obscurantism' was anathema to the PCF and a major step on the path to total Communist control of *Les Lettres Françaises*.

Yet the issue which contained the Vittorini interview showed how far *Les Lettres Françaises* had progressed since its appearance in September 1944. Its first page, in addition to the beginning of the interview, contained a short story by Gorbatov, 'Le Chasseur Taiane', and an article by Delteil on 'La Révolution verbale'. On the second page, the Des vérités nécessaires' section dealt hardly at all with the Occupation and the *épuration*, and was almost entirely devoted to 'Indochine 1947'. Inside, there were articles on Braque, 'Du côte des poètes', the Zurich congress of the PEN clubs, and reviews by Sadoul on the film version of *For Whom the Bell Tolls* and on the Brussels Film Festival, and by Pol Gaillard on theatre. Serialisations of fiction included, not only Elsa Triolet's *Les*

Fantômes armés, but also Christopher Isherwood's *Prater Violet*. The issue, which had not yet discovered the 'Rire!' rubric, nevertheless concluded with a humorous article by Jean Effel, 'Les Chevaliers du Tastevin', and the message 'Vacances 47: elles seront courtes et bonnes'.

By December 1947, however, this experiment in ideological independence within the Left and artistic openness, was over, and *Les Lettres Françaises* was brought under direct PCF control, with the replacement of Loys Masson by Pierre Daix. The reasons for this, and their consequences, are interesting in that they illustrate a conjunction of external historical and economic circumstances and the intellectual evolution within the PCF itself. The Liberation press in general was characterised by a combination of enthusiastic optimism and a lack of managerial realism which served it ill when it came to confront the austerity of the postwar period and the complex ideological debates which issued from it. In particular, *Les Lettres Françaises*, like the whole of the Liberation press, was crippled by the long printers' strike, the 'Grève du Livre', which prevented the journal from appearing from 14 February 1947 until 21 March. Thereafter, naturally enough, opinions differ as to the immediate causes of the review's financial difficulties. For Pierre Daix:

> Like most of the papers which came out of the Resistance, *Les Lettres Françaises*, basking in its initial success, had become accustomed to a fairly luxurious existence. However, administrative incompetence, the economic crisis and the long printers' strike of Spring 1947 rapidly created a deficit.[27]

For Claude Morgan, these difficulties were often deliberately provoked by the PCF as a means of sabotaging an independant left-wing press,[28] and in any case were due to incompetence elsewhere, particularly in the administration of the 'Messageries Françaises de Presse', set up to replace Hachette at the Liberation and incompetently managed, and which collapsed during the summer of 1947, owing *Les Lettres Françaises* two million francs.[29] The ensuing financial crisis obliged Morgan to float a personal loan, guaranteed by a delux edition of a work by Gongara illustrated by Picasso, but this was ultimately not enough and he was forced to turn to the PCF for help.[30] As Daix records:

> The Party agreed to refloat *Les Lettres* on conditions of which I was never informed but which I gradually deduced. I believed I

had been appointed on merit, but I had to recognise that I had been one of those conditions, in other words, the guarantee of the political control of the review by the Party.[31]

The decision was taken at a meeting in November with Laurent Casanova, 'in charge of Communist intellectuals since the Strasbourg Congress',[32] and in the new year Daix replaced Loys Masson as editor, with Pierre Leschemelle as Administrator, and the review moved into the offices of *Ce Soir*, at 37, rue du Louvre. As Daix commented: 'Once Leschemelle and I had repulsed the enemy offensive against *Les Lettres Françaises*, there remained the task of reconstruction':[33] in identical circumstances to the PCF takeover of *Europe* in 1935, *Les Lettres Françaises* had lost its independence.

One key factor in the removal of Masson was the ambiguous role of Aragon. Morgan constantly asserts that Aragon was acutely displeased at the independance of the review: 'Once Paris was liberated and I found myself by force of circumstances at the head of *Les Lettres Françaises*, I had to deal with Aragon. This review was slipping out of his control and he took it fairly badly',[34] and recounts numerous battles with both Aragon and Elsa Triolet over adverse book-reviews, one of which led to the intervention of Thorez himself and the dominance of Casanova: 'The result of this meeting was that Laurent Casanova, a member of the Central Committee, was designated to take charge of intellectual problems.'[35] In the light of this, it is surprising that Morgan should so disingenuously underestimate Aragon's role in the dismissal of Loys Masson: 'Aragon, who had the power, did nothing to prevent his departure',[36] whereas Daix is quite clear in asserting that he was offered the post of editor by Aragon himself.[37] This seems plausible in the light of the fact that Aragon himself had been somewhat under a cloud with the PCF since the publication of *Les Voyageurs de l'Impériale* and *Aurélien*, judged unorthodox, and needed to buy himself back into the Party's favour.[38]

Much more important, however, than the role of Aragon in the takeover of *Les Lettres Françaises* was the rapid evolution of PCF thinking on intellectual and cultural matters under the impact of the Cold War. At the beginning of the Liberation period, the Party appears to have been genuinely relaxed and open to pluralism in cultural and intellectual matters, crystallised in the political domain by Thorez's declaration, in November 1946, to the London *Times* and *Daily Mail* that: 'the progress of democracy in the world allows us to envisage for the advance of Socialism ways different from those taken by the Russian Communists'.[39] This openness in Party cultural policy contributed considerably to the vitality of the French postwar 'Renaissance' in the years 1944–6, particularly since it brought to the fore a number of talented young Communist writers and intellectuals, such as the group around the review *Action*, including Pierre Hervé, Roger Vailland, Pierre Courtade, Edgar Morin, Jean Prouteau, Jean-Francis Rolland, Robert Scipion and Claude Roy, and the 'Rue Saint-Benoît Group', of which Marguerite Duras was the centre. Commenting on *Action*, Claude Roy points to the same eclecticism which characterised *Les Lettres Françaises* in its best years:

> It was perhaps useful to the Party that we were able to produce a Communist review which was vibrant and without jargon, and which could publish Georges Limbour and Jacques Prévert, Simone de Beauvoir and Jean Duché, Alexandre Astruc and Raymond Queneau between Wurmser and Garaudy.[40]

The inclusion of the name of Simone de Beauvoir alongside of that of Roger Garaudy in this list is significant, because it points to an ability of the Party at that time to tolerate genuine differences of opinion: Garaudy's famous denunciation of Sartre as a 'false prophet' in *Les Lettres Françaises* in December 1945[41] was an isolated critique, though with hindsight it now appears as the beginning of an orchestrated campaign which saw the Existentialists as serious rivals.

Yet, if the PCF in 1946 was able to reconcile differences, with the onset of the Cold War and the rise in the Soviet Union of Zhdanov to supreme responsibility for cultural affairs, the mood changed drastically. As David Caute comments: 'Zhdanovism seemed to suit well the French Party in its bitter, post-Republican unity mood of 1947–8.'[42] In this respect, *Les Lettres Françaises* under Loys Masson rapidly found itself diverging from official Party cultural policy. Even before Zhdanovism, the PCF had a particularly materialist and utilitarian concept of the postwar 'Renaissance'. In a speech to the Tenth Party Congress in 1945, entitled 'Les Intellectuels et la Renaissance Française', Roger Garaudy, after a number of by now traditional side-swipes at Sartre and Gide, spoke of the necessarily utilitarian aspect of intellectuality and unveiled the project for the Party's *Encyclopédie de la Renaissance Française*, which would constitute 'the basis for a vast synthesis of our knowledge and technology which will continue the Encyclopaedia of the eighteenth century, that of Diderot and D'Alembert'.[43] This project was elaborated on further by Georges Cogniot in a later speech at the same congress, when he referred to the mission of the PCF, 'the Party of the elite and of intelligence', as that of 'continuing France', but continuing in a certain sense: 'As inheritors of Voltaire, of the Encyclopaedia with its fervent technical thought, of Cartesianism inspired by noble practical concerns, the intellectuals will unite to co-operate in the reconstruction of the country.'[44] It is interesting to what extent the eighteenth century dominated French culture in the late 1940s, whether in the forms of the detached cynicism of a Nimier, the libertinism of a Vailland, or, as in this case, a return to the practical traditions of the *Encyclopédie*. Clearly, however, this particular concept of the continuity of a certain utilitarian French tradition militated against experimentation and innovation in the arts, particularly in the domain of literature.

This point was made clearly by Jean Kanapa in his well-known article, 'Les Mots ou le métier d'écrivain', which appeared in Pierre Séghers' *Poésie 47*, one of the most successful cultural reviews of the postwar period, in the August/September number of 1947. What concerned Kanapa was the growing interest amongst writers in 'écriture', with a proportional diminution of content: 'Perhaps philosophers will say that the danger of the sign lies in the fact that one is tempted to take the word for the object.'[45] On the contrary, 'Words are not either privileged or disadvantaged instruments, they are utensils, like other utensils.'[46] In his subsequent generalised attack on 'rhétorique', in which 'son Emminence J. Paulhan'[47] and Brice Parrain, and not Sartre and Simone de Beauvoir, were the main targets, Kanapa even singled out Queneau: 'And Queneau, quite incomprehensibly, brings his contribution with his *Exercices du style*, which lower the narrative to the level of a meaningless formal grammar.'[48] This attack, which in itself does no more than look forward to the criticism levelled with equal violence during the 1960s and 1970s against Structuralist poetics, forms part of a global strategy which denied to literature, not merely the autonomy of its own language, but also the choice of its subject-matter, and here, Kanapa opposed Socialist Realism, with its task of 'denouncing scandal',[49] to bourgeois realism, with its emphasis on the individual, which led it all too often into the realm of sexuality and, inevitably, pornography. In this respect, it is vital to see that Communist cultural policy, in spite of Kanapa's protestations to the contrary, coincided with a general return in post-Liberation France to sexual puritanism, of which the major example was the closure of the brothels. This puritanism, however, directly affected literature through the courts: as J. Galtier-Boissière records in his diary for March 1947:

> We are now back in the terrible age of 'Father Modesty', Senator Bérenger. Four publishers are being prosecuted for obscenity: Gallimard because of *Black Spring*, Vox because of *Tropic of Cancer*, Gérodias because of *Tropic of Capricorn*, and Jean d'Halluin for *J'irai cracher sur vos tombes*.[50]

What is significant about these prosecutions is that they were directed against one of the major targets of the PCF, Henry Miller, who was anathema both because of the sexual explicitness of his work and because of his American nationality. In other words, if, by 1947, the Party was beginning to roll back the freedom accorded to its writers and intellectuals, to severely limit the flexibility and autonomy of literary language, to support the wave of sexual censorship, it was also in the process of abandoning its receptivity to foreign literature, particularly as concerns the United States. As Guy Besse argued, in an article 'L'Expansionnisme idéologique des Yankees', in the Party's *La Démocratie nouvelle* of February 1948, France was the victim of an American cultural invasion, designed to poison French morals:

> Look at Miller, an export commodity, and his books, lined up in the shop-windows like SS troops on parade. He's banned in America, but he is welcome here because he pays compliments to Gide, yesterday a collaborator, now a Nobel Prize winner.[51]

For the Americans

> can count on this government of riot police who have strangled the French cinema in order to make way for witches, singing clergymen and pin-up girls. This unhealthy bric-a-brac is certainly good enough for the French, thinks the Hollywood mogul.... The Americans keep the atomic bomb back in America, because it's a state secret, but they send us Faulkner instead.[52]

And: 'It's in the very centre of Paris, at the Café de Flore, that the most deadly poisons are concocted.'[53]

In the last half of 1947, therefore, the official policy of the PCF and of its cultural spokesman Laurent Casanova hardened considerably, with the result of an appreciable narrowing of cultural perceptions and the beginning of the 'exclusions' of dissident or merely unorthodox intellectuals: it was the Saint Germain-des-Prés cell, notably, which effected the expulsion of the 'Rue Saint Benoît Group' and most of the early collaborators to *Action*. In the case of *Les Lettres Françaises*, it led not only to the takeover of the journal by the Party and the replacement of Masson by Daix, but to the implicit repudiation of some of the journal's past successes: the serialisation of Queneau's *Loin de Rueil*, articles by Miller, serialisations of American novels, careful attention to developments in the American cinema, to say nothing of Loys Masson's *New Yorker* cartoons.

Les Lettres Françaises, under the editorship of Georges Adam and then, especially, under that of Loys Masson, was a genuine reflection of the diversity and openness of cultural life in the early post-Liberation period. It is fair, broadly, to lay the blame for the review's demise at the door of the postwar economic situation, particularly in 1947, but also at that of the PCF, no longer officially able to tolerate non-utilitarian art or independent intellectual debate. At the same time, *Les Lettres Françaises* was the victim of its own ambiguities and, particularly, of its inability to break away from the immediate past: like Georges Cogniot, the review tended all too often to see 'Reconstruction' in terms of re-establishing continuity with a certain essentially French tradition which went back to the eighteenth century of the *Encyclopédie* or the seventeenth century of Descartes. This combined with an obsession with the Occupation period from which the review drew its legitimacy. As Jean Cassou wrote as part of his contribution to the Paulhan debate in 1947:

For four years, our country found itself in a special situation. It continued to exercise its literary function. It did so in the conditions and the state of mind imposed upon it by that situation. During that period, French writers were soldiers, prisoners, deportees, victims, wounded, dead. Their writings were the writings of soldiers, prisoners, deportees, victims, wounded and dead. These writings expressed the continuity in spite of everything of French life.[54]

Such an assertion is blatently false, and whilst imprisonment and deportation may have been a vital, even major, element in the French literary experience of the period 1940–4, they were not exclusively so, and there remained other areas of intense creativity which were tacitly ignored. Not only was this unfortunate for the literary tone and content of the review itself, which remained dominated by the Resistance experience and, above all, by the Resistance aesthetic, but it led, through its concern with *épuration*, to the pattern of 'exclusions' to which it itself was to fall victim in December 1947.

Notes

1. See Pascal Ory, *Les Collaborateurs* (Paris: Seuil, coll. 'Points', 1976).
2. See Claude Morgan, *Les 'Don Quichotte' et les autres* (Paris: Editions Roblot, coll. 'Cité Première', 1979) p. 162.
3. See Jean Galtier-Boissière, *Mon Journal pendant la grande pagaïe* (Paris: La Jeune Parque, 1950) p. 100. Galtier-Boissière, the editor of *Le Crapouillot*, sets the sales, in April 1947, of *L'Humanité* at 450,000, *Le Figaro* at 399,000 and *France-Soir* at 578,000.
4. *Les Lettres Françaises*, 9 September 1944, p. 1.
5. See Laurent Casanova, 'Le Parti Communiste et les intellectuels', in his *Le Parti Communiste, les intellectuels et la Nation* (Paris: Editions Sociales, 1949) p. 13.
6. See, for example, David Caute, *Communism and the French Intellectuals, 1914–1960* (London: André Deutsch, 1964); David Caute, *The Fellow-Travellers: A Postscript to the Enlightenment* (London: Weidenfeld & Nicolson, 1973); J. E. Flower, *Literature and the Left in France* (London: Macmillan, 1983); Herbert R. Lottman, *La Rive Gauche* (Paris: Seuil, 1981).
7. See Jacques Debû-Bridel (ed.), *La Résistance intellectuelle* (Paris: Julliard, coll. 'La Résistance par ceux qui l'ont faite', 1970), Ch. 3: 'Jacques Decour, le CNE, Jean Paulhan, *Les Lettres Françaises*'.
8. See Caute, *Communism*, p. 151; Claude Morgan, *'Don Quichotte'*, pp. 129ff.
9. Morgan, *'Don Quichotte'*, p. 138.
10. See ibid., pp. 148ff.
11. George Adam, *L'Epée dans les reins, roman: Chronique des années quarante* (Paris: Editions des Trois Collines, 1944).
12. André Lhôte, 'Un Eternel malentendu', *Les Lettres Françaises*, 28 October 1944, p. 7.

13. See Morgan, 'Don Quichotte', p. 163.
14. 'Pierre Benoît rayé de la liste noire', *Les Lettres Françaises*, 22 November 1946, p. 5.
15. Roland Dorgelès, 'Pour verser au dossier des criminels de guerre: Marsoulas', *Les Lettres Françaises*, 16 December 1944, pp. 1, 3.
16. See André Gide, 'La Délivrance de Tunis', *Les Lettres Françaises*, 18 November 1944, p. 1; Aragon, 'Retour d'André Gide', *Les Lettres Françaises*, 25 November 1944, p. 1.
17. 'Sans pouvoirs: Les Dernières pages de Giraudoux', *Les Lettres Françaises*, 23 September 1944, p. 1.
18. Claude Roy, *Nous* (Paris: Gallimard, coll. 'Folio', 1980) p. 469.
19. See Morgan, '*Don Quichotte*', pp. 65–6.
20. Pierre Daix, *J'ai cru au matin* (Paris: Robert Laffont, coll. 'Vécu', 1976) p. 197.
21. Claude Roy, 'Esquisse d'un portrait de Loys Masson', in Loys Masson, *Des Bouteilles dans les yeux* (Paris: Robert Laffont, 1970) pp. 22–3.
22. Roy, *Nous*, p. 469.
23. Morgan, 'Don Quichotte', p. 67.
24. Daix, *J'ai cru au matin*, p. 197.
25. Ibid., p. 197.
26. Edgar Morin and Jean Gratien, 'Une Interview d'Elio Vittorini', *Les Lettres Françaises*, 27 June 1946, pp. 1, 7.
27. Pierre Daix, *J'ai cru au matin*, p. 197.
28. See Morgan, '*Don Quichotte*', p. 181: 'It was total sabotage'.
29. See ibid., p. 182.
30. See ibid.
31. Daix, *J'ai cru au matin*, p. 197.
32. Ibid., p. 197.
33. Ibid., p. 201.
34. Morgan, '*Don Quichotte*', p. 178.
35. Ibid., p. 180.
36. Ibid., p. 67.
37. See Daix, *J'ai cru au matin*, p. 191.
38. See ibid., p. 193.
39. Quoted in Galtier-Boissière, *Mon Journal*, pp. 28–9.
40. Roy, *Nous*, p. 120.
41. Roger Garaudy, 'Jean-Paul Sartre, un faux prophète', *Les Lettres Françaises*, 29 December 1945, p. 1.
42. Caute, *Communism*, p. 327.
43. 'Discours de Roger Garaudy', in Roger Garaudy and Georges Cogniot, *Les Intellectuels et la Renaissance Française* (Paris: Editions du Parti Communiste Français, 1945) p. 9.
44. 'Discours de Georges Cogniot', ibid., p. 23.
45. Jean Kanapa, 'Les Mots ou le métier d'écrivain', *Poésie 47*, 40 (August–September 1947) p. 94.
46. Ibid.
47. Ibid., p. 96.
48. Ibid.

49. Ibid., p. 110.
50. Galtier-Boissière, *Mon Journal*, p. 71.
51. Guy Besse, 'L'Expansionnisme idéologique des Yankees', *La Démocratie Nouvelle*, 2 February 1948, p. 76.
52. Ibid., p. 76.
53. Ibid.
54. Jean Cassou, 'La Littérature de ces quatre années', *Les Lettres Françaises*, 20 May 1947, p. 4.

8

The Reconstruction of Culture: Peuple et Culture and the Popular Education Movement

BRIAN RIGBY

Peuple et Culture has recently been described as 'the major cultural organisation of the Liberation'.[1] It called itself a 'national movement of popular culture',[2] and its central ambition was to 'give culture back to the people and give the people back to culture'.[3] The movement was begun by a small group of people in Grenoble after the Liberation and emerged from the Commission Education of the Comité de Libération de l'Isère.[4] The name 'Peuple et Culture' is said to have been taken from a Collège du Travail formed in 1935.[5] The principal members of Peuple et Culture had played an important part in the Ecole des cadres at Uriage and then in the maquis of the Vercors. Before that, the founding president of Peuple et Culture, Joffre Dumazedier,[6] had formed the Collège du Travail at Noisy-le-Sec in 1936,[7] and had been deeply involved in the Auberges de la Jeunesse movement at the time of the Popular Front and afterwards.[8] It was during his activities in the Resistance that Dumazedier conceived the idea of Peuple et Culture as an organisation to be formed after the Liberation. Throughout this period Dumazedier was closely involved with Bénigno Cacérès, a master carpenter from Toulouse, who had shared the same experience at Uriage and in the maquis, and who was to play a crucial role in the movement, both as 'animateur' and as chronicler of its history.[9] Others joined the group at Grenoble at the time of the Liberation, for example Paul Lengrand who was principally responsible for drawing up the movement's 1945 manifesto *Un peuple, une culture*.[10] Peuple et Culture immediately began to play a key role in initiating several projects in Grenoble: the Centre d'Education Ouvrière de Grenoble, the Centre Interfacultés, the Centre Sanitaire and the Maison de la Culture.[11] At the time he created Peuple et Culture Dumazedier had also been appointed

'Inspecteur principal de la Jeunesse et de l'éducation populaire' in the Grenoble *académie*.[12] Towards the end of 1946 the association moved to Paris,[13] where the headquarters are still to be found.[14] The movement is still very much alive and has many regional associations and many international connections.[15]

The movement has never ceased to retrace its own historical beginnings. Cacérès, in particular, has always been ready to wax lyrical at the memory of the Golden Age of 1942–6, when the seeds of the movement were planted at Uriage and in the 'équipes volantes' of the maquis, and when the movement actually came into being in Grenoble after the Liberation. Cacérès had been a carpenter in Toulouse, keen for self-improvement, and had gone along to lectures given by the left-wing Abbé de Naurois, with whom he became acquainted.[16] The Abbé de Naurois invited Cacérès to give a talk on 'la condition ouvrière'. Later, when the Abbé de Naurois was at Uriage, he invited Cacérès there to give another talk. After other occasional visits, Dunoyer de Segonzac asked Cacérès to stay on at Uriage, which he did. Cacérès continued his connections with Uriage when the group moved on to La Thébaïde, a large isolated manor-house near the Vercors, from which Resistance activities were organised. In La Thébaïde the working-class autodidact Cacérès found a highly cultured and highly intellectual setting, and one which for him was a kind of cultural paradise. From this base, as a member of one of the 'équipes volantes', Cacérès would go out into the countryside to visit the camps of Resistance fighters.[17] Here was a model of the links between political struggle, fraternity and culture which deeply marked Cacérès and others of his generation, and it was a model which they were determined to pursue after the Liberation. It was Cacérès's job to take culture to the 'Resistants'. First, they would pillage the library at La Thébaïde for relevant and morale-raising passages, and then they would transport the appropriate books in their rucksacks to the camps, to read them by the camp-fire:

> Reading took on then its full meaning. Here, passages from Michelet, Hugo, Saint-Just, Apollinaire, François la Colère, assumed their true significance. The great poets came amongst men in order to help them to live, in order to teach them to hope.[18]

It is not difficult to imagine how powerful such an experience must have been, and Cacérès tells us that it determined the whole direction of his life:

> By communicating this portion of Man to other men, I came to believe for ever that in certain circumstances culture could really be shared. . . . There, in that clearing of the Vercors, was revealed to me the incantation of words, the power of language. Reading meant the preparation for the long road to change. We had to continue that enrichment.[19]

This heroic spirit and cultural idealism were not surprisingly also to the fore in Grenoble at the time of the Liberation, when again cultural idealism was to thrive on scarce resources and difficult physical and material conditions:

> You had to have lived through that genuine cultural epic in order to imagine the enthusiasm which at that time infused our country. During the hard winter of 1944, when the snow was blocking the roads, when food was never guaranteed, in buildings, with improvised equipment, these 'animateurs' managed to create an extraordinary centre of cultural activity. They established institutions which the whole of France and, rapidly, foreign countries, came, not to admire, but to see in action, in order to attempt to reproduce them elsewhere. And yet everything was still disorganised. The simple fact of going for the continuation of this activity, constituted an expedition. Means of transport, worn out by four years of Occupation, had given up the ghost. You had to fight for a place for long journeys in frozen coaches. You crossed the Loire on a wooden bridge, on foot, carrying your suitcase.
>
> Finding premises in Grenoble was a problem. There were still problems of food, of lodging and of money.
>
> The workers went back to the 'Bourse du Travail'. A 'Centre d'éducation ouvrière' was created. Fraternally united, the members of the CGT and the CFTC attended evening courses and training sessions. The workers were so numerous that we had to repeat courses. A thirst for culture had taken hold of these men who wanted to actively participate in the future of their country in every sector.[20]

In both the Resistance and the Liberation experiences Cacérès describes what he regarded as the perfect coming together ('la rencontre') of intellectuals and the people.[21] Cacérès himself had already achieved his own personal reconstruction during these years and he wanted his fellow French workers to share this experience. This notion of cultural sharing ('le partage culturel') was crucial for Cacérès and for the Peuple et Culture movement. It was assumed that the workers had a 'thirst for culture',[22] that they had cultural needs and aspirations which could be satisfied to a significant degree by being given 'access' to culture. The Resistance movement offered a privileged model of how intellectuals and workers could come together in a shared experience of culture, in a 'culture commune'.[23] This 'culture commune', or 'culture populaire' as it was also called, was what had to be fought for after the war and extended to the whole nation. This was the cultural struggle which now lay ahead and which was described in the heroic, virile vocabulary of the Resistance mixed with the traditional rhetoric of the working-class movement. It was a 'cultural struggle',[24] but it was also a 'cultural conquest by the people',[25] and the 'cultural emancipation of the people'.[26]

Peuple et Culture's aim was to develop certain specific pedagogical methods in the service of specific ideals, in order to bring about this cultural emancipation. It saw itself as a movement of 'popular education' or 'popular culture' which signified a vague mixture of adult education and working-class education. Peuple et Culture wanted not only to educate the working class which had lost out in the educational and cultural stakes, but also to modernise and perfect the educators, that is, it wanted to create a class of skilled, professional educators and 'animateurs', who in turn could carry on the work of 'permanent' education. Cacérès has, in fact, called Peuple et Culture 'the first French movement for the training of "animateurs"'.[27] The words 'populaire' and 'peuple' are notoriously ambiguous and one can already see how, like so many other organisations and individuals at the time of the Liberation, Peuple et Culture was caught between at least two definitions of the 'people'. On the one hand the 'peuple' was the exploited working class who lived in a state of cultural deprivation ('dénuement culturel')[28] and on whose behalf radical steps needed to be taken in order to change this. On the other hand, the 'peuple' was the whole nation, on whose behalf a unified and common culture needed to be forged at this great moment of national freedom and solidarity, in order to ensure the future health and efficiency of the nation. It was without doubt this latter definition – the 'peuple' as

unified nation – which dominated Peuple et Culture discourse in
the early postwar years. There was, of course, at this stage, an
enormous desire on the part of all groups to achieve unity and
consensus, and in this atmosphere Peuple et Culture, like others,
was led to think not only that future unity and a common culture
were the major priorities, but also that this unity actually already
existed, that in fact the 'peuple' was already a unified nation. Thus
we have Cacérès claiming: 'The Liberation was ... the historical
place and moment of the reintegration of the proletariat into the
nation.'[29] But although Peuple et Culture largely adhered to this
'unanimist' line, a close reading of its literature shows that there
were unresolved conflicts and ambiguities. This is hardly surprising when we know that the movement was made up of men
with significant differences in their political and philosophical
views, which were likely to surface even in this period of willing
compromise. In the early postwar period, for instance, both
Dumazedier and Cacérès joined the Communist Party for a year, a
move which deeply disturbed other members and put the movement under severe strain. This more radical commitment was
intermittently apparent. For example, in the first issue of the
movement's periodical in June 1946 we are told that the class
struggle is still an incontrovertible reality,[30] and in the second issue
in May 1947 we find an attack on 'bourgeois culture'.[31] In the 1945
Manifesto we are told that a 'fraternal and collective civilisation' is
about to replace 'bourgeois individualism'.[32] And, despite the
close links with Uriage, Personalism and progressive Christian
groups, Dumazedier in 1948 criticises Christian youth organisations quite violently and makes a traditionally passionate and
traditionally divisive plea in support of 'l'école laïque'.[33]

One of the most interesting and revealing sources for Peuple et
Culture at this period is a dramatic spectacle entitled *La Vraie
Libération*, produced in Annecy in the Summer of 1945 by a Peuple
et Culture theatre group, the text of which was published by
Peuple et Culture in Grenoble in 1945. The spectacle was called a
'celebration' and is a most peculiar production, but no doubt is
very characteristic of the period, from both an aesthetic and an
ideological point of view. It is a kind of Greek dramatic piece, full
of portentous rhetoric and clearly aspiring to the sublime and
prophetic modes. It was performed by a team of youths and girls
from the 'Jeunesses communistes de la CGT, des Auberges de la
Jeunesse et de la JOC'.[34] It re-enacts, with the help of songs,

dances and gestures, the process of defeat, occupation and resistance. The 'Voix des ondes' tempts the chorus ('men and women of France') into collaboration. The chorus, after internal dissension, refuses the call to collaboration and chooses to resist. The enemy is conquered and expelled, and an exultant cry goes up from the leader of the chorus: 'Without delay we must rebuild the house. To work, my children, for reconstruction.'[35] But then a note of warning is struck. The invader may have been expelled, but not the old enemy – the 'patron'. The men and women of France are ready to rebuild the house of France but not in the form of the 'old prison': 'If the workers took to the maquis, it was in order to liberate the country, in order to liberate work.'[36] What must now be created is 'la République du Travail'.[37] Such a consciousness of class antagonism and of the need for radical change continued to surface, as I have already indicated, in the next few years, but was by and large successfully repressed at this moment of 'rassemblement populaire'. There is no doubt that what dominates the postwar discourse of Peuple et Culture is an overwhelming desire for cultural unity, either based on the fusion of classes, or the happy coexistence of classes.

If the words 'peuple' and 'populaire' are slippery notions, then the word 'culture' is no less so. In much French usage at this time, and certainly in the specific context with which I am dealing, the word 'culture' often means exactly the same as 'education'. But the term certainly can carry far wider implications, and it is by no means by chance that the movement chose to call itself Peuple et Culture and not, for example, simply 'Peuple et Education'. It was typical of the period that the founders of Peuple et Culture had in mind not only a narrowly pedagogical revolution, but beyond that a whole moral, social and cultural one. When in the 1945 Manifesto the central question is asked: 'Can the spirit of the Resistance finally bring about a genuine popular culture?',[38] 'culture populaire' does not only, nor even principally, mean education, but points to the ideal of a whole shared life of a nation. Like their fellow idealists at Uriage, the founders of Peuple et Culture were aiming at the creation of a new 'style of life', a 'new man', a new 'revolutionary Humanism' – in other words they were aiming at nothing less than a reconstruction of culture.

Cacérès has said that the major work at La Thébaïde, apart from finding texts to read in the maquis, was the preparation of the 'summa' *Vers le style du XXe siècle*, a work directed by Gilbert

Gadoffre and published in 1945.[39] The connections between this text and the documents of the Peuple et Culture movement are too extensive to be investigated and set out here. It is enough, in the present context, to say that Dumazedier, Cacérès and others applied to the specific field of 'culture populaire' more or less all of the major elements of the ideology of Uriage. Peuple et Culture also set out to put into practice specific cultural and educational projects that had been sketched out in *Vers le style du XXe siècle* ('Project de Centre d'Education ouvrière', 'Projet de Maison de la Culture').[40] Not least, of course, Uriage stressed the need to create a professional elite of educators and cultural 'animateurs', a militant avant-garde, with a profound sense of mission to undertake the cultural reconstruction of postwar France,[41] based on the new civic faith of 'revolutionary Humanism'.[42] The founders and cultural militants of Peuple et Culture certainly saw themselves as this committed avant-garde, and set out consciously to put into practice the teachings of *Vers le style du XXe siècle*.

Together with the high moral intentions there was a very practical and concrete dimension to Peuple et Culture's desire for cultural reconstruction, and, if anything, this dimension came to outweigh other considerations. Following on from the Popular Front's notions of cultural and leisure needs, Peuple et Culture worked for the improvement of the cultural infrastructure of the country – that is to say, it believed in the prime need to provide equipment, installations and institutions, for in this it saw the surest way to put into practice a genuinely democratic cultural policy, one which would permit all people to have *access* to culture. So we read in the Manifesto: 'We shall fight unceasingly for the general institution in our own country of organisations such as the Russian "Palais des Pionniers", the American "Clubs de jeunesse" and the Swedish "Maisons du Peuple" '.[43] The notion of achieving cultural democracy primarily by improving the cultural infrastructure of the country was in many people's minds at the end of the war, and in the specific context of France it can be seen, as already mentioned, as an extension of the work of the Popular Front in this field.[44] This direct link with the period of the Popular Front is evident in the fact that it was Jean Guéhenno who in 1945, was put in charge of the section of the Ministry of Education devoted to youth movements, popular education and sport. Guéhenno's vision of postwar cultural reconstruction was made clear in a speech he gave at the Palais de Chaillot in March 1945:

I can see in each village a schoolhouse which has been transformed and expanded, where there would be several large
rooms, for games, for work and for reading as well. You can call
it what you like: a village club, a 'maison de culture', a 'foyer de
la nation'. It will be a 'foyer', the 'foyer' of the modern spirit,
I mean a beacon, where people will go until they are sixteen in
order to begin to learn to think, certainly, but where people will
continue to go afterwards, for their whole lives, because they
will be sure of finding there joy and knowledge, every means to
think even better and to live better. The establishment will be
run by a specially trained teacher, specifically appointed to that
post, the post of teacher of men, of teacher of adults, equally
capable of helping them and informing them in their professional life as in changing the quality of their leisure activities ...
And this country will begin to sing again, as it used to sing, as
gaily, as solemnly, according to its rhythm, according to its style,
according to its faith. And culture and the people will finally be
reconciled.[45]

In Guéhenno's speech there is a marked similarity with the ideas
of Peuple et Culture. Guéhenno stressed the need to provide
culture and leisure institutions for the community, where above all
the young, but also people of all ages, could be educated to attain a
higher quality of life (Guéhenno talks of changing 'the quality of
people's pleasures'), and where there could occur a genuine
coming together, a 'reconciliation' of 'peuple' and 'culture'. As was
the case at the time of the Popular Front, Peuple et Culture tended
to lump together culture, education and leisure, and much of the
time these terms are interchangeable. Peuple et Culture certainly
held very firmly to the prewar and Vichy belief in sport as a
privileged means of attaining the civic ideal, and was highly
suspicious of sport being commercialised or being regarded as an
'escapist' activity, as part of a 'culture d'évasion'.[46] A key element
of Peuple et Culture's policy was its ambition to set up 'healthy'
leisure and cultural clubs, to combat the pernicious effects of city
life and especially of café life:

Popular leisure clubs in order to attract into a healthy and
educative environment the great number of people for whom the
main 'foyer' is the café: factory clubs, district clubs, new army
clubs, film clubs, youth clubs or 'maisons du peuple'. It doesn't
matter what they are called: that varies with the age, the milieu

and the technical particularity which defines them. Here, education takes place especially in a healthy environment, in collective celebrations (civic or artistic), film shows, exhibitions of posters, exhibitions in general, etc. .... For the mass of young people we must cover the entire country with a dense network of youth-hostels and organise popular tourism on a vast scale.[47]

Above all, Peuple et Culture seems to have wanted to find ways of protecting the nation against what it considered to be the evils of mass culture. At one point mass culture is even called the new 'occupying force', in the face of which the militants of popular education must organise a stubborn resistance.[48] Against what it saw as the commercialised anarchy of mass culture, Peuple et Culture offered the alternative of a 'popular culture' based entirely on these cultural and leisure clubs, a 'popular culture' which would be guided and controlled by high-minded civic educators and 'animateurs'. What is, however, also evident is that Peuple et Culture wanted the state to be eventually responsible for this 'popular culture', as one can see from this statement made in 1945: 'Militants, do not let us forget that the final goal of our activity remains the creation of a public service in charge of workers' leisure and culture'.[49] At this early postwar stage, the state did not in fact include 'cultural development' in its planning process, something that was to only happen in years to come. But it seems clear that Peuple et Culture at the time of the Liberation laid much of the groundwork for later debates on cultural development, and it continued to make significant contributions throughout the 1950s and 1960s to the increasingly important area of 'cultural planning'.[50] It also provided many of the key figures who became the professional 'animateurs' and managers of cultural institutions. Gabriel Monnet, who ended up by being in charge of the Maison de la Culture at Bourges, is perhaps one of the most famous examples.[51] Peuple et Culture also went on to contribute significantly to the work of international cultural organisations, most notably UNESCO.[52]

From the very beginning Peuple et Culture's high-minded moral and cultural aims went together with a desire for 'la culture populaire' to play its role in the postwar economic effort and in the modernisation of France in all its sectors. Peuple et Culture believed it could contribute to the process of training and transforming individuals and of 'adapting' them to the modern society which lay ahead. It believed its contribution was perfectly geared to the new scientific and industrial society of the future. This explains its absolute obsession with, and faith in, such notions and practices as 'functional pedagogy' and 'mental training'.[53] It prided itself on its scientific 'technique' and insisted that its educators and 'animateurs' were 'technicians'.

Contrary to what one might at first think, given much of its high cultural and high moral stance, Peuple et Culture was also only too ready to apply economic models to the area of culture and education. This can be seen most strikingly in a rather startling assertion in the Manifesto: 'We want to be educators, to PRODUCE EDUCATION, as others produce bread, steel or electricity.'[54] And a later passage in the Manifesto states that the educational project to produce a 'true common culture' (a necessity for a healthy economy) should be pursued with the same efficiency that one expects from the military and industrial sectors.[55] Faced with such statements, it becomes difficult not to conclude that, in the end, Peuple et Culture's grand discourse on culture and education comes down to being an apology for economic modernisation and an exhortation to the state to deploy culture and education in this process of modernisation.

This seems a harsh conclusion to draw on the generous and idealistic project of 'éducation populaire', but it is a rather inescapable one. In fact, it has become rather difficult not to have a similarly disabused view of other major aspects of the popular education movement at this time. I am sure that Peuple et Culture did good work on the ground in its numerous clubs, but one has to say that its cultural, intellectual and political premises were always too naive and muddled. Culturally, it focused too much on the figure of the working-class autodidact, eager for knowledge and culture; it was too respectful of high culture and too suspicious of mass culture. It was too willing to limit future thinking about culture to questions of material conditions and facilities, and no doubt more seriously, it was too ready to allow culture and education to serve economic ends. Intellectually, it was a victim of the hybrid ideology of Uriage, with its inextricable mix of Socialist and Christian rhetoric, which was in part responsible for the impossibly vague and ambiguous terminology with which Peuple et Culture dealt with cultural matters. Politically, it was caught between, on the one hand, attachment to archaic notions of class and work, and, on the other hand, enthusiasm for the classless, technological society of the future. But even given all these criticisms, it still appears to me to be one of the most illuminating and characteristic projects to have come out of the period of postwar Reconstruction. What is more, many of its illusions, naiveties and confusions were to persist long after this period, and one could even say that they still dominate the cultural field in education and in politics.

Notes

1. E. Ritaine, *Les Stratèges de la culture* (Paris: Presses de la Fondation Nationale des Sciences Politiques, 1983) p. 58. Another cultural organisation which deserves close study is Travail et Culture, which in the early postwar years was intimately linked with Peuple et Culture, and with which it shared the periodical *Doc.*
2. *Peuple et Culture (Cahiers de la culture populaire)*, I (June 1946) title-page.
3. *Un Peuple, une Culture* (Grenoble, 1945) p. 10 (reprinted Paris, 1972).
4. J.-P. Saez (ed.), *Peuple et Culture: Histoires et mémoires (Entretiens avec Bénigo Cacérès, Joffre Dumazedier, Paul Lengrand, Gabriel Monnet, Joseph Rovan)* (Paris: Peuple et Culture, 1986). Hereafter referred to as *Entretiens.*
5. *Grenoble, ville d'expériences* (Grenoble: n. d. [1946?]) p. 4. See also *36 en Corrèze, aux jours ensoleillés du Front Populaire* (Tulle: Peuple et Culture, 1976) p. 1.
6. The well-known sociologist, whose most famous study remains, perhaps, *Vers une civilisation du loisir?* (Paris: Seuil, 1962).
7. *Entretiens*, p. 32.
8. Ibid., p. 28.
9. See, for instance, B. Cacérès, *Histoire de l'éducation populaire* (Paris: Seuil, 1964); B. Cacérès, *Les Deux rivages: Itinéraire d'un animateur d'éducation populaire* (Paris: La Découverte, 1982).
10. *Entretiens*, p. 55.
11. On all these, see B. Cacérès, *L'Espoir au coeur* (Paris: Seuil, 1967) pp. 158–9.
12. *Entretiens*, p. 37.
13. *Peuple et Culture 1945–1965* (Paris: Peuple et Culture, 1965) p. 29.
14. 108–10, rue Saint-Maur, Paris 11eme.
15. See the bulletin *Peuple et Culture*, 1 (March 1983) 'Supplément à *Culture*, no. 4'. *Culture* is now the title of the movement's periodical. For an interesting view of the contemporary French adult education scene from an English point of view, see W. S. Toynbee, *Adult Education and the Voluntary Associations in France*, Nottingham Working Papers in the Education of Adults, 7 (Nottingham: University of Nottingham, 1985).

16. *Entretiens*, pp. 1–2.
17. Cacérès, *L'Espoir au coeur*, pp. 39–41.
18. Ibid., pp. 40–1. François la Colère was Aragon's name during the Resistance.
19. Ibid., p. 41.
20. Cacérès, *Histoire de l'éducation populaire*, pp. 157–8.
21. Cacérès, *L'Espoir au coeur*, pp. 136–7.
22. *Peuple et Culture*, I (June 1946) pp. 27–8.
23. *Un Peuple, une Culture*, p. 10.
24. *Peuple et Culture*, October 1947, p. 3.
25. Ibid.
26. Ibid., I (June 1946) pp. 9–10.
27. Cacérès, *Histoire de l'éducation populaire*, p. 157.
28. *Peuple et Culture*, I (June 1946) p. 16.
29. Cacérès, *Histoire de l'éducation populaire*, p. 147.
30. *Peuple et Culture*, I (June 1946) p. 99.
31. Ibid. (May 1947), pp. 11–12.
32. *Un Peuple, une Culture*, p. 14.
33. *Peuple et Culture*, October 1947, pp. 3–4.
34. B. Bing, *La Vraie Libération. Voix de la France. Voix du Travail* (Grenoble: Peuple et Culture, 1945) p. 37.
35. Ibid., p. 31.
36. Ibid., p. 32.
37. The call for 'La République du Travail', has itself a distinctly archaic feel, and this sense is confirmed by the fact that the call also goes up for 'la République Universelle', and that the piece ends with the singing of 'La Ronde des Saint-Simoniens'. This impression of archaism is also evident in Cacérès' *L'Espoir au coeur*, in which he describes the Resistants singing the 'Chant des canuts' and Pierre Dupont's 'Chant des ouvriers' round the camp-fire. It is important to remember that Cacérès was a 'compagnon charpentier', an active member of a 'compagnonnage', and a writer of an historical novel on 'le compagnonnage'.
38. *Un Peuple, une Culture*, p. 9.
39. Equipe d'Uriage, sous la direction de Gilbert Gadoffre, *Vers le style du XXe siècle* (Paris: Seuil, 1945).
40. Ibid., pp. 135ff and 194ff.
41. Ibid., p. 203.
42. Ibid., pp. 156–7.
43. *Une Peuple, une Culture*, p. 25.
44. *Peuple et Culture* always saw itself as building upon the example of the cultural policy of the Popular Front. See B. Cacérès, *Allons au devant de la vie. La Naissance du temps des loisirs en 1936* (Paris: La Découverte, 1981).
45. Quoted in M. Crubellier, *Histoire culturelle de la France, XIXe–XXe siècle* (Paris: Armand Colin, 1974) pp. 325–6.
46. *Peuple et Culture*, October 1947, p. 4.
47. *Un Peuple, une Culture*, p. 24.
48. *Peuple et Culture*, October 1947, p. 3.

49. *Peuple et Culture*, I (June 1946) p. 25.
50. See, for example, the 1964 *Colloque de Bourges*, organised by Peuple et Culture and the Association pour l'expansion de la recherche scientifique with the help of the Bureau d'études du ministère des Affaires Culturelles. The proceedings were published in *L'Expansion de la recherche scientifique*, 22 (April–May 1965).
51. Cacérès, *L'Espoir au coeur*, p. 74. See also *Entretiens*.
52. See *Entretiens*, for the international work of Dumazedier, Lengrand and Rovan.
53. See *Un Peuple, une Culture*, pp. 20–1; and *Peuple et Culture*, I (June 1946) pp. 55ff.
54. *Un Peuple, une Culture*, p. 2.
55. Ibid., p. 27.

9

The Chameleon Rearguard of Cultural Tradition: the Case of Jacques Laurent

COLIN NETTELBECK

In retrospect, it can be seen that the cultural changes of postwar France did not prevent the survival of many of the individualistic values of the Third Republic. And rather than a phenomenon of cultural 'lag' – the time it takes for a collectivity to react to the impact of new events or currents of thought – it would appear more realistic to acknowledge the powers of adaptation of the bourgeoisie, and its ability to absorb new ideas and influences – those from within the French political spectrum, as well as those from abroad. It is this resilience, irritating though it may be in the presence of so much obvious decadence, that commanded the cultural mainstream and that directed the major developments of French Reconstruction. The insight that the case of Jacques Laurent offers into the persistence of the individualistic ethos is broad enough to serve as a model, and possibly an illuminating example of the relationship – or lack of it – between explicit ideological discourse and the defence of the high ground of cultural tradition.

One of the labels that Jacques Laurent claims to have found most sticky and most irritating is that of the 'écrivain de droite' – the right-wing writer. In a recent interview, he sides with Cocteau, who said: 'We are members of the literary Right because we side with the singular against the plural.'[1] His simultaneous denial that such a position has any political implications, on the grounds that he does not vote and has no party affiliations, is not, of course, especially convincing. Although his long career as a polemist has included attacks on people like Mauriac and De Gaulle, most of his targets have been identifiably left-wing, whether individuals like Sartre, or issues like the independence of Algeria, and indeed, as we shall see, if Laurent's individualism and contentiousness carry his attacks across most of the political spectrum, his home-base is always well to the right of centre. Jean-François Josselin, whose attitude towards Laurent seems to vacillate between benign scorn and grudging admiration, sums him up as: 'a cocktail with a base of anarchy and reactionary impulses, whose tastes and distastes may seem strange, exotic, or even odious'.[2] One might quibble about the proportions of these various ingredients, but there is no doubt about the anarchistic spirit or the reactionary tropisms, and it is also true that Laurent's quirky taste and imagination may just as easily shock or intrigue a reader. One thinks of the adolescent sexuality that permeates many passages of his writing, sometimes tiresomely insistent, at others indulgently erotic, even softly pornographic, as in the scene in *Les Corps tranquilles*, where the hero Anne Coquet follows Andrée Bourgthéolde up the stairs, his eyes glued on her underwear.[3]

But one thinks, too, of the movingly spare meditation of Antoine's heartbroken and impotent father in *Le Petit canard*, at the time of the boy's execution as an LVF volunteer; or again, one thinks of the intricate structure of *Les Bêtises*, which expands as the novel develops, embracing an increasing number of social, philosophical and literary issues central in postwar France, and creating a context in which the 'Did he scream?' of the ending acquires the dimensions of a metaphysical cry of anguish.

Despite the paradoxes, there is a great deal of substance in the Laurent corpus, and whether or not one considers him to be a major writer, or a lesser one who sometimes reaches into greatness, he is clearly an author of sufficient significance to merit more attention than he has so far attracted, especially outside France. Part of that significance lies in his wide involvement in political and literary affairs, so that his career and work can be seen as important indicators of how some of the values of the Third Republic have persisted through the great cultural shifts of the postwar era.

An overview of his opus shows it falling into three broad periods, of which the most recent is that of the successful established man of letters – beginning with the Goncourt Prize for *Les Bêtises* in 1971, leading to the *Grand Prix de l'Académie Française* in 1981, and to the height of recognition represented by his admission as a member of the *Académie* in 1986. A very different situation attended him during the Gaullian era, when his persistent musketeering opposition got him into serious trouble with the regime, to the point that he was charged with offences to the Head of State. The earlier period, from the end of the war until the return of De

Gaulle in 1958, is marked by the multiple forms taken on by a daring, if undisciplined talent. This was the heyday of the little group that became known as the 'Hussards' – which as well as Laurent, included Nimier, Déon and Blondin.[4] For Laurent himself, it was the time of the creation of Cécil Saint-Laurent and various other pseudonyms,[5] and of the genesis of a populist, commercial output of quite prodigious proportions.[6] Prodded by his publisher to imitate the success of *Gone with the Wind* and placing such heroines as Caroline, Guillemette and Clothilde in diverse historical settings, some from other eras, others more contemporary, Laurent aimed, with great accuracy moreover, at a mass audience. But it was also the time when, beyond the gadfly activity that kept up busy attacks on Sartrian orthodoxy or the modishness of the *nouveau roman*, he was involved in theatre, cinema, and a number of boldly conceived periodicals, as well as his two 'serious' novels, *Les Corps tranquilles* and *Le Petit canard*.

Before looking at Laurent's first period in detail, to examine how his production offers insight into some attitudes and tensions of French Reconstruction, it is worth sketching in the author's background and early life and making some comments on them. In *Histoire égoïste*[7] and various other statements,[8] he furnishes ample documentation about his family and early activities, and when one pieces it together, it provides not only a psychological explanation of his own contradictions and combativeness, but also a mosaic of many of the divergent forces more generally at work in the France of the 1930s.

His mother's family, of Catholic and aristocratic origins, was nationalist and anti-British in the tradition of French naval officers to which it belonged. Its most startling member was the fanatically antidemocratic Eugène Deloncle, Laurent's maternal uncle, founder of the Cagoule and of the Mouvement Social Révolutionnaire, one of the major public collaborationists of occupied Paris, as well as one of the Occupation's more shadowy cloak-and-dagger figures.[9] On his father's side, Laurent evokes the peasant stock of his forebears, half-Bonapartist, half-Republican, gradually transformed into a collection of anticlerical lawyers, parliamentarians and high-level public servants. To these influences must be added a natural teenage rebelliousness and the discovery of a whole range of literature and philosophy, as well as the impinging presence of the portentous events of the 1930s. The young Laurent – as presented by the older one – reminds one in part of the Olivier of Bernanos's *Un Mauvais rêve* – 'born like that, in little pieces'[10] – and obliged, in his search for some overarching sense of unity or purpose, to put his trust in his own temperament rather than in any principled choice. In this respect, his steady drift towards a nationalist stance in the Action Française movement and as a journalist for *Combat* is less significant in itself than in what it reveals of an intellectual already inclined to skeptical detachment vis-à-vis the external world and to an investment of sensibility in the world of literature.

If what appears to be an irreducible individualism will sometimes take the explicit form of ego- and/or Gallo-centric positions, Laurent's mocking pessimism will also prevent him from taking anything too seriously – anything except the literary tradition, that is, which emerges in his ethos as the only guarantee of freedom and the only reliable conduit for the transmission of culture.

What tradition and what culture? Although his faith in literature embraces a wide range of forms, eras and national origins, he makes it clear in *Le Roman du roman*[11] that his predilection was always for the novel, because of its complexity, its flexibility, its capacity for rendering the sensual as well as the cerebral, the grand as well as the trivial, the individual as well as the social, the present as well as the past. He never gives any tight definition of what he means by a 'novel' – precisely because it is variety that he values and wishes to emphasise – but in his reflection, there is a small cluster of notions that recur: freedom, the ability of the genre to produce new forms, to be the vehicle of a certain social reality, and to suggest the existence of an infinite universe. He also enumerates some conditions antipathetic to the novel – in particular, rigid social conventions or fashions, or totalitarian political regimes. Thus, he will praise Dumas, and defend his own *Caroline* series, but attack the narrowness of the medieval *roman* and what he sees as the dogmatism of the French *nouveau roman*. These ideas, sometimes banal enough in themselves, constitute in Laurent's case a counterbalance to his ideological leanings, the almost religious zeal with which he defends open-ended creativity reinforcing his scepticism as an additional brake on his political prejudices.

It is a historical coincidence, but a nice one, that Jacques Laurent's military service class was chosen, after the 1940 débâcle, to be kept in uniform in the Armée de l'Armistice, and that he should have had the task of helping guard the Demarcation Line as a corporal. This personal experience of being at the interface of the Free Zone and the Occupied Zone, and in the intermediate position between leaders and followers, would appear central to the young writer, and symbolically representative of the collective experience of the French population. Similarly, his modest activity, later in the war, as an intermediary between Vichy and the maquis, which would lead to his joining an FFI unit and from there to a brief stint in the regular army's Liberation sweep, is presented not as something glorious, but as being based on typical attitudes of residual patriotism, in which respect for Pétain and his government were natural ingredients. There is no doubt about Laurent's belief that his kind of attitudes and actions were widely shared, and that there was broad validity in his picture of a French population living the Occupation as uncommitted either to collaboration or Resistance, essentially unaware of official government collaborationism or its extreme manifestations in military aid, paramilitary repression or racial persecution. And indeed, if one knows that such a view is flawed by complacency and selective blindness, one also knows that such failings were themselves common enough in the period – and certainly more so than the heroic bravery of the Resistance fighters, or the dramatic and treacherous cruelty of French Gestapo agents or the Milice. However, Laurent's very accentuation of the mundane aspects of the Occupation is symptomatic of the same pessimistic disillusionment about political and social reality that he had already experienced before the war. The only thing that really mattered to him, it would seem, during this period, was his novel *Les Corps tranquilles*, whose writing was begun during his time on the Demarcation Line and sustained throughout the Occupation, and then well into the beginning of the Fourth Republic.

In summary, the environment in which Laurent grew up imposed on him many of the conflicts and disillusionments common in French society at the time, to which he responded by adopting the generally nationalistic and traditionalist outlook of his class, but one which was tempered both by a pragmatic scepticism about politics and ideology, and by an idealistic belief in the power of literature to transcend the vicissitudes and contingencies of history. The faith in literature as a metaphysical value is in itself traditionalist, and it will be the driving force of the writer's whole career after the war, for, in a context where France's internal disarray and collapse as a great power appeared as an insurmountable and irreversible trauma,[12] it was in that tradition that he saw the only possibility of a continuous French identity.

The social and political ferment of the Liberation and the early years of the Fourth Republic was a climate to which Laurent readily adapted. Jean-Pierre Rioux, in his analysis of the major trends and tensions of the period, opines that if no unifying vision of a new national identity or purpose was able to impose itself, either from the Resistance movements or from the reconstituted institutions of Republican Government, it was principally because the French population as a whole was not yet ready for the necessary effort of regeneration.[13] In reaching this conclusion, Rioux recognises the inevitabilities with which the nation was faced: how the costs of military and economic reconstruction – necessary to the mainten- ance of national sovereignty – made acceptance of the Marshall Plan aid unavoidable, which in turn led to the removal of the Communists from the government; and how the country's weak- nesses rendered it especially vulnerable to the postwar colonial problems. None the less, what remains striking about the period is its astonishing vitality and the equally astonishing range of diver- gent viewpoints on almost everything – and not the least on those matters where there were the most conscious efforts to create the basis for consensus: the *épuration*, for example, or the attempts to forge the three major post-Liberation parties into a viable govern- ment.

But if this diversity was a source of weakness in terms of political unity and social cohesion, it was a stronger force in the literary and intellectual worlds, where the release of energies repressed during the Occupation produced an explosion of new philosophical movements and artistic experimentation. Sartre, Camus, Mounier, Barthes, Lévi-Strauss; Adamov, Genet, Beckett, Ionesco; Sarraute, Robbe-Grillet; André Bazin and the *Cahiers du Cinéma* – the established monuments of the first postwar decade have perhaps, to borrow an image from Starobinski, been 'too rapidly engraved in tablets of stone'; and our view of the time too quickly, and too narrowly delimited by so much attention being focused on Existen- tialism and the Absurd, on Structuralism and semiotics, on the genesis of the 'new' theatre, novel and cinema. Even so, it is an impressive list, and when one adds to it phenomena like the opus of Boris Vian or the immense variety of novel writing, from Jean-Louis Bory, Romain Gary and Roger Vailland, through Jean Dutourd and the 'Hussards' to Françoise Sagan, or yet again, the songs of Georges Brassens, it becomes obvious that from the Liberation until at least Dien Bien Phu, France's cultural revival – and modernisation – was on a very large scale indeed.

There are plenty of teasing paradoxes about the period, many of them resulting from the conflicting claims of a ground-swell of freedom on the one hand, and, on the other hand, various attempts to harness it into old or new orthodoxies. In the political arena, it is not always easy, moreover, to distinguish the new from the old: by 1947, for example, while the government was trying to rebuild itself, the nation and France's place in the world, the veneer of the 'united Resistance' concept had worn so thin that the prewar divisions were again showing through in the big political groupings – with the Communists and Socialists harking back to December 1920, and the MRP and the Gaullists even further, to Pope Leo XIII and Barrès, as all tried to capture positions of influence in a world whose prewar shape had been dramatically altered by the Soviet and American bulldozers.

In the literary and intellectual world, the complications were just as great. There is the well-known case of 'Existentialism' being seen less as a fine philosophical balance of freedom and responsibility than as a kind of extended orgy in the jazz cellars of Saint-Germain-des-Prés. But Sartre offers much more in the way of embodying and creating contradiction. The mellow autobiographer who, in *Les Mots*,[14] portrays himself as devoid of any authoritarian impulse, and declares: 'Throughout my life, I have never given an order without laughing, or being laughed at', has his counterpart in the bemused signal-corps soldier of the *Carnets de la Drôle de guerre*.[15] Yet it is hard to find a more didactic ambition, or a more dogmatic tone, than in *Qu'est-ce que la littérature?*,[16] or in the murderous attack on Céline in his 'Portrait de l'antisémite',[17] or in the savage 1952 liquidation of his friend Camus.[18] Boris Vian's Jean-Sol Partre, pontiff of *L'Ecume des jours*,[19] parodies the double reality of Sartre's appeal to youth being based on many elements quite alien to his philosophy, and on his own vulnerability to the enjoyments of stardom.

There is another interesting example in Robbe-Grillet. When one thinks of the impact of his famous essay of 1957, 'Sur quelques notions périmées',[20] with its assumptions about a non-anthropocentric world-view and its rejection of character, story, commitment and the form–content distinction, one tends to see it as central to the whole development of the novel in France. Now, without denying the real long-term contribution of the *nouveau roman* to the evolution of French fiction and to the modernisation of gallic aesthetic sensibility, the movement's initial success was much greater in the export market than domestically (a phenomenon in which vigorous promotion activities by some producers matched up nicely with the curiosity of avant-garde academics, especially in the USA). However, when *Les Gommes* appeared in 1953,[21] the convoluted narrative quest and the implosion of the self-destructing form were a long way from the centre of literary activity, which was expressing the general climate of renewal in more concretely realistic and more traditionally thematic terms. *Bonjour tristesse*[22] is a case in point: and there is no doubt that the rebellious self-liberation of the young heroine of Sagan's novel, which is written in a classical language and form – including the use of the *passé simple* – was far from being regarded in any way obsolete: and of course, Robbe-Grillet's *dicta* notwithstanding, the character and her story remain perfectly vital today.

Given that for France, as distinct from Italy and Germany, the general prewar social order was not Fascist, or even overtly repressive, it is understandable that the experience of Fascist rule should not in itself have sufficed to dissipate the memory of the earlier atmosphere, and that the Liberation should have revived it. It is in this atmosphere of chaotic fertility, dominated by a quite undifferentiated urge for freedom – as polymorphous and perverse as Freud's descriptions of infant sexuality – that one can best situate the young Jacques Laurent. Indeed, his work reflects that atmosphere perhaps better than any other single author, Boris Vian being the possible exception. (It is not intended to suggest that Vian and Laurent have much in common – despite their early pastiches of American detective thrillers.[23] Vian was both purer in his artistic motivation and more extreme in its expression, afflicted as he was with a despair as sharp-edged as Kafka's, that slices through the commonplaces of language and experience to produce symbols of haunting universality, such as the water-lily in the lung that kills Chloé in *L'Ecume des jours*, or the conflicting construction of hotel and tunnel in *L'Automne à Pékin*.[24]) Laurent's directly political comments at this stage were fairly rare: certainly in his essays in *La Table Ronde*, he attacked the moral bankruptcy of the French authorities during the Occupation – what he called the 'legal' government – as well as pouring scorn on the 'other' master across the Channel. But these attacks were couched in terms that express a general loss of respect for authorities that have lied too much, and a complete disaffection with politics. Against the encroachments of a state power that he perceives as dangerously inquisitorial, he rejects the idea of sacrificing good judgement or human warmth on the altar of 'le Burlesque Show de la politique'. In 1947–8, at the same time that Sartre was calling for 'engagement', Laurent was seeking literary *'démilitantisation'*:

> In politics, there is at present no value, no idea, no party (either recognised or clandestine), no doctrine, which is not either voluntarily or involuntarily complicit in a lie, an injustice, a crime or retraction.
>
> It is a question of knowing whether the role of intellectuals consists in using their talent in order to better camouflage these faults (which is called 'engagement') or whether they should refuse to sacrifice the slightest fragment of their integrity to the lies which are inherent in the political struggle, however pious they may be.[25]

It is the same general anti-authoritarianism that is at work in *Le Petit canard*, rather than any attempt to rehabilitate the memories of young people who stumbled into the LVF: Laurent does not defend the 'choice' of his young protagonist, but, rather, asserts the absence of any reliable guidance principles in society, and castigates the system that condemns the boy to die.

If it were just a retrospective attack on the *épuration*, *Le Petit canard* would be of limited interest. By the time it appeared, the purge had well and truly run out of steam, with the suppression of the special courts in 1951 and the proclamation of the general amnesty law in 1953.[26] However, the novel is also an attack on the 'Resistance' mentality, and as such, part of a movement of significant dimensions, which began with Aymé and Nimier, and has remained ever since as a permanent stratum in the field of French narrative – driven somewhat underground during the Gaullian decade, but otherwise very much in evidence. Covering writers as different in age and background as Céline, Marguerite Duras, Jean Dutourd and Patrick Modiano, this is a vast phenomenon, and it would require a vast study to do it justice.[27] However, there seem to be three characteristics of the movement that were already present in its early manifestations and to which it is worth drawing attention. As simple narratives, one might bear in mind *Le*

Petit canard, Nimier's *Les Epées*, Aymé's *La Tête des autres*, Blondin's
Les Enfants du Bon Dieu, Dutourd's *Au Bon Beurre*, Anouilh's *Pauvre
Bitos*, Duras's *Hiroshima mon amour* and Céline's *D'un Château
l'autre*.[28]

The first shared characteristic of these works is their concern to
bring into the open some of the less glorious or welcome truths of
the French experience of the war and its aftermath – not so much
to judge them, but simply to affirm their right to be told: to say, for
instance, that a rebellious young man might have joined the *Milice*
on an impulse; or that a *milicien* might have managed to slip into
the Liberation army, changing from 'occupied' into 'occupier'; or
that some who exploited the misery of their compatriots during the
Occupation became figures of power and respect during the
postwar period; or that a young girl who fell in love with a German
soldier could have her head shaved, be paraded naked, and be
brutally traumatised by people whose own comportment was not
especially honorable; or that there were some noble-minded
people in the Vichy Government, etc.

The corollary of this individualistic truth-telling – and this is the
second common characteristic – is a rejection (sometimes implied,
sometimes explicit) of any tendency to 'doctrinalise' the Resistance
experience, and to turn the truths of the experience of a handful
into an exclusive vision of history, or into a criterion of what might
be judged as good or bad for the nation. The operative motives
here appear to be not in any disrespect for authentic Resistance
activities (although there is a widespread suspicion about how
such authenticity might be validated), but, once again, in the spirit
of individualism, and in a more specific erosion of credence in the
authoritarian and paternalistic discourse with which official Resistance pronouncements – whether Communist or Gaullist – are so
heavily overlaid, with models of leadership and responsibility very
much confused with that of the *paterfamilias*.

The third characteristic is the most interesting. It is that portrayal
of the 1940–7 period, however important *anecdotally* – that is, in
terms of the new information or insight it may provide – is also
emblematic, a sign of a deeper need and determination to maintain
a link between narrative and the direct emotional experience of life
in its individual and diachronic dimensions. That is, the telling of
the diverse experiences of the particular events or circumstances of
the Occupation and Liberation is predicated on a more fundamental belief in the inherent value of story-telling as a way of

coping with what Paul Ricoeur calls 'the aporia of time',[29] both in terms of individual lives and as a way of understanding social change. On this level, it is obviously a universal tradition that this group of narrative writers is working to maintain – a fact which tended to get lost in the polemical flurries in postwar Parisian intellectual circles.

In his effort to delineate literature – and in particular narrative literature – as an activity worthy of pursuit in its own right, free of political interference, and even of political orientation or interpretation, Jacques Laurent allowed himself the indulgence of facile formula-writing – an indulgence, in that what began as a way of making money to finance his 'serious' writing revealed itself as an irresistible pleasure.[30] It needs to be observed, however, that if the huge output of novels signed Cécil Saint-Laurent is unashamedly intended for middle-class entertainment, relying on sex and intrigue to push the story forward and playing, through various historical settings, on the reader's enjoyment of *dépaysement*, both background and plot are well crafted – certainly not challenging any of the well-established parameters of narrative art, but within the conventions of popular fiction sustained by an out-of-the-ordinary talent. Laurent is no Guy Des Cars.

This talent is more controlled, though still very eclectically applied, in Laurent's work for the literary reviews to which he contributed – the already mentioned *La Table Ronde*, and also *La Parisienne* and *Arts*, which he directed. The first thing that strikes one about the last two is how very committed Laurent was to variety – accommodating Bachelard and Gustave Cohen as well as that young demon of cinema criticism, François Truffaut. This openness, in a broad sense, reflects the way in which the period as a whole, for all its competing doctrines, was able to tolerate the coexistence of its differences. While denying any doctrinal affiliation, Laurent had his obsessional themes and was thus involved in the general struggle, rather than being above it. His own articles reveal an urbane and witty commentator, but one whose motivation was thoroughly consistent: when he tilts at the greats – at Mauriac, Sartre, Malraux, Gide or Camus – it is always to tax them for subordinating their literary talent to a political aim. The text of presentation of *La Parisienne* is illuminating in this regard: 'our ambition is not to guide, but to seduce. Neither a witness, nor a director of conscience, *La Parisienne* is imprudent and touches everything out of the love of art'.[31] Underlying the demand for an art free of commitment is a hedonism that can have its dangers – not only in the sense that the pleasure-impulse can be just as tyrannical as any other criterion of evaluation, but because pleasure is dependent on sensibility, which in Laurent's case, as we have seen, was set very early in a conservative mould. As a result, although his quick intelligence is well-trained for seeking out flaws in an argument or inconsistencies of behaviour, his own judgement is inconsistent, leading him to praise René Massip's *La Régente*, for example, at the expense of Simone de Beauvoir's *Les Mandarins*.[32] Even more tellingly, his praise of Paul Morand's *Flagellant de Séville*, of 1951, is based on Morand's return to traditional syntax, which Laurent imputes to a reaction against postwar abuse of the French language:

> There was ... no longer any interest in teasing out the finer points of syntax when the jargon of the philosophical novelists, the ignorance of the American novelists and the enumerative facility of Prévert-like poets were in the process of murdering it by pedantry, error or omission.[33]

This is the heart of Laurent's conservatism, and the point at which he most clearly illustrates his identification with a certain phase in the development of the French language, and the implication that it should not, or need not, evolve – or not very much – as if it had reached some kind of inherent and universal perfection that would allow it to continue to exist as a reality independent of the political and social world – and, in particular, unaffected by the great changes brought about by the war.

The opposition, in Laurent's ethos, between a fatalistic pessimism about France's future and an untiring defence and illustration of Stendhalian or Proustian French, throws light on another of the dynamic paradoxes of postwar France, namely the coexistence of linguistic traditionalism and the linguistic revolution that has challenged classical syntax and the register hierarchy. Laurent's conservatism marks his writing as progressively more *arrière-garde* as French usage has changed, but it remains well within the broad base of affirmation of the French language as a significant national resource. This linguistic confidence has played an important role in the rebuilding of French self-image and self-esteem. The linguistic policies that have emerged as quite central in contemporary France's global geopolitical strategies are worth extensive study in themselves, but it is clear that linguistic traditionalism is as powerful a factor as any other trend. It is no historical accident that the bastion of tradition, the Académie Française, should experience the need to offer seats to both Ionesco and Laurent.

Laurent has spoken of *Les Corps tranquilles* as the work to which he is most attached, with *Les Bêtises*.[34] Of very considerable length – almost a thousand pages in the standard hardback edition – and elaborated over a period of seven or eight years, it is the best example of the author's artistic motivations and goals during his first period. Laurent's own often-repeated assertion that the novel was the product of an instinctive need, and not of conscious planning, is worth bearing in mind, since it sits well with his general rejection of the idea of writing *for* something; though at the same time, however unconsciously his choices were made, the book does reveal a certain coherence of vision.

An obvious aspect of this is the setting of the novel in the period March 1937–March 1938. There is a footnote warning us that the novel does not seek to render the 'teneur historique' of 1937.[35] But even if it is not deliberate, the choice of a time of trough in the build-up to the war, and a time when the disintegration of the *Front populaire* Government and the internal problems of France were more significant, momentarily, than what was happening in the rest of the world, allows Laurent to express symbolically his view of the *postwar* climate, and to insinuate an idea of cultural continuity that he finds congenial: namely that of a weak and divided central government that allows the greatest possible freedom of individual behaviour.

The slice-of-life approach is as classical as the five-part structure, but in fact, the real driving forces of the novel are in the intertwined adventures of clusters of characters, most of them young; and in the eclectic experimentation with a wide variety of narrative forms and techniques. As far as the characters are concerned, the author's vision is resolutely individualistic. Social collectivities are presented in systematically negative terms, and more or less indiscriminately: that is, because they are collectivities, and not because of what the collectivities represent. Thus, the parliament carried around in his head by Toussaint Rose[36] – a kind of Socialist Amédée Fleurissoire, and just as tragi-comically touching – is represented as being of the same order as say, the Jeunesses nationales group that turns the young Gilbert Duruy into a sexual bully and a proto-Fascist thug. The collectivist impulses are considered only in terms of their impact on individuals. It needs to be said, however, that behind the action, collectivist values loom like the demon in a shadow-play, seldom in focus, but menacingly present. Whether it be the obviously identifiable police force that closes in on Bataillère's club – using enormous powers of coercion and repression for quite trivial reasons – or the Bataillère lonely-hearts club itself, which reduces business and literary talent to a crass exploitation of people's solitude, there is an underlying assumption of necessary corruption as soon as the limits of individual experience are forced. At its most mythical, the collective assumes the guise of Goribon – the mysterious person or international entity behind the Antisuicide institute whose activities dominate the novel's first half, in a grand swindle involving government and police. Evocative of the prewar Stavisky scandal and the postwar Joanovici, 'Goribon' is above all an incarnation of Laurent's distrust of collectivities.

No single character monopolises the narrative. On the contrary, Laurent displays a large number of individuals – which in itself indicates another of his basic tenets. His readers follow characters, lose sight of them, are brought back to them in a loose, if not random fashion. Links between characters, too, are made in a quite free-wheeling way: we meet the adolescent Jacques because he is Monique's brother, but he becomes a significant figure in his own right; similarly with Maurice, who enters the story-line first as Frédérique's husband, but whose mathematical reflections are taken into the narrative as an illuminating symbol. There is, none the less, a central protagonist – Anne Coquet – whose adventures form a loose network of bonds between the various places and people, and whose experience receives a quantitatively greater treatment than any other character's.

Coquet is a modern fictional hero with a Laurentian twist. A writer of popular novels, and a professional ghost-writer for other authors, he is self-conscious to the point of being ridiculous, but at the same time as tragically alienated as a Meursault, unable to believe in anything – in his work, in his love affairs, in his own physical illness. Haunted by a lingering fear of death and of 'les maladies ignobles', but detached from it, his super-bright intelligence darts about, lighting up the external details of his undirected experience, registering the conventionally important things (such as love and death and suffering) on the same flat surface as the ephemera of everyday life – such as snippets of conversation overheard in a park or café, or the graffiti on the walls of a restaurant toilet. Coquet is less a self-portrait of the artist Laurent, one suspects, than an exorcism of the aimlessness into which Laurent might have fallen had he not pursued the 'serious' side of his literary vocation – a person whose superior and penetrating intellect allows him no repose, even in his exhaustingly frequent sexual encounters, to which he submits with conscientious resignation.

Let it be said in passing that the erotic side of Laurent's writing, to which he gives a lot of attention, is not always the best controlled. There is no doubt an element of realism in the ways in which the youth of the late 1930s went about shaking off their sexual fetters – and this would be equally true for the late 1940s. And Laurent also does some fine psychological analysis of the erotic: the sexual awakening of young Jacques, and the rendering of his perception of his older sister's affair with Anne Coquet, is very delicate; as is the sequence that shows Anne's ambivalent feelings towards his mistress Frédérique, as he begins to discover the worth of her husband. Furthermore, Laurent is capable of treating the erotic with great humour: Gilbert's desperate need to lose his virginity is the subject of some very funny parodic scenes. None the less, there is a certain obsessiveness in the approach to the theme, and one might be forgiven for opining that too many of the characters spend too much time either in some form of erotic activity, or in planning on how to produce some.

That much having been said, *Les Corps tranquilles* is very much a young man's novel, and it is perhaps natural that Eros should dominate Thanatos. As has been suggested already, the fear of death is one of the powerful organic aspects of Laurent's personal ethos, becoming more dominant as his opus progresses and with his own ageing, but its role in *Les Corps tranquilles* is very much a background one. There is a striking example of its subordination in the sequence of the death of Monique's grandmother, who not only goes on her way in a most serene manner, but clad in a dress which she has had regularly updated to be sure that it is in the latest fashion when she is finally laid in her coffin. Or again, there is Sabine's Aunt Alexandrine, who is having all the dead of all the branches of her ancestral family transhumed from their graves all over France to a single cemetery in each region – an operation which she carries out with military precision, with the aid of detailed maps, train timetables, etc.

It is the male characters who have the predominant roles in the novel – Coquet, young Jacques, Toussaint Rose, the entrepreneur Bataillère, the stuffy professor Lafontaine-Pialat, the Communist Beige, the proto-Fascist Gilbert, etc. But Laurent is fascinated by his numerous women figures, too, from demure young schoolgirls like Jackie, to sophisticated social manipulators like Mme Hallein, and he tries to come to terms with their perception of the world. The women are just as vigorous in exploring their freedom as the men, and Laurent even has his main female protagonist, Monique, tackle Anne Coquet on his double standards in matters of sexual fidelity. In short, Laurent's celebration of youth and individuality includes a recognition of women as independent and equal members of society, a fact worth mentioning in the context of his generally conservative values, since it suggests a wide acceptance of the October 1944 decree giving women the right to vote.

His large number of individual characters offers Laurent an opportunity to play with many different narrative voices, and he uses it extensively. If the range of interior monologues is impressively broad, however, the novel's technical interest depends on much more. Laurent uses his novel as a place to experiment with all sorts of discourse forms and registers, creating a multiply-layered text that contains everything from straight omniscient narrative to the 'collage' effect of quoting an external document in a footnote (one of the latter being an excerpt from the *Larousse du XIXè Siècle*'s article on the dangers of onanism). In between, there are passages of Anne's schoolboy diary, there are exchanges of letters, reproductions of newspaper articles, brochures and police reports (authentic and invented), there are speeches; and there is a clever theatrical scene (with appropriate typography) in which the pre-curtain chatter of the school-children players of *Le Misanthrope* merges into the actual performance. In one instance, Laurent uses stream-of-consciousness, and at the same time mocks it by providing footnoted directions about how it can be read. On the other hand, he demonstrates a mastery of the Dos Passos simultaneist technique in an emotionally strong section on Christmas 1937.

What does all this add up to? It is obvious that Laurent's idea of a 'roman-laboratoire' is not the same as that of a Butor.[37] His approach is much more lucid. Unlike the 'nouveaux romanciers', he does not believe that the novel needs revolutionising, simply because, in his view, it is a form capable of infinite adaptation: and *Les Corps tranquilles* is, in a sense, an illustration of that capacity.

There is one very funny episode that epitomises Laurent's attitude: Aunt Alexandrine, worried that the masses are being lured away from the Church by the direct discourse of Marxism, is sponsoring and organising a project to have the gospels translated into *argot*, and seeking out authentic *argot*-speakers, in the cafes or in prison, to ensure the authenticity of the translation.[38]

If Laurent is being serious at all here, it is not to save the masses from Marxism. It may be that he is satirising the populist mode, but principally, he is having fun, and demonstrating the novelist's right to be playful. His approach to narrative strategy is a coherent reflection of the rest of his vision: an eclecticism free of doctrinaire compulsion.

Does it all hold together? There does not seem to be any mechanism to structure the use of all the different techniques, other than Laurent's obvious aesthetic commitment to diversity. But it is in this that he seems to reflect the climate of contradiction so typical of the Fourth Republic. In taking on the colours of the modernisation of the post-Liberation era, Laurent does not foresake the traditional novelist's omniscience, and his fractious rejection of all forms of authoritarianism does not make him question his own authorial powers as story-teller. In portraying the coexistence of smug frivolity and alienated bewilderment among the young middle-class generation, he seems to assume that life in France will continue pretty much as before the war, subject only to the laws of natural entropy.

Under De Gaulle, Laurent became increasingly embittered as the spirit of the Fourth Republic was squeezed aside by the powerful centralism of the Fifth. Reduced to defending lost causes, such as the French retention of Algeria, he ended up pushing the untenable and self-defeating view that De Gaulle, although a consumate showman, had had no effect at all on history, either in 1940, or in 1944, or after his return in 1958. If Cécil Saint-Laurent survived the Gaullian era, the creative momentum that Jacques Laurent's *esprit frondeur* had generated during the previous decade was lost. None the less, with *Les Bêtises*, in 1971, he would begin to rebuild his broken career. That is a story in its own right, whose telling would require, among other things, an examination of degrees of vitality and atrophy in some of France's major cultural institutions, such as the Prix Goncourt and the Académie Française, and of their relationship to the development of mass culture.

Notes

1. Interview with Josyane Savignon in *Le Monde*, 28 February 1986.
2. Jean-François Josselin, 'Les Confidences de Monsieur Laurent', *Le Nouvel Observateur*, 5–11 September 1981, p. 57.
3. The original text reads as follows:

   > Dans ce jeu des voilures et des gréements, la croupe et les cuisses, se tendant et se compressant au rythme de l'escalade, se martelant et s'attirant mutuellement selon un enclenchement mecanique, enchassés dans une architecture de courroies, de focs, de boucles, de câbles, tiennent prisonnière, entre leurs fûts et leurs meules, la languette de soie du slip qui tantôt disparaît, entortillé dans un chaton de chair obscure, tantôt, apres avoir été élonguée par une tension extrême, se relache au point de livrer à la vue les bruns contreforts du sexe. (Jacques Laurent, *Les Corps tranquilles* (Paris: La Table Ronde, 1958) pp. 602–3)

4. The name came from Nimier's novel, *Le Hussard bleu*, of 1950. The group, as such, was christened in a very hostile article by Bernard Franck, 'Grognards et hussards', in *Les Temps Modernes*, December 1952, pp. 1005–18. Franck does not, however, mention Déon.
5. The following list is probably not exhaustive: Cécil Saint-Laurent, Jacques Laurent-Cély, Laurent Lebattu, Jean Parquin, Albéric Varenne, Edgar Vuymont....
6. There are dozens of titles, J.-L. Ezine, in *Les Ecrivains sur la sellette* (Paris: Seuil, 1981) calculated eighty or ninety. I have verified about three dozen different titles, of which the most popular are *Caroline chérie*, of 1947, and the three volumes of *Hortense 14–18* (1963–7).
7. Jacques Laurent, *Histoire égoïste* (Paris: La Table Ronde, 1976).
8. Jacques Laurent has always been generous with his interviews, and, in addition, many of his essays are sprinkled with autobiographical data. There is a useful supplement to the family information contained in *Histoire égoïste* in 'Jacques Laurent est-il français?', in *Le Monde*, 11 July 1985.
9. See Pascal Ory, *Les Collaborateurs* (Paris, Seuil, 1976) pp. 98–100.
10. Georges Bernanos, *Un Mauvais rêve*, in *Oeuvres romanesques* (Paris: Gallimard, coll. 'Editions de la Pléïade', 1961) p. 966.
11. Jacques Laurent, *Le Roman du roman* (Paris: Gallimard, 1977).
12. C. W. Nettelbeck, unpublished interview with Jacques Laurent (January 1980).
13. See J.-P. Rioux, *La France et la Quatrième République*, vol. I (Paris: Seuil, 1981) pp. 259–65.
14. Jean-Paul Sartre, *Les Mots* (Paris: Gallimard, 1964).
15. Jean-Paul Sartre, *Carnets de la Drôle de guerre* (Paris: Gallimard, 1985).
16. Jean-Paul Sartre, *Qu'est-ce que la littérature?* (Paris: Gallimard, 1947).
17. Jean-Paul Sartre, 'Portrait de l'antisémite', *Les Temps Modernes* December 1945, p. 462.
18. Jean-Paul Sartre, 'Réponse à Albert Camus', *Les Temps Modernes*, July 1952.

19. Boris Vian, *L'Ecume des jours* (Paris: Gallimard, 1947).
20. Alain Robbe-Grillet, *Pour un nouveau roman* (Paris: Gallimard, 1963) pp. 29–53.
21. Alain Robbe-Grillet, *Les Gommes* (Paris: Editions de Minuit, 1953).
22. Françoise Sagan, *Bonjour tristesse* (Paris: Julliard, 1954).
23. Compare Boris Vian (alias Vernon Sullivan), *J'irai cracher sur vos tombes* (Paris: Editions du Scorpion, 1946) and Jacques Laurent, *La Mort à boire* (Paris: Froissard, 1947).
24. Boris Vian, *L'Automne à Pékin* (Paris: Editions du Scorpion, 1947).
25. Jacques Laurent, 'Pour une stèle au Docteur Petiot', *La Table Ronde* (May 1948); reprinted in J. Laurent, *Au contraire* (Paris: La Table Ronde, 1967) pp. 17–25. This is a most useful anthology of Laurent's review essays.
26. See Rioux, *La France*, I, p. 57.
27. Some aspects of this have been examined in C. W. Nettelbeck, 'Getting the Story Right: Narratives of World War II in Post-1968 France', *Journal of European Studies*, XV (1985) pp. 77–116; and in A. Morris, 'Attacks on the Gaullist "Myth" in French Literature since 1969', *Forum for Modern Language Studies*, XXI, 1 (January 1985) pp. 71–91.
28. Roger Nimier, *Les Epées* (Paris: Gallimard, 1948); Marcel Aymé, *La Tête des autres* (Paris: Grasset, 1952); Antoine Blondin, *Les Enfants du Bon Dieu* (Paris: La Table Ronde, 1952); Jean Dutourd, *Au Bon Beurre* (Paris: Gallimard, 1952); Jean Anouilh, *Pauvre Bitos* (Paris: La Table Ronde, 1958; first performed 1956); Marguerite Duras, *Hiroshima mon amour* (Paris: Gallimard, 1960; written 1956–7); Louis-Ferdinand Céline, *D'une Château l'autre* (Paris: Gallimard, 1957).
29. Paul Ricoeur, *Temps et récit*, vol. I (Paris: Seuil, 1983).
30. Compare Laurent, *Histoire égoïste*, pp. 403–4.
31. Quoted in Laurent, *Au contraire*, p. 295.
32. See ibid., p. 219.
33. Ibid., p. 184.
34. 'Pour moi, n'aurais-je fait que ces deux livres, la justification de mon existence, en tant qu'écrivain sur la terre, serait faite' (unpublished interview with C. W. Nettelbeck, January 1980).
35. At the end of the text.
36. This technique is taken up again in *Les Bêtises*.
37. See Michel Butor, *Répertoires*, vol. I (Paris: Editions de Minuit, 1960) pp. 7–11.
38. The original text is as follows:

> Actes des Potes. Paulot, X, I. Y avait à Césarmuche un pitaine de griffetons ritals qui en pinçait pour Dieu et qui, rien cave, égrenait son artichaut au populo. A neuf plombes, voila que le pitaine y bigle un angelot qui se ramène en l'appelant par son blaze. L'autre, les miches à zéro, y jacte: De quoi, Seigneur? Et l'angelot lui rétorque: Tes salades et les colibards que tu donnes aux purées, ça lui botte, au Seigneur. (Laurent, *Les Corps tranquilles*, p. 846)

10

German Literature in 1945: Liberation for a New Beginning?

HELMUT PEITSCH

The prevailing opinion in the Federal Republic is that 8 May 1945 was not, in fact, a liberation from Fascism, but, according to CDU/CSU Party Whip Alfred Dregger, a 'catastrophe' for the German Reich as it is supposed to survive today within the boundaries set in 1937.[1] Furthermore, the editor of the *Frankfurter Allgemeine Zeitung*, Joachim Fest, has said that it was 'a defeat for the principle of democracy', since the Soviet Union ranked among the victors in the coalition against Hitler.[2] A counterpart to this attitude is to be found in the debate over postwar literature. Here too, the question as to the 'Liberation for a new beginning' is flatly refuted. A basic element of continuity and a certain orientation towards the West are the essential features of the political and corresponding literary historical significance of the 8 May.

In the words of Hans-Peter Schwarz, in the *History of the Federal Republic of Germany*:

> this continuity was really quite natural – after all, the 3rd Reich only lasted twelve years! – and contemporaries were perfectly aware of it. It was somewhat forgotten over the following decades, however, when the image of the literary scene ... was increasingly formed by the generation of writers and literary scholars who had only begun to write after 1945. They created the impression, quite incorrectly, that German literature had had to begin anew from a spiritual and intellectual 'Nullpunkt' ['Year Zero'] in 1945. At that time, in fact, the continuity had been quite obvious.[3]

In his positive evaluation of continuity (to which he adds Western values of 'pluralism' and cosmopolitan openness[4] as new features of literature after 1945), Schwarz is alluding to those critical,

172

literary historical works which had been seeking since the mid 1960s to expose such 'uncritical platitudes' (Wolfgang Emmerich)[5] as the notions of 'Nullpunkt' and the 'Stunde Null' ('Zero Hour'). Hans Mayer declared categorically in 1967: 'There can be no question of a "Nullpunkt" or of a beginning from scratch in German literature'.[6] Later studies by Frank Trommler, Hans Dieter Schäfer and Volker Wehdeking gradually built up the picture of a uniformly restorative period[7] in literary history between 1930 and 1960, in which neither 1933 nor 1945 represented an interruption. In 1967, however, Hans Mayer still emphasised the existence of an *impulse* towards a new beginning, which had been released by the military victory over Fascism.

Mayer referred at that time to 'a number of books based on personal experience of the immediate post-war period', in which the 'linguistic and literary "Kahlschlag" ("clean sweep")' demanded by Wolfgang Weyrauch and others was seen to be realised, as well as to the 'speeches about construction and renewal ... whose serious intent and democratic motivation is beyond question'.[8] Hans Mayer only retracted this partial recognition of a tendency towards a 'Neubeginn' in 1978. At a conference of the newly founded Cultural Circle of the Committee for an Undivided Germany, he delivered the heading 'Restoration and New Unity', describing the literary development in both German states as equally restorative and putting the 'withdrawal of the expectations and goals, and the Utopian enthusiasm' of 1945 on the same footing as that of 1968.[9]

This uniformly black picture of 'deutscher Misere' was popularised one year later by Fritz J. Raddatz, in his article in *Die Zeit* entitled 'We will go on writing, even when everything is in ruins', which was based in particular on the research of Hans Dieter Schäfer. Raddatz bombastically declared: 'The theory until now was: 1945 was "Kahlschlag" and "Nullpunkt". The theory is wrong. Postwar German literature began during the war.'[10] Even if the conservative Hans-Peter Schwarz refers us to the consciousness of contemporaries, the theory of continuity becomes problematic when it denies the significance of the break made by the 8 May.

The foreigners in our country are now seeing that everything is put in order.... They are now doing what we should have done long ago. They are removing the military rule of the Nazis, country squires and industrial barons. Why? In order to make us peaceful. But we were not belligerent. It was instilled into us. . . . Let us get moving. Let us seize this moment. . . . The way which we could not open has been opened up, our way. . . . We have been beaten. Let us take heart. No longer a great power, no longer do we want power, but – a new construction of our society. Finally, after centuries, German freedom.[11]

It was with this very direct linking of individual with social change that Alfred Döblin closed his pamphlet *The Nürnberg Lesson*. In the expectation that he would be able to contribute to the 'new construction' of German society and to the 'pacification' of Germans after the military destruction of Fascism, the writer who had fled the Wehrmacht from France into American exile was motivated to return to the ruined Germany quickly, and even in French uniform as an official of the military government of occupation: 'I can do something useful here',[12] he wrote to American friends in his first letter from Baden-Baden. His optimism was confirmed by the existence of literary organisations, newspapers and periodicals, and publishing projects: 'there is a "cultural council" made up of native anti-Fascists',[13] whose lectures Döblin praised; he prepared his periodical *The Golden Gate* 'on the job', by writing to authors all over the world ('for of course I must open up again the door shut to them in 1933');[14] he also wanted to promote the publishers' contribution to the renewal with his own books: 'over there my drawer lay full of manuscripts; that too will change'.[15]

The problem with Döblin's expectation at an individual level is revealed by the statement of a writer who, unlike Döblin, had remained in Nazi Germany. The difference is all the more striking since Wilhelm Hausenstein, former director of the features pages of the *Frankfurter Zeitung*, shared the principal expectation for change. On 9 May 1945 he wrote in his diary: 'the change in events has not produced a change in spirits'.[16] In Hausenstein's eyes, the importance of literature was increased because of this: since people had not learned from their own experience, literature must come to their assistance. Hausenstein, however, to whom the Americans had offered the direction of the soon-to-be-founded *Süddeutsche Zeitung* did not think much of the contribution that the literature of the 'exiles' could make to the spiritual and intellectual change. For Hausenstein, 'helpful'[17] books came from Hans Carossa, Ernst

Jünger, Werner Bergengruen, Emil Barth or Ernst Penzoldt: not only, therefore, from Christian or bourgeois Humanist 'Inner Emigrants', but also from authors who had been helped on by Fascism. Whilst Hausenstein was very generous in this respect, his objections to exile literature were much more pointed. He turned against Klaus Mann's point of view, which he saw as 'the collective attitude of those in exile': 'all of us who did not live in emigration during these years have contributed to the "cultural facade" of the Third Reich'.[18] In response to this, Hausenstein asserted in his diary-entry of 15 May 1945 that:

> all emigrants simply withdrew from Germany and its conflicts during these twelve years: THERE IS NOTHING POSITIVE IN SIMPLY RUNNING AWAY FROM A SITUATION. – Yet there was surely something worthwhile in striving for twelve years as a journalist TO PRESERVE THE PURITY OF GOODNESS FOR ITS OWN SAKE, and in such a style as though Hitler and his scoundrels DIDN'T EVEN EXIST, despite the danger. No future generation will even SUSPECT, from the literary and women's pages of the *Frankfurter Zeitung* during the ten years that I edited them, that they were produced under Hitlerism: they were so thoroughly edited above and beyond the regime, not even at a tangent. I believe that THIS means something, and it leaves me with a perfectly clear conscience. 'Cultural facade': if this notion were to make any sense, there would have to have been a LINK between the supposed facade and the house behind it: but this link did NOT exist: my work, and any similar work, existed QUITE ON ITS OWN, TOTALLY ISOLATED.[19]

On three points, Hausenstein's record from May 1945 anticipates the debate over exile and Inner Emigration which took place in the summer of 1945 in the Allied-controlled radio stations and in the newly founded newspapers of the occupying powers: first, as a moral/political criticism of exile; second, as a justification of the writers who published in Nazi Germany; and third, as a description of the change that was sought in favour of intellectual continuity. Hausenstein accused the exile writers of cowardice, contrasting their 'simple escape' with the 'daily peril' under National Socialism; he exonerated the literature of Inner Emigration by asserting the autonomy of literature that was 'good for its own sake', 'pure', and 'on its own, totally isolated', and in doing so undermined questions as to social function. Hausenstein's third point is particularly important for the problem of change: in Hausenstein's view of things, change should mean the widespread adoption of the behaviour demonstrated by him, and by other members of the intelligensia like him, under Fascism. Change thus appeared to be a matter for others, but not for oneself.

Two examples illustrate the connection between the moral vilification of exile and the justification of Inner Emigration with arguments of literary autonomy and change as continuity. They stem from two very different representatives of Inner Emigration: Elizabeth Langgässer, a Catholic who was banned from writing in 1936, and Frank Thiess, a conservative who had welcomed Hitler's election to the Chancellorship of the Reich in 1933. In her letters of 1945, Elizabeth Langgässer criticised the literary life emerging in postwar Berlin as lifeless and lacking culture, because people were 'unchanged after all their ordeals and suffering'.[20] People were 'stuck in 1933' and eating out of 'tin cans': that is to say, relying for inspiration and guidance on figures like Ernst Toller, Kurt Tucholsky and Bertolt Brecht, 'instead of looking out for the true young elite'.[21] Elizabeth Langgässer emphatically claimed continuity for herself. She suggested that even during the bombardment of 1943 she had found 'inner freedom and liberation'[22] in her faith and literary production: 'This period must be regarded as one of asceticism, involving spiritual reflection, silence, practice, and inner experience and visions. Only in this way can a meaning be found and monstrousness be tolerated.'[23] Precisely because of this preoccupation with the continuity of values, she failed to notice the change in the Socialist exiled writers whom she had pronounced dead with the macabre tin-can image. In their place, she claimed for herself a position of spiritual leadership on behalf of the 'young generation'.

Frank Thiess laid false claim to the creation of the concept of Inner Emigration, to describe those non-Nazi writers who remained in Germany. He it was, though, who engaged in a momentous public dispute with Thomas Mann. Originally, the term Inner Emigration had emphasised the common ground of anti-Fascism which united opponents of Hitler inside and outside Germany. Thiess changed this by extending the notion of Inner Emigration in such a way as to justify any behaviour under Nazism. Inner Emigration was equated with spiritual and intellectual resistance, and the purely internal, often only private, rejection of National Socialism came to be seen publically as the only true 'spiritual' and 'German' form of opposition. According to Frank Thiess: 'Wherever one met like-minded people, a word or a glance was often enough to recognise each other as allies against a world of terror and as Germans against the un-German spirit of arrogance and nastiness.'[24] The Socialist exiled authors endeavoured to bring together exile and Inner Emigration, and therefore rejected the 'ugly and senseless squabbling over each other's burden of suffering and persecution'.[25] The tacit premise in this dispute was that greater suffering meant superior understanding, and therefore precedence as spiritual and intellectual leaders of a new Germany. Frank Thiess asserted that Inner Emigrants had had to 'stand by their posts'[26] and had not gone into exile for the reason that:

> if I should manage to survive this dreadful era, I will have won so much for my spiritual and human development that I will emerge from it richer in knowledge and experience than if I had watched the German tragedy from the seats of the boxes and stalls abroad.[27]

In his *Farewell to Thomas Mann*, Thiess pursued his argument against this representative of exile literature:

> what will carry us to new shores . . . will be in a new hope and a new certainty of indestructible inner worth. It cannot be the message of an 'American citizen of the world' writing in German; it can only be the fruit grown from the bloody seeds of German and European suffering.[28]

The experience of suffering and the preservation of the spiritual values of the West, of Christianity and bourgeois Humanism, were, for Thiess,[29] as for Langgässer, justification enough for a spiritual leadership which they denied the exiled writers, be they liberals or Socialists.

Johannes R. Becher belonged to the latter. He, like Döblin, returned quickly to Germany in order to assume cultural-political responsibilities. He had said in his suggestions to the KP working committee on the reordering of Germany, which met in Moscow on 29 September 1944, that:

> peace is the continuation of the war against Fascism by other means . . . Total defeat will call for total criticism in all spheres. It

would be disastrous if this criticism were to be limited to the political and military leadership. It would be equally disastrous if the Nazi clique were the only ones branded with guilt. Certainly they are the main offenders, but the fact that they ever managed to become the main offenders means that our whole historical development must come open to criticism.[30]

Becher therefore defined re-education as a 'process of politicisation and democratisation'[31] and as a 'task of liberation and construction'.[32] He took up the *Bündnispolitik* of the German KP in the 1930s, the policy of united action and of a Popular Front, illustrated when he set literature the following goal: 'Anti-Fascist literature will become the dominant German literature; it will become a new national literature'.[33] Becher justified the leading role of his party and its writers by showing the scientific nature of the historical criticism which would have to be achieved in a national self-criticism of Fascism and the German traditions expressed in it. Brecht, observing Becher's national pathos and his speeches and writings imploring the 'new German Man',[34] noted in his work journal, on the occasion of Becher's article 'Death and Resurrection': 'at least the Pied Piper of Hamlin must have been able to whistle'.[35] Becher's insistence on historical materialism is nevertheless remarkable, when he repeatedly based his thinking on the premises of Lenin's analysis of imperialism and Marx's and Engels' concepts of base and superstructure: 'We cannot be satisfied with superficial anti-Fascism, we must endeavour to deepen the collective mood against Fascism and broaden it to include conscious anti-imperialism'.[36] Scientific, historical criticism provided the foundation for the claim to leadership made by the forces of Communist anti-Fascism, who envisaged a new order and a new beginning, a change in social conditions and, as Becher put it, 'a fundamental transformation in feeling and thought' in the individual German 'in an effective context'.[37]

If we summarise the expectations of a new beginning linked to 8 May 1945, important differences are already revealed in these hopes for change. The more spiritual and individual the change is seen as, the more clearly conservative and liberal ideas differ from those of the Socialists. Bernd Hüppauf characterised 'somewhat schematically' the three main groups at work in literary life as follows: '(1) The expropriation of the means of production and reordering of society under the leadership of the working classes;

(2) Humanist Socialism in a representative democracy; (3) recollection of the true values of the European tradition: Humanism and Christianity.'[38] Most of the ideas on the 'new beginning' to be found in the literature of 1945–6, and particularly in the newspapers and periodicals which dominated publishing activity, can easily be attributed to one of the three currents of literary thought established and selected by contemporary writers:[39] the literature of Inner Emigration, represented by Ernst Wiechert, Reinhold Schneider or Ricarda Huch; exile literature, represented by Alfred Döblin or Johannes R. Becher; and the literature of the 'young generation', represented by Hans Werner Richter and Alfred Andersch. To the extent that the descriptions of these three literary tendencies reveal the age or place of residence during the years of National Socialism, they certainly lie on different conceptual planes. Yet they all focus on the same problem. All three try to deal with the question of German guilt: the exiled writers fled Hitler's regime, the Inner Emigrants remained in Germany whilst remaining at odds with National Socialism, and the 'young generation' was too young to be guilty of anything. It is a telling fact that the problem of guilt, at the heart of politics in the postwar years, seems totally absent from the self-definitions of the different literary tendencies, despite the fact that the definitions are not in fact literary, but almost exclusively political in character.

Of the authors quoted up to now, only Elizabeth Langgässer, who was 46 at the time, counted herself as one of the young generation. For them, it was not spiritual values preserved under Fascism, as it was for the conservative Inner Emigrants, nor was it the scientific critique of Fascism as imperialism, as it was for Socialist exiles, which provided the basis for a claim to leadership after the war. The exponents of the thesis of the 'young generation' employed a very broad definition of youth, including everybody between 15 and 45 years of age, which covered about half the population.[40] This breadth certainly says a lot for the function of the term in lifting the burden of guilt, but the difficulties involved with it are less obvious. The thirty-year span of this generation is only unified by the common bond of eligibility for military service, and the basis for the legitimacy of the literary young generation was, consequently, the experience of war. On the authority of this experience, Alfred Andersch and Hans Werner Richter rejected as equally ideological the conservatives' offer of reorientation according to long-established truths and the Communists' plan for the reordering of social conditions. Through 'the experience of the battlefront and of imprisonment . . . and of having "laid one's life on the line" ',[41] Andersch saw young Germans as being linked to the French Resistance and to Existentialism: 'They have in common their attitudes and experience, independent of any ideology or ethos'.[42] Andersch wrote about 'young Germany': 'They stood up for something wrong. . . . But they did stand up'.[43]

In the different periodicals founded around 1846, such as *Der Ruf, Ende und Anfang, Horizont* and *Pinguin*, the writers of the young generation presented themselves as a band of common soldiers, sceptical and disillusioned. In his *Statement on the Nürnberg Trial*, Andersch drew a clear distinction between the guilty generals and the innocent 'young Germans':[44] just as Hausenstein could see no functional connection between Fascism and the *Frankfurter Zeitung*, so Andersch saw no link between Fascism and military service:

> There is no connection whatsoever between the astonishing acts of valour by young Germans in this war and the 'acts' of somewhat older Germans who are now standing trial at Nürnberg. The warriors of Stalingrad, El Alamein and Cassino, who were accorded every respect even from their opponents, are innocent of the crimes of Dachau and Buchenwald.[45]

Unlike some of the conservative Inner Emigrants and liberal, as well as Socialist, exiled writers, for whom the 8 May was undoubtedly a liberation, the authors based primarily around *Der Ruf* used the idea of the collapse of all traditions as the premise for a new beginning. In their eyes, conservatives, liberals and Socialists were old simply because they wanted to preserve any traditions at all. In a critical analysis of 'the attempts of a few groups of young Germans to take up the question of generation consciousness in print',[46] particularly in the Munich periodical *Der Ruf*,[47] Werner Krauss, a Resistance fighter and Professor of Romance Studies at Marburg at that time, pointed out that: 'the experience of a generation only assumes historical relevance if the fetters of tradition no longer exist'.[48] For Krauss, the extraordinary feature of the attempt to politically revive a generation consciousness after 1945 lay in the inner contradiction of its youthfulness:

> It is a fine thing that sons are here again to sit in judgement on their fathers. But the 'betrayed generation' has passed the death

sentence on the bond between generations with its outcry: they are in fact accusing the fathers because they couldn't stop their sons from fulfilling their wildest dreams, because they were unable to protect these young people from themselves![49]

Johannes R. Becher saw the connection between swimming with the current and disillusionment in a similar way: 'the man who believed everything is the man who now no longer believes anything'.[50]

In the literary-programmatic articles of Alfred Andersch and Hans Werner Richter, who later founded the Gruppe 47, the polemical distancing from the literature of exiled writers was much more pronounced than that of the Inner Emigrants, with whom they at least shared the experience of war in the service of Fascism. It is no coincidence that Andersch singled out Carl Zuckmayer's drama *Des Teufels General* as the sole exception to the rule that exile literature was an aesthetic failure. Andersch detected 'a hidden artistic defect in this whole current in German literature' in the 'tendentious realistic novels' of Heinrich Mann, Arnold Zweig, Franz Werfel, Feuchtwanger and Becher: 'They are electrically loaded with a particular tendency which is harmful to the true artistic concerns of realism',[51] and 'In this day and age, when the fragility of all the objective systems of values is becoming ever more apparent, and when nothing remains but man's bare existence, it seems doubly absurd to offer us a form of realism carrying the symptoms of propaganda'.[52] Andersch's essay *Deutsche Literatur in der Entscheidung* [*German Literature at the Crossroads*], of 1947, is one of the many descriptions of the literary situation which, in the postwar period, replaced manifestos and political programmes. In it, it is not only the experience of Nazi Germany from the inside that makes him feel an affinity to the Inner Emigrants, but also the conception of literary autonomy:

> German literature, insofar as it merits an individual identity, was synonymous with emigration, and with a geographical and mental distance from the dictatorship. It must be established once and for all that any literature which saw the light of day under Nazi rule was a form of opposition by virtue of the very fact that it was literature.[53]

Despite this proximity to liberalism and conservatism, the literary publicists of the young generation saw themselves as Democratic

Socialists, and aligned themselves critically within the sphere of the SPD. The declaration of their belief in Socialism, which Richter and Andersch, and even more assertively Walter Heist and Walter Mannzen, laid down, firstly in *Der Ruf*, and later in the now-forgotten periodicals, *Neues Europa* and *Deutsche Stimme*,[54] is indicative of an anti-Fascist tendency that can also be detected in the literary life of 1945 and 1946.

The anti-Fascist orientation of these first two years after the war was determined by the occupying powers and by the anti-Fascist German parties and social organisations. This 'spontaneous' tendency towards the Left in political and literary life is, along with the impulse towards a new beginning examined already, a second argument against the simple theory of continuity mentioned at the start of this chapter. Anti-Fascist hegemony was more than just the sort of pluralism admitted by Hans-Peter Schwarz.

The Allied Offices of Information Control[55] forbade the publication of anything considered militaristic or Fascist; anti-Fascist enlightenment was encouraged through the provision of licences. Depending on the military governments' understanding of Fascism, different expressions of enmity to Fascism were promoted in literature and the press. In the French zone, for example, twenty-two of the first eighty-eight books published were by the Catholic Inner Emigrant Reinhold Schneider, six were by the Archbishop of Freiburg, Conrad Gröber, and there were others by Lenin, Stalin and Pope Pius XII.[56] The Americans not only asked of the newspapers licensed by them (such as the *Frankfurter Rundschau* and the *Rhein-Neckar-Zeitung*) that they employ Liberals, Social-Democrats and Communists, but also demanded the same of the cultural-political periodicals which were so influential at a time when books were scarce. *Die Wandlung*, published in Heidelberg, was one such periodical. It was edited by Karl Jaspers, by former *FZ* editor Dolf Sternberger, and by Werner Krauss, at that time a member of the KP section of the parliament for Gross-Hessen.[57] Theodor Heuss, who was active as a journalist for the *Frankfurter Zeitung* and later *Bundespräsident*, was one of the editors of the *Rhein-Neckar-Zeitung*, which printed a number of essays by Werner Krauss. Heuss' own record of events in May 1945 reveals the extent to which left-wing anti-Fascism was dominant in the first months after Liberation. 'There are not only Communist martyrs', noted Heuss.[58] Before going on to praise the Church and the 20 July as forces of resistance, he conceded: 'Social Democrats and Communists certainly represented the largest proportion of Germans in the concentration camps'.[59] By tracing left-wing anti-Fascism back to the suffering of the camps and by turning the fighters into victims to use as evidence of liberation from guilt[60] against Allied reproaches of collective German guilt, he aligned anti-Fascism more closely to those who justified themselves on the grounds of experience and moral integrity. This point of view allowed Heuss to draw two conclusions. In his report, aimed at readers within the military government, he demanded that the intellectual and spiritual confrontation with Nazism should not be put in the hands of emigrants, but of such Germans 'who have experienced life's afflictions at first hand. The opportunity must also be provided for intellectual and cultural forces to find expression and take effect outside the political arena.'[61] Heuss pointedly rejected the 'instruction' of the population by exiled writers, because 'we have lived through innumerable tragedies' and 'have had enough propaganda after twelve years of Goebbels'.[62] The second conclusion he drew was a prediction of the decline of anti-Fascism. In the curriculum vitae which accompanied his application as licencee of the *Rhein-Neckar-Zeitung*, Heuss formulated the express desire to see the authorisation of political activity deferred until anti-Fascism had died down: 'Anti-Nazism will lose its binding strength as inevitably as Nazism itself, which is effectively over with, has been eradicated or has fled the soul.'[63] As long as anti-Fascism included a tendency towards Socialism, no party-political activity should be permitted, for Heuss thought that Marxist 'ideological chatter' was 'rubbish',[64] though of Socialism he wrote: 'Few words are bandied about so much'.[65]

Heuss's hopes for the disintegration of left-wing anti-Fascism were based on the idea of the supposed autonomy of unpolitical culture and the tenet of first-hand experience. The first books published and read in 1945 in no way met these expectations. The tremendous and overwhelmingly positive response generated by Theodor Plievier's novel *Stalingrad*,[66] written in Soviet exile and publicised by the radio and the press since May 1945, actually confirmed the strength of left-wing anti-Fascism in finding spontaneous approval as the model for interpretation of personal experience. Plievier worked from the form of national self-criticism embodied in the Nationalkomitee Freies Deutschland, and was nevertheless accepted by disillusioned front-line soldiers. In the first months after Liberation, however, the reading public was not only prepared to see its own experiences portrayed in literature, but also to take a good look at the experiences of others.

In 1945–6, autobiography[67] occupied a leading position among the different literary genres, despite the fact that the authors' standpoints, and the experiences about which they wrote, were not those of the majority of the German population. Such reports based on personal experience were published mainly by Christians and Communists, and sought to offer a further form of enlightenment about Nazi crimes and to stimulate the recognition of personal responsibility. Five of the ten personal reports from concentration camps and prisons printed in 1945 were written by Communists; by 1946, reports from concentration camps represented 75 per cent of all autobiographical literature about Fascism, their authors being mainly Communists and Catholic priests. In 1946, the few books of this genre written by bourgeois Humanist Inner Emigrants, and which are still available today, appeared: Luise Rinser's *Prison Diary* and Ernst Wiechert's *The Forest of the Dead*. The autobiographical literature of resistance fighters and victims of persecution was gradually replaced, to begin with, by the books of the Inner Emigrants, who had, since 1946, mainly been publishing diaries, and then from 1948–9 onwards, by the memoirs of activists, major culprits and those who had gone along with the regime. This major change was worked out in advance by literary critics, who saw themselves as 'unpolitical' and who, in accordance with a 'creative' aesthetic norm, rejected the mere description or interpretation of experience. The apparently only aesthetic rejection of concentration-camp literature could, however, have been based on a distaste for enlightenment, arising from a sense of guilt.

Such an unfavourable reaction to concentration-camp literature could already be detected quite early on. The Berlin journalist Margaret Boveri, for example, who had read Plievier's novel with interest, expressed her outrage over the *Deutsche Volkszeitung*, the central organ of the German Communist Party: 'One third to a half of the space is given over to Nazi atrocities, concentration camps and self-accusations.'[68] She became particularly touchy, though, when Emigrants ventured to express their experiences. Margaret Boveri was especially radical in expounding the dogma of the immediacy of experience, describing it as 'one of the principal realisations of this period':

even those who sympathise with us are clueless and therefore loaded with false judgements because they didn't live through what we lived through here. It is surely one of the principal realisations of this period, that no amount of being told about something and no amount of empathy, however intensive, can ever replace the experience of having gone through something oneself. A fairly hopeless realisation, as far as the problem of understanding between peoples is concerned.[69]

Remarkably, another literary genre, the poetics of which were described by contemporaries as 'the Realism of the Immediate',[70] became the preferred example to support the case for the possibility of the literary 'understanding between peoples'. The short story became the leading genre in newspapers and periodicals in 1946, stimulated by special competitions and a little later by short-story anthologies, and it is this which, to this day, best illustrates postwar German literature's orientation towards the West and the impression that the United States made as a model for emulation.

One element in the promotion in status of the short-story genre has not yet been considered, yet it says a great deal for anti-Fascist hegemony in the realm of literature. Because of its association with the journalistic media, the short story was held in contempt, just as autobiography was scorned because of its documentary character. Many conservative attempts to determine the concept of culture reverted to Ortega y Gasset and openly stood up for an aristocratic form of culture centered on art, contrasting its 'spiritualisation' and 'internalisation'[71] with the Nazi past. In one such example, it was declared: 'National Socialism didn't even have time to read a good book that went beyond the limited scope of a "short story" or "documentary" and could be digested intellectually.'[72] In response to such conservative condemnation of genres as being unartistic, simply because they satisfied the tastes of the masses, postwar writers justified the maligned short story by highlighting its democratic character. The publisher Walter Kahnert, for example, tried to locate the short story in the context of a 'German reform of style'.[73] For him, the exemplary character of the short story lay not least in its narrative approach, which he formulated in the following rule: 'Limit yourself to portraying people as you meet them in real life, without passing personal judgement on them; leave this to the reader.'[74] By renouncing the urge to 'make up the reader's mind', the short story would be particularly suited to stimulating the 'sober' 'stock-taking' needed in Germany.[75] And in no way was the democratic character of the genre related exclusively to the United States, as later research categorically asserts, but also to the Soviet Union, remarkably enough. A further sign of the hegemony is the periodical *Story*, produced by the Rowohlt publishing house, whose role in popularising the 'modern short story'[76] can hardly be over-estimated. The first issue in August 1946 did not just contain Americans: along with Hemingway, there was Maugham, Marcel Aymé, Gorki and the Czech writer Capek.

When Ernst Schnabel wrote about the 'Form and material of future literature' in the British-run newspaper *Die Welt*, he predicted that French and English literature would not have much influence on postwar German literature of the future: 'Our literature will probably be more akin to that of America and Russia, whose passionate new strength was also born of upheaval'.[77] Schnabel drew the comparison between America's Black Friday, the October Revolution and Germany in 1945, insofar as 'young Americans awoke to reality from the dream of prosperity' and that in the 'catharsis of Russia's revolution', not only had 'the vessels been shattered, but their contents too had become meaningless'.

The genre which had been dismissed as aesthetically inferior because it appeared in the press, was paradoxically restored by the discovery of traditions which actually anticipated the break with tradition. When Schnabel asserted: 'Our writers will probably not make much of art-forms passed on from literary traditions', he was expressing the credo of the Realism of the Immediate, as Wolfgang Weyrauch, in 1946, had named the new style drawn from the short story: 'They will have to choose forms which themselves contain their subject matter. These will be new forms.' Only in 1949 did Weyrauch retrospectively give to this literary expression of the new beginning the label 'Kahlschlag'. The concept turns up in the afterword to his anthology *Tausend Gramm*, which once again documents the significance that the anti-Fascist impulse also had for the short story genre. *Tausend Gramm* arose from Weyrauch's editorial work on two periodicals that were licensed by the Soviets: *Ost und West* and *Ulenspiegel*. Weyrauch gave precedence to an international range of established stories over the short stories of authors from the four zones of occupation: here too, as in the first issue of *Story*, a Russian stands next to an American.[78]

Both autobiography and the short story, as leading genres in the years 1945 and 1946, emphasise the misleading nature of Hans-

Peter Schwarz's idea of pluralism and cosmopolitanism quoted at the beginning, especially when he fails to point out that the variety of postwar literature was attributable to anti-Fascism, and that when German literature opened itself up to international influences, it also looked to the East – at least for one-and-a-half years.

Notes

1. Alfred Dregger, 'Katastrophen kann man nicht feiern', *Frankfurter Allgemeine Zeitung*, 27 December 1984.
2. Joachim Fest, 'Sieg und Niederlage', *Frankfurter Allgemeine Zeitung*, 20 April 1985. In addition, see Hagen Schulze, 'Schwierigkeiten mit einem Gedenktag: Zum 8 Mai 1945', *Der Tagespiegel* (Berlin), 5 May 1985; Michael Stürmer, 'Keine Angst vor gemischten Gefühlen: Trauer und Bitternis, Aufatmen und Dankbarkeit prägen die Erinnerung an den Tag, als der Krieg zu Ende war', *Die Zeit*, 25 January 1985. For critical accounts of this 'Historiker-Debatte', see Jürgen Habermas, 'Entsorgung der Vergangenheit', in *Die Neue Unübersichtlichkeit: Kleine politische Schriften*, vol. v (Frankfurt, 1985) pp. 261–8; Wolfgang Fritz Haug, 'Die neuen Deutungskämpfe um Anti-Faschismus: ein Untersuchung zur neokonservativen Offensive im Spiegel der *Frankfurter Allgemeine*', *Das Argument 28*, 158 (1986) pp. 502–26; 'Vergangenheit, die Zukunft werden soll: über den Historiker-Streit', *Das Argument 29*, 161 (1987) pp. 9–23.
3. Hans-Peter Schwarz, *Die Ära Adenauer: Gründerjahre der Republik 1949–1957* (Stuttgart, 1981) p. 422.
4. Ibid., p. 424.
5. Wolfgang Emmerich, 'Nullpunkt', in *Kulturpolitisches Wörterbuch Bundesrepublik Deutschland/DDR im Vergleich* (Stuttgart, 1983) p. 538.
6. Hans Mayer, *Deutsche Literatur seit Thomas Mann* (Reinbek, 1968) p. 55.
7. Hans Dieter Schäfer, 'Zur Periodisierung der deutschen Literatur seit 1930', *Literaturmagazin*, 7 (1977) p. 112. This special issue 'Nachkriegsliteratur' includes summaries of earlier research done by Frank Trommler and Volker Wehdeking.
8. Mayer, *Deutsche Literatur seit Thomas Mann*, p. 53.
9. See Günther Rühle, 'Restauration und neue Einheit', *Frankfurter Allgemeine Zeitung*, 23 September 1978.
10. Fritz J. Raddatz, 'Wir werden weiterdichten, wenn alles in Scherben fällt', *Die Zeit*, 12 October 1979.
11. Hans Fiedler (Alfred Döblin), *Der Nürnberger Lehrprozess* (Baden-Baden, 1946) p. 32.
12. Alfred Döblin, *Briefe* (Olten, Freiburg im Breisgau, 1970) p. 327.
13. Ibid., p. 327.
14. Ibid., p. 326.

15. Ibid., p. 327. See Friedhelm Kröll, ' "und die ich nicht in die Wolken geschrieben hatte": Warum Alfred Döblin in der westdeutschen Nachkriegsliteratur nicht angekommen ist', in Jost Hermand *et al.*, *Nachkriegsliteratur*, vol. II: *Autoren, Sprache, Traditionen* (Berlin, 1984) pp. 65–72.

16. Wilhelm Hausenstein, *Licht unter dem Horizont: Tagebücher von 1942 bis 1946* (Munich, 1967) p. 348.

17. Ibid., p. 179.

18. Ibid., pp. 356–7. For the term 'Kulturfassade', see my article 'Kulturfassade vor der Barbarei?', in Hans Werner Heister and Hans-Günter Klein (eds), *Musik und Musikpolitik im faschistischen Deutschland* (Frankfurt, 1984) pp. 57–74.

19. Wilhelm Hausenstein, *Licht unter dem Horizont*, p. 357.

20. Elisabeth Langgässer, ... *soviel berauschende Verganglichkeit: Briefe 1926–1950* (Hamburg, 1954) p. 138.

21. Ibid., p. 131.

22. Ibid., p. 119.

23. Ibid., pp. 116–17.

24. 'Frank Thiess antwortet Thomas Mann', in Hans Ludwig Arnold (ed.), *Deutsche Literatur im Exil 1933–1945*, vol. I: *Dokumente* (Frankfurt, 1974) p. 265.

25. Arnold Bauer, 'Verbannte und verkannte Literatur', in Arnold (ed.), *Deutsche Literatur im Exil*, I, p. 271.

26. Frank Thiess, 'Innere Emigration', ibid., p. 249.

27. Ibid., p. 248.

28. Frank Thiess, 'Abschied von Thomas Mann', ibid., p. 259.

29. See Frithjof Trapp, 'Logen- und Parterreplätze. Was behinderte die Rezeption der Exilliteratur?', in Ulrich Walberer (ed.), *10 Mai 1933: Bücherverbrennung in Deutschland und die Folgen* (Frankfurt, 1983) pp. 255–9.

30. Johannes R. Becher, 'Bermerkungen zu unseren Kulturaufgaben', in his *Publizistik*, vol. II: *1939–1945* (Berlin and Weimar, 1978) p. 362.

31. Ibid., p. 362.

32. Ibid., p. 363.

33. Ibid., p. 365.

34. Johannes R. Becher, 'Erziehung zur Freiheit', in *Publizistik*, II, p. 517.

35. Bertolt Brecht, *Arbeitsjournal*, vol. II: *1942–1955* (Frankfurt, 1974) p. 479.

36. Johannes R. Becher, 'Zur Frage der politische-moralischen Vernichtung des Faschismus', in *Publizistik*, II, p. 406.

37. Johannes R. Becher, 'Deutsches Bekenntnis', in *Publizistik*, II, p. 495.

38. Bernd Hüppauf, 'Krise ohne Wandel. Die kulturelle Situation 1945–1949', in his '*Die Mühen der Ebenen.' Kontinuität und Wandel in der deutschen Literatur und Gesellschaft 1945–1949* (Heidelberg, 1981) pp. 93–4.

39. See Alfred Döblin, *Die literarische Situation* (Baden-Baden, 1947); Hans Werner Richter, 'Literatur im Interregnum', *Der Ruf*, I, 15 (1946/1947) pp. 10–11.

40. See, as an early example of criticism, Henning Martell, 'Ein Weg

ohne Kompass. Neubeginn am Beispiel der Zeitschrift *Der Ruf'*, *Kürbiskern*, 2 (1975) pp. 105–19.

41. Alfred Andersch, 'Das junge Europa formt sein Gesicht', *Der Ruf*, I, 1 (1946/1947).
42. Ibid.
43. Ibid.
44. Alfred Andersch, 'Notwendige Aussage zum Nürnberger Prozess', *Der Ruf*, I, 1 (1946/1947).
45. Ibid.
46. Werner Krauss, 'Das Ende der Generationsgemeinschaft', in his *Literaturtheorie, Philosophie und Politik*, ed. Manfred Naumann (Berlin, Weimar, 1984) p. 399. The article was first published in *Padogogik* in 1947.
47. Ibid., p. 409, n. 1.
48. Ibid., pp. 401–2.
49. Ibid., p. 409.
50. Johannes R. Becher, 'Erziehung zur Freiheit', p. 528.
51. Alfred Andersch, 'Deutsche Literatur in der Entscheidung', in Gerd Haffmans (ed.), *Das Alfred Andersch Lesebuch* (Zürich, 1979) p. 124.
52. Ibid., p. 125.
53. Ibid., p. 114.
54. See Helmut Peitsch and Hartmut Reith, 'Keine "innere Emigration" in die "Gefilde" der Literatur. Literarische-politische Publizistik im Umkreis der Gruppe 1947–1949', in Hermand *et al.*, *Nachkriegsliteratur*, II, pp. 135–8.
55. See, for details, Helmut Peitsch, 'Politisierung der Literatur oder "Freiheit des Geistes"? Materialien zu den Literaturverhaltnisse in den Westzonen', in Jost Hermand *et al.*, *Nachkriegsliteratur in Westdeutschland 1945–1949: Gattungen, Schreibweisen, Institutionen* (Berlin, 1982) pp. 168–72.
56. See *Das Goldene Tor*, I, 2 (1946) p. 207.
57. See Manfred Naumann's account of Krauss's editorship in his 'Prolegomena zu einer Werner-Krauss-Biographie', *Sinn und Form*, 35 (1983) pp. 954–5.
58. Theodor Heuss, *Aufzeichnungen, 1945–1947* (Tubingen, 1966) p. 85.
59. Ibid., p. 84.
60. Ibid., p. 75.
61. Ibid., p. 83.
62. Ibid.
63. Ibid., p. 106.
64. Ibid., p. 175.
65. Ibid., p. 176. For the general interest in literature, see Reinhard Rösler, 'Beiträge der Publizistik für die Entwicklung der Literatur in den westlichen Besatzungszonen Deutschlands während der Jahre 1945–1949 (Rostock: Doctoral dissertation, 1980).
66. See my analysis in 'Theodor Plieviers *Stalingrad*', in Christian Fritsch and Lutz Winckler (eds), *Faschismuskritik und Deutschlandbild im Exilroman* (Berlin, 1981) pp. 83–102.
67. See, for a typology of postwar autobiographical writing, Helmut

Peitsch, 'Methoden der Medienanalyse am Beispiel von Selbstzeugnissen über den Faschismus in den Massenmedien der Nachkriegszeit', in Karl-Heinz Braun (ed.), *Subjektivität als Problem psychologischer Methodik* (Frankfurt, New York, 1985).

68.   Margaret Boveri, *Tage des Überlebens* (Berlin, 1945; Munich, 1968) p. 272.

69.   Ibid., p. 328.

70.   For this term, see my interpretation 'Wolfgang Weyrauch und der Kahlschlag', in *Stadtansichten. Jahrbuch für Literatur und kulturelles Leben in Berlin (West)*, 2 (1981) pp. 135–43.

71.   Georg Dörge, *Vom kulturellen Lebensstandard: Versuch einer nüchternen Umschau* (Stuttgart, 1947) p. 16.

72.   Ibid., p. 14. See Francisco Sanchez-Blanco, 'Ortega y Gasset: Philosoph des Wiederaufbaus? Anmerkungen zu einer unbeachteten Rezeption', in Hermand *et al.*, *Nachkriegsliteratur*, II, pp. 101–11.

73.   Walter Kahnert, *Objektivismus: Gedanken über einen neuen Literaturstil* (Berlin, 1946) p. 10.

74.   Ibid., p. 25.

75.   Ibid., p. 8.

76.   This was the subtitle of *Story* from its fourth number, in 1950.

77.   Ernst Schnabel, 'Form und Stoff künftiger Dichtung', *Die Welt* 17 May 1946.

78.   Weyrauch's anthology was published in all four zones of occupation: see Wolfgang Weyrauch (ed.), *Tausend Gramm. Sammlung neuer deutscher Geschichten* (Hamburg, Stuttgart, Baden-Baden, Berlin, 1949).

11

Continuity or Change? Aspects of West German Writing after 1945

KEITH BULLIVANT

Until well into the 1960s, the prevailing conventional wisdom was that for West Germany the capitulation of 8 May 1945 marked an absolute caesura, a radical break with the Third Reich: this is the substance of the myth of the 'Nullpunkt' or 'Stunde Null'. More recent studies have revealed an astonishing degree of continuity in the area of capital before 1948, the year of the currency reform and the Marshall Plan, which in turn marked a large-scale return to power and influence of a compromised generation. Over and above this, the rapid development of the Cold War situation led to the Western allies, in their fear of Communism, rushing through and reducing to a farce the process of so-called denazification, so that the key positions of responsibility in the legislature and in commerce could be assumed only by the only people with appropriate experience, in many cases former Nazis. The revelations about the Nazi past of leading West German politicians and industrialists in the 1960s and 1970s were but the tip of the iceberg.[1] A rather similar comforting view of the development of West German literature – encouraged both by literary historians and by semi-official pronouncements – was that here too a new beginning had taken place: a new generation of writers was said rapidly to have realised the extent to which language had been corrupted by the Nazis and to have determinedly set about cleansing it, as the starting-point for a true new beginning in literature. This was, in the term coined by Wolfgang Weyrauch, the 'Kahlschlag', the clearing away of the dead wood. Closely linked to this was the idea that the new writers turned for their literary models not to the tradition of their own country, but to – for them – hitherto unknown American realist models, such as Dos Passos, Saroyan and Hemingway, whose works only now became available, as the basis for a Realist literature of a critical, humanitarian kind, the major theme of which was a reckoning with the Nazi past (the so-called 'Bewältigung der Vergangenheit').[2] 'Kahlschlag' and the New Realist literature were associated, in their turn, with Gruppe 47, born out of the short-lived periodical *Der Ruf*, which was seen as standing for a non-dogmatic, 'humanist-socialist' aesthetic. This group was, in the comforting picture that was drawn, seen as *the* representative group of West German writers.

It was not until well into the 1960s, in pioneering studies of the immediate postwar literary situation by Urs Widmer and Heinrich Vormweg, that this myth was eventually nailed. Since then there has been, in fact, considerable academic debate as to whether the real caesuras in German literature are not 1930 and the end of the 1950s, rather than 1933 and 1945.[3] This is not a discussion into which we can or should enter here, the important thing is the way in which the myth of the fresh start needed severe qualification in at least four areas. First, the extent of, and the achievement represented by, 'Kahlschlag' literature, despite the bold words of the late 1940s, was greatly exaggerated: no real linguistic break took place in German literature in the immediate postwar years. Second, despite the early publication of a few important novels, very little of the New Realist literature was produced and the claims made for the status of its major practitioner, Heinrich Böll, in the 1940s and 1950s had been inflated. With the onset of the Cold War after the Berlin Blockade the climate in the country was such as to lead to any critical realism being equated with Socialist Realism and thus viewed as near-treasonable. Third, the idea – so central to the role that Gruppe 47 ascribed itself – of a young generation assuming responsibility for the moral regeneration of the country, a process in which literature was allotted an important part, was quickly hindered by the American obsession with collective guilt, the delicate balance in the relationship between the occupying forces and then, with the intensification of the Cold War, the subsequent hostile attitude towards any form of critical realism. Finally, although some of the writers that constituted Gruppe 47 are central to what was later to become the mainstream of West German literature from the late 1950s onwards, their role in the early years, important though it is as the pre-history of the major literary tradition of the Federal Republic, was greatly exaggerated. Not only did the work of a number of its major writers hardly adhere to the programmatic line put forward by Hans Werner Richter, but to equate the development of West

German prose and poetry – the position with regard to drama is more complex – was to ignore the prominent role played in the literature of the 1940s and 1950s by an older generation of writers, by conservative critics, scholars and journals, in the re-establishment of a type of writing that had its roots back in the period before 1933 or in the so called 'Inner Emigration' of the Nazi years.

The most immediately striking aspect of the continuity represented by this, the more dominant group of writers in the postwar years, is that they conceived of the aftermath of the war in the same aesthetic categories as the German right-wing intelligentsia had used to view the dangers of Fascism – indeed, they were in some cases the same people. In the early 1930s Karl Jaspers had analysed the threat to traditional German values of the 'spiritual condition of the age' (the 'geistige Situation der Zeit'), while Ernst Robert Curtius had written of 'the endangered German spirit' ('deutscher Geist in Gefahr'). They, like the majority of German writers at the time, had not been able to understand and appreciate the dangers of National Socialism as a *political* movement. In the aftermath of the war their solutions to the crisis of the German people were expressed in similarly spiritual terms: the rediscovery of the true meaning of the legacy of Goethe was now seen as the path that would lead to Germany's re-discovery of its true self. Friedrich Meinicke, who held similar views, went as far as to suggest in his *Die deutsche Katastrophe* [*The German Catastrophe*] of 1946 that national regeneration lay in the creation of a chain of Goethe communities. Perhaps the most revealing statements indicating the German propensity for interpreting political developments in essentially aesthetic categories is found in the postwar writing of Thomas Mann. In Autumn 1945, Mann, while in no way trying to excuse what had happened, described National Socialism as resulting from a secret alliance of the German soul with the demonic, as reflecting the German rejection of the rational thought of the Enlightenment in favour of the 'chthonic, irrational and demonic, that is to say the *real* life-forces'.[4] After the horrors that had happened, Mann was still, in other words, explaining National Socialism in the same non-politial terms that he had used in the 1920s and 1930s. It should be said, in fairness, that Mann was one of the first German writers to identify the threat posed by the Nazis and there is no doubting his opposition to it in exile; it is precisely that stature that throws into relief the peculiarly German inability to understand social and political developments other than in terms of the ebb and flow of the spirit.

Given the essentially aesthetic understanding of the war and its consequences amongst German writers and intellectuals, it is not surprising that it is reflected in the way in which imaginative writing deals with these matters. There is, of course, no better example than Thomas Mann's *Dr Faustus* (1947), his literary exploration of Fascism in terms so familiar to us from his essays and novels over the preceding decades. Perhaps more important examples, given the particular status of Mann as someone who chose to remain in exile, are two writers, who – together with Hermann Hesse – were in 1948 termed by Hans Egon Holthusen, the major literary critic of the period, the most important German writers of the age: Ernst Jünger and Gottfried Benn.[5] Although Jünger had an ambivalent attitude towards the plebian Nazis, his militaristic poetic evocations of the First World War had a prominent role to play within the Nazi concept of literature, and he had continued to publish during the Third Reich. Moreover, for all his contempt for the Nazis, his conservative philosophical writings and trenchant anti-Republicanism had helped to prepare the intellectual ground for their political takeover. Gottfried Benn, a prominent member of the Expressionist generation had, in 1933, expressed his faith in National Socialism and joined the sanitised literary section of the Prussian Academy of Art. While democratic realist writers, like Alfred Döblin, who had gone into exile and who could, at the end of the war, have represented a fruitful continuity were ignored, Jünger and Benn were praised by Holthusen for continuing with the 'Magical Realism' of the 1930s which, far from getting to grips with the immediate past and the problems of the present, was concerned with the inner world of the spirit, in which values threatened in the crude outer physical world were still attainable. Thus, in *Das abenteuerliche Herz* [*The Adventurous Heart*, 1948] Jünger contended that literature itself was the 'highest form' of reality and contrasted it with the 'shallow realities of the bourgeois world', which can be disregarded with disdain by the elite.[6] Benn's notion of 'absolute prose', the theory of which was published in the same year, likewise locates it in the world of the imagination, outside spatial and temporal limits.[7] Both writers represent, in short, the continuance of the idealist tradition in German literature that dominates German writing in the nineteenth and the earlier part of the twentieth centuries and which has always been opposed to the sort of realism demanded by Gruppe 47. Given the strength of this tradition, the stature of the writers who embody it and the weight of critical support that it has always received, it should not be surprising that, far from a New Realism of the type promulgated by Richter and others coming to dominate the writing of a younger generation in the postwar period, this role fell to works in the style of the 'Magical Realists', such as Elisabeth Langgässer's *Das unauslöschliche Siegel* [*The Indelible Seal*, 1946], Ilse Aichinger's *Die grössere Hoffnung* [*The Greater Hope*, 1948] and Hermann Kasack's *Die Stadt hinter dem Strom* [*The City beyond the River*, 1947], which was widely acclaimed as *the* representative novel of its time. Gerhard Pohl described this allegorical depiction of life after the collapse of Germany as a life beyond the river of death as 'a mirror-image of our "lost" age . . . a magnificent poetic vision of the beginning, the course and the end of all life'.[8] Kasack himself wrote of it 'presenting symbols of reality . . . which maintain their "universal validity" quite independent of their specific manifestations'.[9] This literary concern in an essentially symbolic or allegorical style with what were conceived of as timeless problems, rather than the manifestations of a particular society and time, was characteristic not only of the novel, but also of lyric poetry and the radio play, which were in many ways the most significant literary expressions of the period from the end of the war up to the late 1950s. The concern of such writing was in no way to address itself to, and help with, increasing understanding of the social and political problems of the day – as a means of contributing to decisive change that would bring about the establishment and subsequent consolidation of a truly democratic Germany, such as had been demanded by Richter and Alfred Andersch – but a concern 'to *think* order back into a totally disordered world, to restore old truths in new language', as Hans-Egon Holthusen put it.[10]

Alongside the continuity of this sort of thinking, the assertion of the power of 'Geist' (mind or spirit) that had such fatal consequences in the prewar period, we find the existence of other types of German thinking that continued the tradition of bourgeois non-political philosophies. The postwar years saw the renewal of interest in ideas of cultural pessimism, drawing particularly on Nietzschean ideas and on Oswald Spengler's morphological view of history that he put forward in *The Decline of the West*, which underwent a considerable renaissance at this time. The influence of the Conservative Revolution, despite its preparation of much of the intellectual ground for National Socialism and the flirtation of a number of leading Conservative Revolutionaries with the Nazis, re-emerged as a strong influence in conservative circles, and the Youth Movement, drawing its ideas from all of these sources, underwent a remarkable and influential revival. To these established non-political modes of thinking was added another, one which had its origins in Germany, but which now returned via France – Existentialism, which in Germany, despite the homage paid to Sartre, entirely lacked the political engagement it had in French intellectual circles. In Hans Erich Nossack's *Nekyia* it led to but a variant on the apocalyptic view of the war and its aftermath that we have noted in others, while in the work of Alfred Andersch it promoted a concern with an abstract notion of individual freedom rather than social issues and, in stylistic terms, to a propensity for more or less timeless symbols that, again, was not that far away from the writing of more avowedly conservative writers.[11]

The strength of the German Idealist tradition that I have indicated becomes abundantly clear if we go back to the literary criticism of Holthusen, Friedrich Sieburg, Günter Blöcker and Karl August Horst, the major critics of the 1950s, and still significant in the 1960s, all of whom were active before 1945.[12] Recent analyses of this pattern of continuity have produced ample evidence to support the notion that there were many cases of opportunism involved here, and it is with a certain irony that we note how, in one of the very first surveys of postwar literature (1947), Horst Lange drew attention to the way in which the occupants of the 'inner Reich' were astutely portraying their literary activities during the Nazi period as 'Inner Emigration' and thereby diverting attention from the fact that, after 1945, they were still singing 'the same old song'.[13] But we do not need to enter into this tricky debate here. The important thing for us to grasp is that their position throughout was perfectly consistent with German Idealism, in which, as it developed from Hegel's aesthetic theories onwards, not only was literature's real concern with the inner world of the spirit, but this inner world was seen as truer than a now debased outer reality; to such a world view National Socialism, disturbing though it may have been, merely served to confirm the nature of the physical world as profane and the consequent superiority of the inner life in which the writer was truly at home.

Thus, in terms so redolent of the literary theoreticians of German Idealism in the nineteenth century, Frank Thiess, another writer active before 1945 who became an important literary critic of the postwar period and, in the early 1950s, President of the influential Mainz Academy of Sciences, one of the representative cultural academies, was at pains to stress in a treatise on 'literature and reality' that true literature had nothing at all to do with what 'is commonly understood as reality'. Its concern was with a 'deeper level of reality', indeed, 'the *authentic* level of reality' beyond the 'factual domain of bourgeois existence'.[14] In the light of this view of empirical reality and the concomitant task of literature, it is not surprising that the degree of continuity in what was at the time considered to be the major thrust of the literature of the 1940s and 1950s was so great; political change was essentially irrelevant to a literature concerned with eternal problems and values.

The major difficulty for those now coming fresh to West German literature of the postwar period is that, given the change that did come later and, too, the radical re-evaluation of this time that came with, and in the wake of, the student movement of the late 1960s, writers so central to the first phase of West German writing are now relatively forgotten and, quite reasonably, regarded as, at best, interesting minor phenomena. If we look back at the pattern governing the award of the major literary prizes in West Germany then we see clearly just how much the so-called 'Inner Emigrants' and various other lesser practitioners of the Idealist tradition dominated the scene until well into the 1950s. Such a case is Gerd Gaiser, who was awarded a number of major literary prizes and was considered by the conservative critics mentioned to be one of the major writers of the postwar generation. His earliest writing, published during the war in the leading journal of the 'Inner Emigrants', *Das innere Reich*, included some highly jingoistic poetry, but this aspect of his work remained conveniently forgotten until into the 1960s. Gaiser had been a member of the conservative Youth Movement, and so it is not surprising to find ideas derived from it figuring prominently in his work, fused to the clear influence of Schopenhauer, Nietzsche, Moeller van den Bruck and Oswald Spengler. His writing is dominated, above all, by a cyclical view of history that strongly relativises the significance of any individual epoch. In addition, there is the strong presence of a cultural criticism of the modern age, that is to say the nineteenth century and beyond, that draws heavily on Heidegger and

conservative ideas of the 1920s. The modern age poses a fundamental threat to cultural values going right back into antiquity,
which values alone gave human existence meaningful shape and
some sense of purpose and permanence. In keeping with this view
and in a manner so typical of the Idealist novel of the nineteenth
century, Gaiser's novels and short stories make extensive references to Classical literature and also draw heavily on Biblical
symbolism, which has the effect of intensifying the relativisation of
the importance of the specific time at which his work is set. Thus in
Eine Stimme hebt an [*A Voice is Lifted Up*, 1950] Gaiser is only
superficially concerned with the problems facing the soldier
coming home from the war and of a society trying to return to
normal. The book depicts, rather, the quest of the cultured central
figure, and of those like him, for assurance that true culture is not
dead. Oberstelehn is the Odysseus of his age, or a Don Quixote
struggling to keep alive eternal values. The actual postwar world is
sketched with incredible vagueness and the crucial thing is not
survival – death affords, indeed, one form of access to the
supra-reality beyond the physical world – but to be able to
continue to hear 'the ambrosial voice from Lesbos'. Gaiser's next
novel, *Die sterbende Jagd* [*The Dying Hunters*, 1953] was widely
understood at the time as *the* poetic portrayal of the war in the air.
A closer reading of the novel reveals, however, that the pilots –
recognisably either from the 'bündische Jugend' (the 1920s' manifestation of the Youth Movement), and sharing its elitist notions –
and other sympathetically portrayed characters have by now
familiar cultural, rather than military, concerns. Even the actual
description of aerial combat is, in a manner that takes us back to
Gaiser's wartime poetry and to Ernst Jünger's novels of the First
World War, despecified completely: the pilots are the most recent
manifestation of the knightly warrior who has played such a
central role throughout history. Only once in this again amazingly
vague treatment of a theme which seems in itself to be historically
so specific is there a reference to a feature peculiar to this war – to a
picture, almost certainly of Hitler, on the wall of the station office,
but even here this is put over in a way that fits into Gaiser's view of
history as something consisting of a pattern that transcends the
features of individual societies. Referring to this picture, one of the
central characters says: 'God has sent him . . . and he is bound to
destroy us. I understand it and don't understand it. But I can't
escape it and I can't deflect it. *Nemo contra Deum nisi Deus ipse*'.[15]

Hitler is seen not as the product of a particular ideology in a particular political situation, is not even located within a specific society, but as merely the latest manifestation of evil inflicted upon mankind by an unfathomable Will that is behind all of the meaningless suffering that is the surface pattern of human history. Escape from this is not to be found in either the political or the military arenas, but – and this takes us back to ideas of Jünger and Thiess quoted earlier – in the realm of a superior reality. The contrast between 'the true life', access to which can be gained through dreams, through contact with those beyond the grave or through artistic contemplation, and the banality of modern existence is at the heart of Gaiser's best-known novel *Schlussball* [*The Last Dance of the Season*, 1958], which was in its day widely (mis-)understood as *the* socially critical novel of the early years of the economic miracle. The central character is again from the Youth Movement and his concerns, like those of the figures close to him, again exist on a different plain from the drab materialist world of the town of Neu-Spuhl. There is now, looking back, a sense that the war and the privation of the immediate postwar period had suspended the modern age for a time; now it has re-established itself with greater intensity and so the need to turn away from the real world in the quest for authentic life, in the sense of participation in an eternal realm of cultural values that transcend empirical reality, is all the more keenly felt. This theme of Gaiser's, developed most fully in two volumes of short prose, *Gib acht in Domokosch* [*Take Care in Domokosch*, 1959] and *Am Pass Nascondo* [*Nascondo Pass*, 1960] was, inconceivable though it may seem today, so well received in established literary circles that the critic Walter Jens felt compelled to write a lengthy article in the liberal weekly *Die Zeit* specifically attacking the over-enthusiastic response to Gaiser's writing and Marcel Reich-Ranicki devoted a lengthy and highly critical chapter to him in a volume of essays in 1963, in which, for the first time, attention to Gaiser's wartime writings was drawn.[16]

The case of Gaiser, as well as the high standing of other writers of his generation of a similar bent, such as Aichinger, Langgässer and Kasack, together with the resurgence of older conservative writers like Jünger, Hesse and Benn, and the critical stance adopted by major critics and literary journals of the day, all serve to demonstrate the strength of the German Idealist tradition and help to explain to some extent the reasons for the high degree of continuity in West German writing after 1945. Hans Werner Richter, looking back on the immediate postwar period from the 1960s, felt that this – and the concomitant failure of Gruppe 47 radically to change the nature of German literature – represented the literary dimension of a deliberate policy of 'restoration' by the Adenauer Government, the over-rapid normalisation of things in West Germany and the burying of awkward questions about the past. [17] There is something to this, but, nevertheless, it's not quite as reassuringly simple as that. Richter seems unaware of the strength of the Idealist tradition in German literature, but, even within his own terms of reference, he fails, for example, to note that the literary normalisation pre-dates the establishment of the Federal Republic. As soon as the war was over, the major literary figures who had remained in Germany in, as they now termed it – and not always particularly persuasively – 'Inner Emigration' were up and proclaiming the extent of their 'resistance', which, Frank Thiess asserted in September 1945, was so much more meaningful than that of those who went into actual exile. The possibility of a measure of truly meaningful continuity, in the form of a linking up with the literature of the emigrant generation, was rendered almost impossible by the suspicion of, or in some cases downright hostility to, these writers. Some major figures of the Weimar Republic spent the postwar years in obscurity in the West, while others soon quit the West for the Soviet Zone which, however we may now view the early literature of the GDR, laid claim to, and was seen to represent, a conscious attempt to forge the connection with the democratic literature of the period up to 1933. The most striking evidence as to the strength of the resistance to exile writers is provided by the case of Thomas Mann, for the non-German world the major German writer of the twentieth century. Outside Germany his stature is unquestioned, it is doubtful, indeed, if scholars and readers in other countries are even aware of the suspicion with which Mann was viewed after the war and even beyond his death. In 1945, Walter von Molo and Frank Thiess urged Mann to return to Germany, but were very much at pains to stress the superiority of that literature which had been published during the Third Reich over exile writing. Mann's statement as to why he was not yet able to return to Germany included a critical reference to the literature of 'Inner Emigration' and this produced a hostile response, with Frank Thiess going as far as to publish a public leave-taking from Thomas Mann. The future, he proclaimed lay 'in a new hope and a new certainty about the indestructibility of inner values, but this cannot be the message of an "American citizen of the world", it can only be the fruit of the bloody seed that is the suffering of Germany and Europe'.[18]

Mann's own writing is, I would argue, part of the German Idealist tradition and in many ways accords with Thiess's criteria for literature; as such, the attacks on him now seem rather bizarre, but the important thing in this context is the way in which a climate was produced that brought about the lack of attention paid to exile literature after 1945 and the clear break with the critical realism of the Weimar period. The dominance of allegorical writing, of so-called 'Magical Realism', in West Germany until well into the 1950s is, therefore, to a considerable extent the result of the key role played by conservative writers who remained in Germany during the Third Reich and there is, as I have indicated, ample evidence as to the continuity beyond 1945 in the publishing patterns of a host of writers. But, nevertheless, Richter's interpretation of the relative failure of Gruppe 47 in the late 1940s and early 1950s ignores crucial contradictions inherent in the group itself. One of the most important critical pronouncements on literature, a paper given by Alfred Andersch, co-founder with Richter of Gruppe 47, brings these out very clearly. In *Deutsche Literatur in der Entscheidung* [*German Literature at the Cross-Roads*, 1947] Andersch not only ascribes 'noble motives' to those writers who went along with National Socialism in an – admittedly misguided – 'attempt to salvage whatever they could', he sees German literature as being synonymous with 'Inner Emigration' and, as such, with resistance to National Socialism.[19] Despite the fact that Andersch wrote a number of articles in 1948 as a professed 'anti-Symbolist' and claimed to be advocating a modern, 'revolutionary' realism, he saw this as being exemplified at its best by the work of Ernst Jünger, whom he clearly preferred to emigré writers like Thomas Mann and Alfred Döblin. These articles, his speech to Gruppe 47 and his own writing indicate the gulf between the public stance of the group and his own sense of literature. If we now look more quizzically at the make-up of Gruppe 47, we discover that this contradiction was by no means peculiar to Andersch. Implicit in its composition and its pronouncements on literature are an ignoring of the potential for a new start inherent in the work of those that fled into exile and, despite the well-known descriptions by Richter, Wolfgang Weyrauch and Walter Kolbenhoff of the new Social

Realism demanded by the postwar situation, we find an equally vigorously expressed opposition to such notions. Thus Wolfdietrich Schnurre, who is still generally regarded as one of the key practitioners of the so-called new writing of the later 1940s, while moving away somewhat from the elitism of his first statements, which allot the artist the task of separating out the 'eternal' from the ephemeral aspects of life, nevertheless continues to regard what we would call realism with suspicion. Rejecting the work of 'reality fanatics' like Walter Kolbenhoff as not getting anywhere near the truth, he identifies the task of literature in the postwar situation as penetrating through the surface of reality to reveal the true nature of the problems of human existence, which lie in the struggle between the physical and the spiritual, the demonic and the divine – a view of life that in its very language is so close to that of conservative writers of the 1920s and 1930s. The ultimate task of his 'Magical Realism' – yes, that is the label he puts on it – is the spiritual penetration of the chaos surrounding the writer and a new awareness of the nature of mankind, terms that are familiar to us from the Expressionists' interpretation of the situation after the First World War, but which hardly square with the demands within Gruppe 47 for literature representing an essentially socialist humanism.[20] If we then look at Wolfgang Weyrauch, who is also regarded as a key early member of Gruppe 47 and as the major proponent of 'Kahlschlag' writing, we find the astonishing central concept of the aftermath of the war being akin to the time after the Great Flood, with Germany being 'in the same situation as Noah' – an allegorical view of things that could easily have come from Ilse Aichinger, whose *The Greater Hope* portrays the war and the immediate postwar time in precisely these terms, or from any other of the conservative writers.[21] As with Gaiser, this not only despecifies the crimes of National Socialism into vague 'sins' for which some vengeful higher force has exacted punishment, but it also locates any concern with the immediate past within a cosmic, rather than a sociopolitical, debate. In a way, this sort of contradiction within Gruppe 47 should not be all that surprising, in that its membership can be traced back in a number of cases to the circle connected with a literary periodical, *Die Kolonne*, published around 1930 in Dresden, which essentially stood for a contemplative, often metaphysical, 'pure' literature.[22] Despite the unambiguous call for 'Immediate Realism' by Walter Kolbenhoff (which is also exemplified by his novel *Von unserem Fleisch und Blut* [*Of Our Flesh and Blood*, 1947]) and early signs of support for this, a general turn against this position seems to have happened by 1950. Günter Eich had by now renounced earlier statements that seemed to go along with the drive for a socially committed literature, now viewing such literature as 'totalitarian'[23] and it is frequently not noticed that his award of the prize of Gruppe 47 in 1950 was for 'Fränkisch-tibetanischer Kirschgarten' ['Franconian–Tibetan Cherry Orchard'], a timeless nature poem that would in no way have been out of place in *Die Kolonne* fifteen years earlier. By the early 1950s Kolbenhoff was an outsider and the writing of the group consisted in the main of the lyrical, contemplative, metaphysical or nature literature that dominates the non-'völkisch' writing of the Third Reich; in 1952 the group even went so far as to award its annual prize to Ilse Aichinger, who just a few years before seemed to stand for the opposite of the literary aims of Gruppe 47. Despite the general claims made for the writing of the group to be seen as representing the authentic tradition of West German literature that came through to triumph over a rearguard defence from an older, conservative tradition, a closer look at its profile in the early 1950s makes it clear that in the shorter prose form, so-called 'autonomous' lyric poetry and the radio play, as represented in particular by the work of Eich and Ingeborg Bachmann, this essentially allegorical sort of literature tended to dominate. Indeed, looking back on the first ten years of the group, Arnold Bauer observed with a certain sense of relief that very few of the old guard, and hardly any of the younger members any longer subscribed to the original tenets of the group.[24] In 1962, in an anthology ranging over its first fifteen years, Fritz Raddatz was by no means displeased to note that, contrary to popular conceptions, 'matters of general public concern' did not feature in its writing, that it could in no way be seen as a politically engaged group; what he relished in its literature was that it represented the successful overcoming of a thankfully short hiatus, the return to 'pure' literature.[25]

These responses tell us a lot about the development of Gruppe 47 and the convergence of views between an older, apparently conservative generation of writers and critics and the younger, postwar one. Let us not, however, lose sight here of those few new writers who do, by and large, mark a new departure in German postwar literature. Heinrich Böll, within Gruppe 47, was clearly a significant exception to the pattern, with his novels and shorter prose of the 1940s and 1950s seeming to plough an, at times, lonely furrow for the compassionate realism demanded at the inception of the group. While we should not forget that much of Böll's earlier writing is marred by an unfortunate tendency to heavy symbolism and that in – even sympathetic – critical circles he tended to be dismissed as merely a popular writer, Böll did attain a degree of public recognition and support from a wider public. The early work of Arno Schmidt and Wolfgang Koeppen, on the other hand, now recognised as some of the most important of its time, went almost unheeded; it was not until well into the 1960s that a new generation of critics rediscovered and commended to the reading public the critical prose of two writers whose place in West German literature is now unchallenged.

There is also a very real danger here in that, in trying to indicate just how little significant change there was in German writing after the war, we are somewhat harsh in our judgement of the writers of the time and fail to recognise the pressure on them of established views of writers and literature. We would, indeed, undoubtedly do well to bear in mind the cautionary words of Günter Grass in *Headbirths or The Germans are Dying Out* (1980), in which he stresses the important factor of the generations in the pattern of postwar literature. With great honesty he speculates on his likely career if he had been born ten years earlier. Taking due note of Wolfgang Weyrauch's admittance of being carried along for a time by the euphoria generated by the Third Reich, he feels it unavoidable that he would have been captivated by the nationalist fervour of the day and would have turned out poetry that reflected that mood. Only after Stalingrad and the gradual change in the shape of the war would he have started to have his doubts, would his writing have tended to the more allegorical distancing of 'Inner Emigration' before, after an appropriate brief silence at the end of the war, taking up a position akin to that of Weyrauch within Gruppe 47. His own generation though, having still been children at the outbreak of the war and hardly mature at the end of it, were granted a different view of things. That different view is, though, born of mere chance, and so he refuses to judge those like Weyrauch and Eich, who in some way came to terms with the Nazi State and then developed in the way that we have observed in the postwar period.[26] His generation, he stresses in *Headbirths* and elsewhere, was able to see, and had a special duty to examine, the burden of National Socialism and its aftermath.[27] It is a persuasive argument and it is undoubtedly significant that the real break with the Idealist literary tradition did not start to happen until the late 1950s, when a younger generation of writers – including Grass, Martin Walser, Siegfried Lenz and Uwe Johnson – joined Heinrich Böll and helped to give Gruppe 47 the prominence and significance it came to have in the early 1960s. Gone at last was the ultimate concern with a transcendental world, gone the allegorical, mystical treatment of the great questions of life as a generality, without regard to those of the day. In their various ways and styles, these writers represented a secularisation of German literature, one that at last could take a critical look at the questions of the past and a quizzical look at the present-day of the Federal Republic, which concerns have been at the heart of West German writing ever since. The contrast between the literary achievements of these writers and what went before in the postwar period, perhaps more than anything else, supports the claim made by Günter Grass in *Headbirths*: 'There was no collapse, no absolute beginning, just sluggish and murky transitions. The full sense of horror at the extent of crimes that had been tolerated, directly or indirectly abetted and for which, in any case, we have to accept our share of the blame, came only later, years after the so-called "clean slate".'[28]

Notes

1. See, in this connection, Georg Hallgarten and Joachim Radkau, *Deutsche Industrie und Politik von Bismark bis heute* (Frankfurt, 1974), and Michael Schneider, 'Wie mann einen verlorenen Krieg gewinnt', in *Die Wiedergutmachung* (Cologne, 1985) pp. 165–354.
2. See, for example, Wilhelm Grellman, 'contemporary realism is one of the key features of the post-war era. It reflects the inhumanity of the "Third Reich" and the last war, as well as the despair of the first years after the German collapse' (see *Deutsche Dichtung der Gegenwart* (Frankfurt, 1955) p. 445).
3. See Urs Widmer, *1945 oder die 'Neue Sprache'* (Düsseldorf, 1966), and Henrich Vormweg, 'Deutsche Literatur 1945–1960: Keine Stunde Null', in M. Durzak (ed.), *Deutsche Gegenwartsliteratur* (Stuttgart, 1981); first published 1971. Of the considerable body of literature on the question of periodisation, see, in particular *Literaturmagazin*, 7 (1977); J. Hermand, H. Peitsch and K. R. Scherpe (eds), *Nachkriegsliteratur* (Berlin, 1982–3) 2 vols, *Argument* 'Sonderbande' 83 and 116; Frank Trommler, 'Der "Nullpunkt 1945" und seine Verbindlichkeit

für die Literaturgeschichte', *BASIS*, I (1970) pp. 9–25; H. D. Schäfer, 'Die nichtfaschistische Literatur der jungen Generation', in H. Denkler and K. Prümm (eds), *Die deutsche Literatur im Dritten Reich* (Stuttgart, 1976) pp. 459–503; Frank Trommler, 'Emigration und Nachkriegsliteratur: Zum Problem der geschichtlichen Kontinuität', in R. Grimm and J. Hermand (eds), *Exil und innere Emigration* (Frankfurt, 1972) pp. 173–98; David Roberts, 'Nach der Apokalypse: Kontinuität und Diskontinuität in der deutschen Literatur nach 1945', in B. Hüppauf (ed.), *'Die Mühen der Ebenen': Kontinuität und Wandel in der deutschen Literatur und Gesellschaft 1945–1949* (Heidelberg, 1981) pp. 21–46.

4. Thomas Mann, 'Deutschland und die Deutschen', in *Werke*, vol. XI (Frankfurt, 1960) p. 1143.

5. See Hans Egon Holthusen, *Der unbehauste Mensch* (Munich, 1951) in which his early essays were collected.

6. Ernst Jünger, *Gesammelte Werke*, vol. IX (Stuttgart, 1979) p. 173.

7. See Gottfried Benn, 'Der Roman des Phänotyp', in *Gesammelte Werke*, vol. IV (Wiesbaden, 1961) p. 132.

8. *Aufbau*, 1949, Heft 8, p. 653.

9. Quoted in Jürgen Manthey, 'Zurück zur Kultur', *Literaturmagazin*, 7 (1977) p. 22.

10. Holthusen, *Der unbehauste Mensch*, p. 33.

11. See here Andersch's novel, *Sansibar oder der letzte Grund* (Olten, Freiburg, 1958). It is interesting in this context that Günter Grass has recently spoken of his anger at this book's treatment of the Nazis and describes *The Tin Drum* as a conscious riposte to it. See Heinrich Vormweg, *Günter Grass* (Reinbek, 1986) p. 22.

12. See Franz Schonauer, 'Sieburg & Co. Rückblick auf eine sogenannte konservative Literaturkritik', *Literaturmagazin*, 7 (1977) pp. 237–51.

13. Horst Lange, 'Bücher nach dem Krieg', in H. Schwab-Felisch (ed.), *'Der Ruf': Eine deutsche Nachkriegszeitung* (Munich, 1972) p. 219.

14. Frank Thiess, *Dichtung und Wirklichkeit* (Wiesbaden, 1952) p. 9.

15. Gerd Gaiser, *Die sterbende Jagd*, rev. edn (Frankfurt, 1957) p. 157.

16. See Marcel Reich-Ranicki, *Deutsche Literatur in Ost und West* (Munich, 1963) pp. 55–80.

17. See for example Hans Werner Richter (ed.), *Almanach der Gruppe 47 1947–1962* (Reinbek, 1962) p. 11.

18. Quoted in Elisabeth Endres, *Die Literatur der Adenauerzeit* (Munich, 1980) p. 49.

19. Alfred Andersch, *Deutsche Literatur in der Entscheidung* (Karlsruhe, n. d. [1948: given as a paper in 1947]) pp. 10, 15ff.

20. The debate between Schnurre and Kolbenhoff is to be found in *Der Horizont* (1947) and *Der Skorpion* (1948). The key articles are reprinted in Berliner Kulturrat (ed.), *Eine Kulturmetropole wird geteilt* (Berlin, 1987) pp. 60–6.

21. Quoted in Dragica Horvat, 'Die "junge Generation" auf der Suche nach der neuen Literaur', in Kulturrat (ed.), *Eine Kulturmetropole wird geteilt*, p. 59.

22. On *Die Kolonne*, see H. D. Schäfer, 'Zur Periodisierung

der deutschen Literatur seit 1930', *Literaturmagazin*, 7 (1977) pp. 98ff.

23. See Helmut Peitsch, 'Politisierung der Literatur oder "geistige Freiheit"?', in Hermand *et al.*, *Nachkriegsliteratur*, vol. I, p. 194.

24. Arnold Bauer, in *Der Kurier* (Berlin), 5–6 October 1957.

25. Fritz Raddatz, 'Die ausgehaltene Realität', in Richter (ed.), *Almanach der Gruppe 47 1947–1962*, pp. 52–9.

26. See Günter Grass, *Headbirths, or The Germans are Dying Out*, trans. R. Mannheim (Harmondsworth, 1984) pp. 22–4.

27. See also Günter Grass, *Widerstand lernen* (Darmstadt and Neuwied, 1984) and Vormweg, *Günter Grass*, pp. 16–23.

28. This is my translation from Günter Grass, *Kopfgeburten oder Die Deutschen sterben aus* (Darmstadt and Neuwied, 1980) p. 23 (see Grass, *Headbirths*, p. 24).

12

West German Theatre in the Period of Reconstruction

URSULA FRIES

It is more true of the theatre than of the field of literature that the years 1945–50 set the course for later developments and influenced events until far into the 1960s. Theatre, more than other arts, is an institution, and institutions are – perhaps especially in Germany – ponderous and only changed with difficulty. Thus, decisions made in the 1940s determined the theatre scene for years: a very simple example is that of the long-term contracts with directors and actors.

In general, the theatre of the early years presented a multicoloured picture. Contrasts and irregularities were not yet levelled out: it was a 'theatre of productive contradictions'.[1] Only at the end of the 1940s – for various reasons – did the cultural scene become more uniform, only to end in the great boredom of the 1950s. Because they were full of contradictions, the early years are difficult to portray and can hardly be reduced to handy formulae. Hence, the question arises as to how the variety of contradictory events in the field of theatre can be presented without succumbing to the temptation to cut the facts to size in order to give them a clear and definite interpretation. In this chapter, I have tried to solve the problem by drafting it as a sort of jigsaw puzzle or kaleidoscope:[2] in other words, without claiming to consider all important phenomena and without a final interpretation. Before beginning to piece together some aspects of the German theatre between 1945 and 1950, I want to make a final preliminary note: writing about Germany in the postwar period inevitably suggests the question as to whether that time was characterised by a new beginning or by continuity. Just because theatre life in the first years was chaotic and colourful, this question can be answered in advance by 'both'; which is not absolutely satisfying, and I will return to this point later in the chapter.

The picture of the defeated German, who, in 1945, humiliated and depressed, spent his day hunting for calories and coal, is – even if it seems self-evident – wrong, or at least only half-correct. There was also a very strong demand for entertainment, amusement and edification, and astonishingly quickly there was a supply of all these. Less than three weeks after the capitulation, the first theatre re-opened in Berlin. The opening performance was Schonthan's *Raub der Sabinerinnen*,[3] an old farce, which perhaps can be compared to *Charley's Aunt*. It is very interesting that, still today, theatre historians claim that 'the real intellectual beginning of the theatre in Berlin' was *Nathan der Weise*,[4] produced by Wisten – as if they just could not accept that the postwar theatre started with trivialities. Berlin was not the only city to start so early: in Vienna, plays were being staged before the war had ended.[5] At the beginning of the season in September 1945, theatres were opened in nearly all the bigger cities, and very often they started with successful old comedies and farces.

At the same time, the starting conditions were very bad indeed: in the Autumn of 1944, all theatres had been closed in the cause of 'total mobilisation'; more than a third of all theatre buildings totally destroyed by air-raids,[6] and nearly all of them damaged. In Bochum, for example, the whole equipment (costumes and decorations, etc.), together with the library, was burnt: play books had to be borrowed and copied. Materials for decoration and costumes (clothing, nails, paints, timber, etc.) could hardly be organised. If it was freezing, the performances had to be cancelled because there was no way to heat the theatres. Like most of the Germans, the actors were starving, and we can hardly find a contemporary publication about theatre that does not quote the negative answer to an application asking for heavy workers' rations for actors: actors, the Board decided, do their work 'while walking around',[7] and could not therefore be considered for special rations.

In addition to these problems, there were difficulties such as the curfew and grotesque handicaps like the ban on wearing a uniform, which was applicable to all Germans. At least in those first months, the Allies did not like making any exceptions to this prohibition, not even for theatre performances.

'It was a great theatre time, a blessed time':[8] these are the words of the actor O. E. Hasse about the first postwar years. The most striking characteristic of that time was an enormous theatre boom: in Berlin, in the spring of 1946, there were theatres open at nearly

200 places;[9] in Nordrhein-Westfalia, there were seventy-four 'standing' theatres, and in addition countless small and tiny theatres, room- and cellar-theatres and touring companies.[10] Two hundred and seventeen registered theatres are listed in a theatre almanac of 1946–7.[11] The centre of this theatre activity was Berlin. Both in the Russian sector of the city and in that part of Germany that was occupied by the Soviet Union, theatre blossomed as vehemently and as hectically as in the other zones of occupation. That was astonishing for those 'who had thought the appearance of the Red Army would mean the ruin of Western Culture'.[12]

Unfortunately, we do not know a lot about the small theatre ventures, which sprung up everywhere as an alternative to the subsidised civic theatres and to the established private ones. These groups had certainly very different standards. The 'serious' theatres looked at them with scepticism and suspicion: they lamented that the touring companies, especially, had become a 'public calamity' and that they would threaten the 'educational work' of the bigger companies.[13] The established theatres were afraid of anarchy and chaos, and asked for stricter controls. They tended to take themselves very seriously: they saw themselves consciously in the tradition of the German 'Bildungstheater', that theatre which had the aim to educate morally and aesthetically, and they regarded themselves as 'moral institutions' in the tradition of Schiller. Remarks like: 'Discussing theatre is caring for the West',[14] can be found frequently in contemporary publications. The jealousy of the big companies with regard to the small ones was unnecessary, however: it is one of the peculiarities of the postwar period that all these theatres, big or small, found their audience.

Very early, the audience of the established theatres preferred 'organised cultural events':[15] in Bochum, for example, 90 per cent of all theatre tickets in the season 1947–8 were sold as subscriptions, for which a very complicated system existed.

The German 'theatrical miracle', this early and unexpected boom, must have had social and psychological reasons: a theatre-visit might have given the impression of normality, human dignity and social prestige in a difficult and often humiliating everyday life. Culture was one of the few fields of activity which was not blocked for the Germans – and it was one of the few goods that was not rationed.

In 1948, the theatre-boom came to an end; the audiences stayed away. The currency reform of June 1948 was certainly the main reason for the sudden German aversion to theatre: in contrast to the time before, people could now buy with their new and scarce money whatever they wanted. The theatre ticket became what it had been before: a superfluous luxury article. Only a quarter of all theatres were able to survive this shock.[16] Nevertheless, looking at the problem in more detail, it seems too easy to blame only the currency reform for killing the theatres and driving away the audience. As early as April 1947, H. Ihering complained about a 'general mental and intellectual slackening ... which was promoted by the political development'.[17] In Munich, the dwindling audience-figures were already noticeable in 1947, while in Bochum it was not until 1949–50 that attendances seriously declined. It seems advisable to be careful about 'chronological commonplaces'.[18]

As expected, the established and institutionalised theatres were able to best withstand the return to normality: the small, or 'die alternativen' theatres and touring companies died. At the end of the 1940s, the subsidised civic theatre had won through and dominated the theatre scene. This theatre stands in the tradition of the equally-subsidised Court and Residence theatre; it is dependent on the paying city council, both because of its legal form and especially because of its finances. In 1949 and 1950, the theatres' income from the sale of tickets accounted for less than 40 per cent of their expenditure.[19]

The theatre boom was tolerated by the Allies, even sponsored. Especially in Berlin, there was a real cultural competition between the four sectors. Each of the four Allies wanted to be represented by its own national drama. The generosity of the Allies in this field was based on the assumption that the intellectuals, the 'Dichter und Denker', had been the 'other Germany', the politically clean Germany in the Third Reich. I cannot deal with this problem in this context, but it has to be said that this assumption was wrong. Nor do I have space to consider the different conceptions of culture and theatre policy of the Allies in more detail. I shall therefore generalise slightly: the Americans and the Russians took theatre very seriously; they both had a strong sense of mission and they believed in the possibility of 're-education' and 'redemocratisation' via theatre. The British looked upon that view more sceptically, liberally and relatively disinterestedly. The French did not really have an opportunity for a vigorous theatre policy because there were very few theatres in their zone.

The competent authorities in the field of theatre were the 'Cultural Officers', who, for example, had to decide about licences for Germans. Until 1949, all theatre directors had to be licensed; the licenses could be revoked without notice. All occupying powers liked to appoint German émigrés: it was thought that they were familiar with the German situation in general and the theatre situation in particular, but they were not always competent. Many of them had left Germany twelve years before and were inclined to set back the clocks to the time of Weimar and to pick up the thread of the 'Golden Twenties'. So the backwardness of the German theatre, which was the result of twelve years dictatorship, was rather encouraged by the Allies. The restorative 1950s also have their roots here.

Of course, the theatre policy could not remain unaffected by the aggravating differences between the Soviet Union and the Western Allies. In the immediate postwar years, there was an agreement between the Allies as far as the aims of theatre policy were concerned: education for democracy and anti-Fascist propaganda. But, with the beginning of the Cold War, these priorities changed: 'anti-Nazism had to take second place to anticommunism'.[20] Integrating the Germans into the Western alliance became more important than educating them. The American theatre officer Van Loon called the aim of the new theatre policy quite plainly: 'Selling America'.[21] This aim was to be achieved by plays that imparted a clean, intact picture of America to the Germans: hence, with trivialities. The theatre practice was in flagrant contrast to the originally ambitious plans of the American occupying authorities, who had wanted to cure the 'sick soul of Germany'[22] by educating the Germans through the theatre. In the end, more than half of the American plays put on stage were shallow entertainment.

Most of the theatre directors, producers and actors, who had worked in the theatre during the Third Reich – and that meant theatre that was acceptable to the National Socialists – could go on working after 1945 without any problems, or, rather, could start their work again. In Munich, sixty-six denazification proceedings were brought against theatre people. Subsequently, two-fifths were released, and the remainder were classified as 'opportunist followers' and got away with a fine.[23] Denazification proceedings were carried out by the Allies with differing rigour and intensity. The Americans took most trouble with them and applied the strictest standards, at least until 1947. The reason for that was their social-psychological theory of Fascism, which – to oversimplify slightly – blamed the German National Character for the rise of Fascism. The Russians, who did not share this theory, conducted denazification – at least in the field of theatre – much more generously, as did the British and French. For the Germans involved in it in the postwar period, the practice of denazification must have been as mysterious as it is for us today. The Bochum director, Saladin Schmitt, was allowed, unmolested, to produce in the British zone, but not in the American. The actor Lothar Müthel was not tolerated in Vienna, but the Russians let him play in Weimar. On the other hand, they thought that the conductor Karl Böhm was too politically incriminated, whereas the Americans did not have any objection to him.

But even among those 'Nazi activists' classified in 'Category 1': 'to be unconditionally dismissed', who received a professional ban, there were very few who could not get a firm footing in the theatre later on. The most famous example was Gustaf Gründgens. Since 1937, he had been *Generalintendant* (i.e. theatre director of opera, operetta and drama) of the Staatstheater in Berlin. He had been courted and sponsored by Goering, and had received the title of *Staatsrat* (Privy Councillor). This title – that, at least, was Gründgens' version – became his doom after 1945. First, the Soviet occupying authorities thought that the title *Generalintendant* was a military rank; then, they regarded the *Staatsrat* as proof of political activity. In any case, Gründgens spent nine months in prison before he was denazified – first only as an actor; later on, as a producer as well. Since 1947, he was in charge of – as *Generalintendant* again – the civic theatres of Düsseldorf, and was the most influential producer of the 1950s. The case of Gründgens does not only show the personal continuity of the postwar German theatre, but also illustrates the problematic nature of denazification proceedings or, more generally, of judging behaviour during the Third Reich. Gründgens' behaviour during the period of National Socialism was ambivalent, as his Communist colleague Ernst Busch claimed. But in no way was his behaviour so clearly perfidious as Klaus Mann suggests in his book *Mephisto*.[24]

The behaviour of artists during the Third Reich is a fascinating, but very difficult field, which is only of interest here insofar as these artists determined the culture of postwar Germany to a considerable extent. 'Inner Resistance', 'Inner Emigration', 'adaptation to the regime', 'opportunism' – all these terms are difficult to define, especially if the professional existence of an individual is at stake. Having said that, it would be impossible to support the idea of a general amnesty for artists, like Alexander Golling, the former director of the Bavarian Staatstheatre, who very clearly argued for an amnesty with the words: 'True artistry and political infantilism ... are normally inseparably united factors.'[25]

The postwar careers of former theatre stars of the Third Reich were morally dubious. Of more importance were the consequences that this personal continuity had for the theatre scene of the 1940s and 1950s. Looking at Berlin, it is very impressive how a clique of politically-incriminated men was able gradually to gain all the important theatre posts by mutually supporting each other. Especially piquant is the story of Ludwig Körner, who can be classified as the 'highest theatre functionary of the NS-State'.[26] After 1945, he became an official of the *Verband Deutscher Bühnenangehöriger* (German actors union). One of his duties was to decide about financial compensation for actors who had been persecuted by the Nazis.

Because nearly all the important posts in Berlin were filled by theatre veterans, young talents or returning émigrés did not get any chance to integrate themselves into theatre life. The returned producers Kortner, Piscator and Wicclair, for example, were not able to obtain a post of director and therefore did not get their own company: they remained outsiders. They were also not sponsored by the Allies, which at first sight seems astonishing. Presumably, the occupying authorities were afraid that the émigrés, with their clear record, might be too self-confident and not submissive enough to Allied dictates.

The increasing insulation of the established theatre in Berlin against new blood was instrumental in the process of the 'provincialisation' of the city. In the 1940s and 1950s, Berlin, having lost its political role as capital, also lost its role as a cultural centre, even though the theatres in Berlin received enormous subsidies. Several factors were responsible: Berlin's new insular position, the political pressures that gave a political meaning to each theatrical event, and the nepotism already mentioned, were especially important. In lieu of one main theatre city, therefore, a number of West German theatre centres developed, with varying importance: Munich, Düsseldorf, Hamburg, Bochum, Darmstadt and, later on, Bremen.[27]

In the Nazi era, the German theatres had mainly been performing the classics and the light successful comedies of the 1920s. Considering the prohibition of foreign drama – except Shakespeare, who could be staged as he had become an honorary German as a result of the attention the mental giants of Germany had bestowed upon him – and considering the miserable quality of new Nazi drama, theatres had no alternative. After 1945, they continued to concentrate on the classics: especially popular were Goethe's *Iphigenie* and Lessing's *Nathan der Weise*. The latter, understandably enough, had been prohibited during the Third Reich. On the other hand, Shakespeare's *Merchant of Venice*, which had frequently been performed before 1945, was now banned from the repertoire. It was considered impossible 'after Auschwitz'. It was not until 1952 that the Bochum theatre was the first to feel capable of coping with the Jew Shylock.

Of course, foreign dramatists were now staged: in the Western zones, the French 'Nihilists' and the English and American 'Surrealists' or 'Magic Realists' – these classifications used by contemporary criticism are extremely rough and reflect a certain helplessness in the attitude of the critics towards the plays. Incidentally, all the performing rights for foreign drama had to be supplied by the Allies, if only because German currency was not convertible up until 1948. The Americans, notably, did not miss this chance of censorship. Arnaud d'Usseau's American successes (*Deep are the Roots*, for example) were not licensed for Germany because of their 'unbalanced accent to the American racial problem';[28] nor were Arthur Miller and Eugene O'Neill (*Marco Millions*). Thornton Wilder's *The Skin of our Teeth*, with its irrational and pessimistic conception of history, became the most successful American 'serious' play. Most frequently performed, however, was the love story *Voice of the Turtle*, by Van Druten, and the comedy *Three Men on a Horse*.[29] Of the French writers, Sartre was able to credit himself with the most performances with his *Respectful Prostitute*. In addition, Anouilh, Giraudoux and Claudel must be mentioned, and among the British Christopher Fry and Priestley's *An Inspector Calls*.[30]

Whereas the German playwrights of the 1920s and 1930s and plays written in exile were returned to only hesitatingly, the 'empty drawers' of the new dramatists became a catch-phrase. The hope that authors had produced plays in the Fascist era proved to be vain: unlike poems, perhaps, plays can obviously only be written if there is hope of performance. Even after 1945, drama production did not match up to expectation. With a certain disappointment, the end of the First World War was remembered, when a young generation of dramatists had made Germany one of the most interesting theatre nations in no time at all. This comparison, however, is unfair. People who had been separated from modern world literature for twelve years and had been fed with pathetic Nazi theatre instead, could hardly have been expected to produce stylistically bold masterpieces in 1945. The only young postwar author who succeeded on the stage, and then with one single drama, was Wolfgang Borchert, with *Draussen vor der Tür*.

Yet the most frequently staged drama was German: Zuckmayer's *Des Teufels General*, written in exile in America, premiered in Zurich in 1946, and the greatest success on the German stage up to 1949. The enthusiasm for this politically unfortunate play is only too understandable. The hero, the airforce General Harras, who, as an enthusiastic pilot, fought and won battles for Hitler out of the pure joy of combat and adventure, provided the Germans with a war hero after all, a muscleman of the old school who fails to conceal his great kindness under a mask of cynicism. At the end of the play, he realises his political error and, consciously starting a defective plane, dies an heroic death. It must be assumed that Zuckmayer was unaware that he was glorifying German military prowess beyond all politics. First the Allies banned the play, because they feared the rise of an officers' legend, but at the end of 1947 it was performed in Hamburg for the first time and began its triumphant career.[31]

As already stated, most of the émigré directors did not obtain their own theatres and companies; thus, they had a very limited influence on stylistic instruction and development. Yet a new orientation of acting style was urgently required. 'What you hear about style of production makes you puke', said Brecht in 1947,[32] and he refused to have his plays performed. The American theatre officer Behr criticised the 'wrong tone'[33] in German theatres: there was too much pathos and everything was much too loud – later the returning producers derisively called this way of acting 'Reichkanzleistil',[34] the style of the Chancellery of the Reich. Emancipation from the Nazi theatre had not yet been achieved. Those who did not adopt that style, of which Gründgens was the most distinctive and artistically most polished representative, fell back into even more remote tradition and borrowed from Expressionism. The stylised stage designs of the Expressionists suited the general shortage of material: 'The old plays were performed on empty, pseudomodern stylised stages; the old texts were recited, deeply moved, intelligently at best.'[35] Demands for a magical, mystical or religious theatre, which can be found in contemporary publications, reflect the search for a more modern style. Gründgens, however, demanded 'soundness' and 'faithfulness to the original'. Thus, he provoked a discussion about how to interpret the classics, with his – conservative – position dominating up to the end of the 1950s. If we return again to the comparison between the situation in 1918 and that in 1945, categorised as unfair, the 1920s appear to be characterised by a young generation of producers performing young playwrights, with a mutual influence, whereas in the late 1940s and 1950s, established and no-longer-young directors performed foreign authors and classics: conservatism is thus a logical consequence.[36]

Out of all the events which form part of the history of postwar theatre, I want to select two which have been chosen deliberately and belong to the complex of questions about continuity or a new beginning. The two events are the setting-up of the 'Ruhrfestspiele' and the 'Werner Krauss Scandal' in Berlin.

The former is not only a nice legend but has the additional advantage of being a true one. In the winter of 1946, freezing actors from Hamburg came to Recklinghausen, a town in the Ruhr area, and made a strange proposal to the local pit: if they could obtain an additional supply of coal for the cold theatres in Hamburg from the miners, they would, as a recompense, make a guest performance in Recklinghausen in the spring. This extraordinary barter actually came off. It attracted considerable attention and went down, first in the press and then in the annals of theatre history, as the alliance of theatre and the working class – of art and coal ('Kunst und Kohle'). It became institutionalised as the Recklinghausen Festival. Since 1949, it has been sponsored by the Deutsche Gewerkschafts-bund, the German Trades Union Congress, and by the City of Recklinghausen. Under its name 'Ruhrfestspiele', it was to mark a new period in German history. There was much optimism and enthusiasm in its establishment. The actual percentage of workers in the audience is controversial: workers have always been in the minority, and their percentage went down in the 1950s. The 'Ruhrfestspiele' became one of the most important events in the theatre season of the Federal Republic of Germany, but the initial meaning disappeared, as did the coal myth. The history of its birth, however, has become a favourite tale.[37]

The second event, probably the biggest theatre scandal of the postwar period, was a guest performance by Werner Krauss in Berlin in 1950. Werner Krauss was one of the star actors of the Third Reich. He played the title role in the film *Jud Süss*, which nationally and internationally had been regarded as the most important and most pernicious antisemitic film. After 1945, Krauss had been denazified in Vienna very early and engaged at the *Burgtheater*. Despite vehement protests from the Jewish community, the Social Democratic Senate of the City of Berlin invited the *Burgtheater* for a guest performance of an Ibsen play in which Krauss played the leading role. A protest demonstration by the Jewish community on the evening of the premiere was prohibited. It took place nevertheless, and ended with brutal police intervention and a street fight. Some theatre visitors were refused admission on the grounds that they looked 'Jewish'. When the performance had to be interrupted because of the loud chorus from outside, antisemitic remarks were heard in the audience. In the end, the performance was completed, but the rest of the run was cancelled. Some days later, there were antisemitic demonstrations in Berlin and the police were not brought into action. In vindication of the Social Democratic Party, it must be added, however, that the Chairman of the SPD, Schumacher, openly and sharply criticised the Berlin Party member Reuter for his behaviour in the Krauss case.[38]

The two examples must not be over-strained, but they mark two points on the spectrum of German theatrical life. It is certainly not pure chance that the idea of setting up the 'Ruhrfestspiele', an enthusiastic and future-orientated project, was born in the early postwar period, in 1946, whereas the Krauss scandal, which reveals the mighty relics of the past, happened at the end of the first Reconstruction period.

If there were opportunities and moments for a new beginning for the German theatre, they certainly lay in the anarchy of the early years: in the touring companies and private theatres, in the forced improvisation and the cultural backlog demands of a stage-struck audience, even if, in the end, this may well have been a compensation for different, more materialistic demands. Even if there was never as much innovation, experiment and trend-setting as it appeared to the contemporary commentators, still there were promises of a more democratic and free form of theatre, less rigid and less exclusively aimed at the traditional theatre-going public – as the 'Ruhrfestspiele' showed.

At any time, however, the conservative forces were in the stronger position. Their influence grew during the postwar years and included: the tradition of the institutionalised, subsidised theatre claiming to educate the public; the Allies and their backward-orientated émigré German theatre officers; the primacy of politics in the beginning of the Cold War; the ability to survive of those who had been great in the world of theatre in the Third Reich – and the consequences of this personal continuity; and the tendency of many Germans to become quickly tired of their past and of denazification, as the Krauss scandal illustrates.

Under these influences, German theatre became increasingly restorative in character, and fitted smoothly into the 'post-totalitarian Biedermeier period'[39] of the 1950s, which was accused by Arnold Schönberg, shortly before his death, of having made comfort its philosophy.[40] 'In the course of time, regret about what had been destroyed was mixed with the regret about what had been preserved.'[41]

Notes

1. Herbert Ihering, quoted in Wigand Lange, *Theater in Deutschland nach 1945: Zur Theaterpolitik der amerikanischen Besatzungsbehörden* (Frankfurt, 1980).

2. See Friedrich Prinz (ed.), *Trümmerzeit in München: Kultur und Gesellschaft einer deutschen Grosstadt im Aufbruch, 1945–1949* (Munich, 1984) pp. 9–19.

3. This occurred on 27 May 1945. See Hans Daiber, *Deutsches Theater seit 1945: Bundesrepublik Deutschland. Deutsche Demokratische Republik. Österreich. Schweiz* (Stuttgart, 1976) p. 11.

4. Henning Müller, 'Theater im Zeichen des Kalten Krieges: Untersuchungen zur Theater- und Kulturpolitik in den Westsektoren Berlins, 1945–1953' (Berlin: Doctoral thesis, 1976) p. 140.

5. See Daiber, *Deutsches Theater seit 1945*, pp. 22–3.

6. See ibid., p. 26. Of 262 prewar theatres, ninety-eight had been destroyed.

7. See Friedrich Domin, 'Die Not und das Notwendige', in *Der Theateralmanach 1946–1947: Kritisches Jahrbuch der Bühnenkunst* (Munich, 1946) pp. 37–54.

8.   Quoted in Daiber, *Deutsches Theater seit 1945*, p. 27.
9.   See Hermann Glaser, *Kulturgeschichte der Bundesrepublik Deutschland: Zwischen Kapitulation und Währungsreform 1945–1948*, vol. I (Munich, 1985) p. 245.
10. See ibid., p. 245.
11. See *Der Theateralmanach, 1946–1947*, appendix.
12. Daiber, *Deutsches Theater seit 1945*, p. 28.
13. See *Der Theateralmanach, 1946–1947*, especially, Ulrich Seelmann-Eggebert, 'Rhein-Main-Neckar-Gebiet', pp. 342–59.
14. Rudolph Adolph, 'Georg Kaiser im Exil', in *Der Theateralmanach, 1946–1947*, pp. 161–80.
15. Henning Rischbieter, 'Theater', in Wolfgang Benz (ed.), *Die Bundesrepublik Deutschland: Geschichte in drei Bänden*, vol. III, *Kultur* (Frankfurt, 1983) p. 78.
16. See Daiber, *Deutsches Theater seit 1945*, p. 90.
17. Quoted in ibid., p. 32.
18. Prinz (ed.), *Trümmerzeit in Munchen*, p. 14.
19. See Lutz Jonas, 'Die Finanzierung der öffentlichen Theater in der Bundesrepublik Deutschland' (Mainz: Doctoral thesis, 1972) p. 54. In 1949, ticket sales accounted for 36.7 per cent of income; in 1951, for 37.7 per cent.
20. Anna J. Merrit and Richard L. Merritt, *Public Opinion in Occupied Germany: The OMGUS Survey, 1945–1949* (Urbana, Ill.: University of Illinois Press, 1970) p. 55.
21. Müller, *Theater im Zeichen des Kalten Krieges*, p. 283.
22. Lange, *Theater in Deutschland nach 1945*, p. 31.
23. See ibid., pp. 150ff.
24. See Gustaf Gründgens, *Briefe. Aufsätze. Reden*, ed. Rolf Badenhausen and Peter Gründgens-Gorski (Hamburg, 1967). See also Klaus Mann, *Mephisto. Roman einer Karriere* (Hamburg, 1980).
25. Quoted from the denazification file on Alexander Golling in Lange, *Theater in Deutschland nach 1945*, p. 169.
26. Müller, *Theater im Zeichen des Kalten Krieges*, pp. 288ff. Boleslaw Barlog, the director of the Schiller- and Schlossparktheater, did not belong to this clique and had a clean record.
27. See Rischbieter, 'Theater', p. 75.
28. Wigand Lange, *Theater in Deutschland nach 1945*, p. 23.
29. See ibid., p. 742.
30. See Deutscher Bühnenverein (eds), *Was spielten die Theater? Bilanz der Spielpläne in der Bundesrepublik Deutschland, 1947–1975* (Cologne, 1978) p. 56.
31. See Henning Müller, *Theater im Zeichen des Kalten Krieges*, pp. 243ff.
32. Quoted in Hans Daiber, *Deutsches Theater seit 1945*, p. 71.
33. Walter Behr, 'Gefahren des Darstellungstils', in *Der Theateralmanach, 1946–1947*.
34. See Rischbieter, 'Theater', p. 82.
35. Benjamin Henrichs, quoted in Herbert Hohenemser, 'Introduction', to Eugen Schöndienst, *Geschichte des Deutschen Bühnenvereins seit 1945* (Frankfurt, 1981) p. 43.

36. This same conservatism is to be found in the field of opera in postwar Germany, which continued to recycle the classics, Mozart, Verdi, Puccini, Wagner, Lortzing and Bizet. See Volker Bahn, 'Das subventionierte Theater der BRD' (Berlin: Doctoral thesis, 1972) p. 114.

37. See Herbert Hohenemser, 'Introduction', pp. 23–4. See also 'Die Wahrheit ohne Legende', *Frankfurter Allgemeine Zeitung*, 26 May 1977.

38. See Müller, *Theater im Zeichen des Kalten Krieges*, pp. 273ff.

39. Daiber, *Deutsches Theater seit 1945*, p. 116.

40. See ibid., p. 170.

41. Ibid., p. 113.

Bibliography

ITALY

Annuario del cinema italiano 1979–1980, Centro Studi di cultura, promozione e diffusione del cinema.

Calalogo Bolaffi del cinema italiano (Turin: G. Bolaffi, 1973–).

'Libertà neorealista', *Il Mondo*, 10 May 1955.

La spettacolo in Italia (Rome: Societa Italiana degli Autori e Editori (SIAE), annual).

Venti Anni dell'ANICA per il cinema Italiano 1944–1964 (Rome: ANICA, n.d.).

Ajello, Nello, *Intellettuali e PCI 1944–1958* (Bari: Laterza, 1979).

Alicata, Mario and De Santis, Giusseppe, 'Verità e poesia: Verga e il cinema italiano', *Cinema*, 127 (10 October 1941).

Alicata, Mario, 'La corrente "Politecnico"', *Rinascita*, 3:5–6 (May–June 1946).

Alicata, Mario, 'Intervento di Mario Alicata', in *Atti dattiloscitti del V Congresso del partito communista italiano*.

Alicata, Mario, 'Gli intellettuali e la loro liberta', *L'Unità*, 20 May 1955.

Alicata, Mario, *Scritti letterari* (Milan: Il Saggiatore, 1968).

Andreotti, Guilio, 'Open Letter to Vittorio De Sica', *Libertas*, 24 February 1952.

Antonielli, Sergio, 'Sul neorealismo, venti anni dopo', in *Saggi di letteratura italiana in onore di Gaetano Trombatore* (Milan: Instituto editoriale Cisalpino-La goliardica, 1973).

Antonioni, Michelangelo, 'Per un film sul fiume Po', *Cinema*, 68 (25 April 1939).

Apra, Adriano and Carabba, Claudio, *Neorealismo d'appendice. Per un dibattito sul cinema popolare: il caso Matarazzo* (Florence: Guaraldi, 1976).

Argentieri, Mino, *La Censura nel cinema italiano* (Rome: Editori Riuniti, 1974).

Aristarco, Guido, 'È realismo', *Cinema nuovo*, 55 (March 1955).

Aristarco, Guido, *Neorealismo e nuova critica cinematografica* (Florence: Nuova Guaraldi, 1980).

Asti, Carlo, 'Popolarità e impopolarità del cinema italiano', *Cinema Nuovo*, v, 93 (1 November 1956).

Bandinelli, R. Bianchi, 'Cultura e popolo', *Rinascita*, 2:2 (1945).

Barbaro, Umberto, 'Limiti di Valéry', *L'Unità*, 4 October 1945.

Battaglia, Roberto, *Un nomo un partigiano* (Florence: Ed. U., 1945).

Bigazzi, Roberto, *Fenoglio: personaggi e narratori* (Rome: Salerno, 1983).

Bo, Carlo (ed.), *Inchiesta sul neorealismo* (Turin: Edizioni Radio Italiana, 1951).

Brunetta, Gian Piero, 'Neorealismo: alle fonti di un mito', in G.P. Brunetta, *Intelletuali, cineam e propaganda tra le due guerre* (Bologna: Patron, 1972).

Brunetta, Gian Piero, 'Il cammino della critica verso il neorealismo', in G. P. Brunetta, *Storia del cinema italiano 1895–1945* (Rome: Editori Riuniti, 1979).

Brunetta, Gian Piero, *Storia del cinema italiano, 1945–1982* (Rome: Editori Riuniti, 1982).

Cadioli, Alberto, *L'industria del romanzo. L'editoria letteraria in Italia dal 1945 agli anni Ottanta* (Rome: Editori Riuniti, 1981).

Calvino, Italo, *Il sentierio dei nidi di ragno. Con una prefazione dell'autore* (Turin: Einaudi, 1978).

Calvino, Italo, *Un pietra sopra* (Turin: Einaudi, 1980).

Caracciolo, Alberto, 'Un'ipotesi di periodizzazione', *Quaderni Storici*, XII (1977) 1: *Letteratura ideologia società negli anni trenta*.

Casetti, Francesco, Frassino, Alberto, Grasso, Aldo and Sanguinetti, Tatti, 'Neorealismo e cinema italiano degli anni 30', in Lino Micciche (ed.), *Il neorealismo cinematografico italiano. Atti del convegno della X Mostra Internazionale del Nuovo Cinema* (Venice: Marsilio, 1975).

Cavallo, Luigi, 'Decadenza di Mauriac', *L'Unità*, 17 September 1949.

Chiaretti, Tommaso, 'Cinema di ventura', *L'Unità*, 17 February 1953.

Chiaretti, Tommaso, 'Dietro lo schermo', *L'Unità*, 23 January 1954.

Chiarini, Luigi, 'Tradisce il neorealismo', *Cinemà Nuovo*, 55 (March 1955).

De Michelis, Mario, *Alle origini del neorealismo: Aspetti del romanzo italiano negli anni 30* (Cosenza: Edizìoni Lerici, 1980).

De Santis, Giuseppe, 'Per un paesaggio italiano', *Cinema*, 116 (25 April 1941).

Falaschi, Giovanni, *La resistanza armata nella narrativa italiana* (Turin: Einaudi, 1976).

Falaschi, Giovanni, *La letteratura partigiana in Italia 1943–1945* (Rome: Editori Riuniti, 1984).

Faldini, Franca and Fofi, Goffredo, *L'avventurosa storia del cinema italiano racconta dai suoi protagonisti, 1935–1959* (Milan: Feltrinelli, 1979).

Fedele, Marcello, 'La dinamica elettorale del PCI 1946–1979', in Massimo Ilardi and Aris Accornero (eds), *Il Partito communista italiano: struttura e storia dell' organizzazione 1921–1979* (Milan: Feltrinelli, 1982).

Fenoglio, Beppe, *I ventitre giorni della città di Alba* (Milan: Mondadori, 1976).

Fofi, Goffredo, *Il cinema italiano: servi e padroni* (Milan: Feltrinelli, 1977).

Fortini, Franco, 'Che cosa è stato "Il Politecnico"', in F. Fortini, *Dieci inverni (1947–1957)* (Milan: Feltrinelli, 1957).

Fortini, Franco, 'Mandato degli scrittori e fine dell'antifascismo', in F. Fortini, *Verifica dei poteri* (Milan: Il Saggiatore, 1965).

Ghini, Celso, 'Gli iscritti al partito e alla FGCI', in Mussimo Ilardi and Aris Accornero (eds), *Il Partito communista italiano: struttura e storia dell'organizzazione 1921–1979* (Milan: Feltrinelli, 1982).

Ginzburg, Natalia, *Lessico famigliare* (Turin: Einaudi, 1963).

Gorresio, Vittorio, *I carissimi nemici* (Milan: Longanesi, 1949).

Gruppi, Luciano, 'Note sulla politica culturale del partito nel dopoguerra', *Critica marxista*, quaderno no. 5, supplement to issue no. 1 (1972).

Gruppo 63, Il romanzo spreimentale (Milan: Feltrinelli, 1980).

Guarini, Alfredo, 'Il neorealismo e l'industria', *Cinema*, 123 (15 December 1953).

Guttuso, Renato, 'Una azione culturale communista', *Rinascita*, 23:4 (22 January 1966).

Isnenghi, Mario, 'Trenta-Quaranta: l'ipotesi della continuita', *Quaderni Storici*, XII (1977) 1: *Letteratura ideologia societa negli anni trenta*.

Lattuada, Alberto, 'Prefazione', in A. Lattuada, *Occhio Quadrato* (Milan: Corrente Editioni, 1941).

Lizzani, Carlo, *Il cinema italiano* (Florence: Parenti, 1953).

Luperini, Romano, *Gli intellettuali di sinsitra e l'ideologia della riconstruzione* (Rome: Edizioni di 'Ideologie', 1971).

Luperini, Romano, *Il Novecento: apparati ideologici, ceto intellettuale, sistemi formali nella letteratura italiana contemporanea*, vol. II (Turin: Loescher, 1981).

Misler, Nicoletta, *La via italiana al realismo: la politica culturale artistica del PCI dal 1944 al 1956* (Milan: Mazzotta, 1973).

Miccichè, Lino, 'Verifica del neorealismo', in L. Miccichè (ed.), *Il neorealismo cinematografico italiano* (Venice: Marsilio, 1975).

Monteleone, Franco, *Storia della RAI dagli alleati alla DC. 1944–1954* (Rome, Bari: Laterza, 1979).

Muscetta, Carlo, '*Metello* e la crisi del neorealismo', *Società*, XII (1955).

Onofri, Fabrizio, 'Irresponsabilità dell'arte sotto il fascismo', *Rinascita*, 1:4 (1944).

Overby, David (ed.), *Springtime in Italy: A Reader in Neorealism* (London: Talisman, 1978).

Panicali, Anna, *Il romanzo del lavoro: Saggio su Elio Vittorini* (Lecce: Milella, 1976).

Passerini, Luisa, *Fascism in Popular Memory: The Cultural Experience of the Turin Working Class* (Cambridge: Cambridge University Press, 1987), translated from *Torino operaia e fascismo* (Bari: Laterza, 1984).

Patuzzi, Claudia, *Mondadori* (Naples: Liguori, 1978).

Pavese, Cesare, 'Il communismo e gli intellettuali', in C. Pavese, *La letteratura americana et altri saggi* (Turin: Einaudi, 1962).

Pavese, Cesare, *La Casa in collina*, in C. Pavese, *Prima che il gallo canti* (Milan: Mondadori, 1972).

Petroni, Guglielmo, *Il mondo è una prigione, Botteghe Oscure*, I (1948).

Pomilio, Mario, *Le fortune del Verga* (Naples: Liguori, 1963).

Potter, Joy Hambuechen, *Elio Vittorini* (Boston: Twayne, 1979).

Pratolini, V., *Allegoria e derisione* (Milan: Club degli editori, 1966).

Quaglietti, Lorenzo, *Storia economic-politica del cinema italiano 1945–1980* (Rome: Editori Riuniti, 1980).

Radice, L. Lombardo, 'Alla scuola della classe operaia', *L'Unità*, 30 November 1944.

Rosa, Alberto Asor, *Scritti e popolo* (Rome: Samona e Savelli, 1965).

Rosa, Alberto Asor, 'La cultura', in *Storia d'Italia*, vol. IV: *Dall'Unità a oggi*, 2 (Turin: Einaudi, 1975).

Rosa, Alberto Asor, 'Lo Stato democratico e i partiti politici', in A. A. Rosa (ed.), *Letteratura italiana*, vol. I: *Il letterato e les instituzioni* (Turin: Einaudi, 1982).

Rossanda, Rossana, 'Unità politica e scelte culturali: Togliatti e gli intellettuali italiani', *Rinascita*, 22:34 (28 August 1965).

Rossanda, Rossana, 'Sulla politica culturale e gli intellettuali', *Problemi del socialismo*, 6 (September–December 1985).

Salinari, Carlo, '*Metello*', *Il Contemporaneo*, 12 February 1955.

Salinari, Carlo, 'Discussioni e conclusioni su *Metello* e il neorealismo', *Società*, XII (1956).

Sanguinetti, Edoardo, *Ideologia e linguaggio* (Milan: Feltrinelli, 1965).

Sereni, Emilio, 'Andrei Zhdanov: modello di combattente per il trionfo del communismo', *Rinascita*, 5:9–10 (September–October 1948).

Sereni, Emilio, 'Gramsci e la scienza d'avanguardia', in E. Sereni, *Scienza marxismo cultura* (Rome: Edizioni Sociali, 1949).

Silverman, Michael, 'Italian Film and American Capital, 1947–1951', in Patricia Mellencamp and Philip Rosen (eds), *Cinema Histories, Cinema Practices* (Los Angeles: American Film Institute/University Publications of America, 1984).

Spriano, Paolo, *Le Passioni di un decennio 1946–1956* (Milan: Garzanti, 1986).

Togliatti, Palmiro, *La Politica culturale*, ed. Luciano Gruppi (Rome: Editori Riuniti, 1974).

Togliatti, Palmiro, 'Programma', *La Rinascita*, 1:1 (June 1944).

Togliatti, Palmiro, 'Antonio Gramsci e don Benedetto', in Togliatti, *La Politica culturale*.

Togliatti, Palmiro, 'La colpa e dell'Anticristo', in Togliatti, *La Politica culturale*.

Togliatti, Palmiro, 'Una lettera di Palmiro Togliatti', *Il Politecnico*, 33–4 (September–December 1946).

Togliatti, Palmiro, *I corsivi di Rodrigo* (Bari: De Donato, 1976).

Trabucco, Carlo, 'Chiediamo disco verde per *Ladri di biciclette* (e suggeriamo un pò prudenza ai nostri communisti)', *Il Popolo*, 7 March 1950.

Trombadori, G., 'Artisti e critici dopo la liberazione', *Rinascita*, 2:1 (1945).

Vene, Gian Franco, 'Per chi suona il piffero', *L'Europeo*, 21:27 (12 September 1965).

Venturini, Franco, 'Origini del neorealismo', *Bianco e Nero*, XI, 2 (February 1950).

Visconti, Luchino, 'Cinema antropomorfico', *Cinema*, 173–4 (25 September–25 October 1943).

Vittorini, Elio, 'Lettera a Togliatti', *Il Politecnico*, 35 (January–March 1947).

Wagstaff, Christopher, 'The Italian Cinema Industry during the Fascist Regime', *The Italianist*, 4 (1984).

Zagarrio, Vito, 'Primato degli intellettuali e neorealismo', in Miccichè (ed.), *Il neorealismo cinematografico italiano. . .*

FRANCE

36 en Corrèze, aux jours ensoleillés du Front Populaire (Tulle: Peuple et Culture, 1976).

'Colloque de Bourges', *L'Expansion de la Recherche Scientifique*, 22 (April–May 1965).

Grenoble, ville d'expériences (Grenoble: n.d. [1946?]).

'Humanisme socialiste', *Temps Présent*, 28 September 1945.

'Il faut reconstruire en pensant à l'homme', *Temps Présent*, 24 November 1944.

'Jacques Laurent est-il français?', *Le Monde*, 11 July 1985.

'L'Heure révolutionnaire', *Temps Présent*, 15 September 1944.

Peuple et Culture 1945–1965 (Paris, Peuple et Culture, 1965).

'Pierre Benoît rayé de la liste noire', *Les Lettres Françaises*, 22 November 1946.

'Sans pouvoirs. Les Dernières pages de Giraudoux', *Les Lettres Françaises*, 23 September 1944.

Un Peuple, une culture (Grenoble, 1945).

'Vers la révolution sociale', *Témoignage Chrétien*, 14 October 1944.

Adam, George, *L'Epée dans les reins, roman: Chronique des années quarante* (Paris: Éditions des Trois Collines, 1944).

Adereth, Max, *The French Communist Party: A Critical History (1920–1984)* (Manchester: Manchester University Press, 1984).

Andler, Charles, *L'Humanisme travailliste: Essais de pédagogie sociale* (Paris: Bibliothèque de la Civilisation française, 1927).

Anouilh, Jean, *Pauvre Bitos* (Paris: La Table Ronde, 1958).

Aragon, Louis, 'Prélude à la *Diane Française*', in Paul Eluard (ed.), *L'Honneur des poèts* (Paris: Les Editions de Minuit, 1943).

Aragon, Louis, 'Retour d'André Gide', *Les Lettres Françaises*, 25 November 1944.

Arbousse-Bastid, Paul, 'Pour un humanisme nouveau', *Foi et vie*, March–April 1930.

Aymé, Marcel, *La Tête des autres* (Paris: Grasset, 1952).

Beauvoir, Simone de, 'L'Idéalisme moral et réalisme politique', *Les Temps Modernes*, November 1945.

Beauvoir, Simone de, 'L'Existentialisme et la sagesse de la nation', *Les Temps Modernes*, December 1945.

Bernanos, Georges, *Un Mauvais rêve*, in *Oeuvres complètes* (Paris: Gallimard, coll. 'Éditions de la Pléiade', 1961).

Besse, Guy, 'L'Expansionnisme idéologique des Yankees', *La Démocratie Nouvelle*, 2 February 1948.

Bing, B., *La Vraie Libération: Voix de la France. Voix du Travail* (Grenoble: Peuple et Culture, 1945).

Blondin, Antoine, *Les Enfants du Bon Dieu* (Paris: La Table Ronde, 1952).

Blum, Léon, *A l'Échelle humaine* (Paris: Gallimard, 1945).

Bulletin de la Coopération Intellectuelle, special issue: 'Vers un nouvel humanisme', 75–6 (March–April 1937).

Butor, Michel, *Répertoires*, vol. I (Paris: Éditions de Minuit, 1960).

Cacérès, Bénigno, *Histoire de l'éducation populaire* (Paris: Seuil, 1964).

Cacérès, Bénigno, *L'Espoir au coeur* (Paris: Seuil, 1967).

Cacérès, Bénigno, *Allons au devant de la vie: La Naissance du temps des loisirs en 1936* (Paris: La Découverte, 1981).

Cacérès, Bénigno, *Les Deux rivages: Itinéraire d'un animateur d'éducation populaire* (Paris: La Découverte, 1982).

Casanova, Laurent, *Le Parti communiste, les intellectuels et la nation* (Paris: Éditions Sociales, 1949).

Cassou, Jean, 'La Littérature de ces quatre années', *Les Lettres Françaises*, 20 May 1947.

Caute, David, *Communism and the French Intellectuals, 1914–1960* (London: André Deutsch, 1964).

Céline, Louis-Ferdinand, *D'un château l'autre* (Paris: Gallimard, 1957).

Chenu, R. P., 'L'Homo oeconomicus et le chrétien: réflexions d'un théologien à propos du marxisme', *Économie et humanisme*, May–June 1945.

Chevalier, Irénée, O. P., *Humanisme chrétien* (Paris: Casterman, n.d.).

Cogniot, Georges, 'Discours de Georges Cogniot', in Roger Garaudy and Georges Cogniot, *Les Intellectuels et la Renaissance Française* (Paris: Éditions du PCF, 1945).

Crubellier, M., *Histoire culturelle de la France, XIXe-XXe siècle* (Paris: Armand Colin, 1974).

Daix, Pierre, *J'ai cru au matin* (Paris: Robert Laffont, coll. 'Vécu', 1976).

Daniélou, Jean, 'H. de Lubac. Le drame de l'humanisme athée', *Études*, May 1945.

Daniélou, Jean, 'La Vie intellectuelle en France: communisme, existentialisme, christianisme', *Études*, September 1945.

Debû-Bridel, Jacques, *La Résistance intellectuelle* (Paris: Julliard, coll: 'La Résistance par ceux qui l'ont faite', 1970).

Dorgelès, Roland, 'Pour verser au dossier des criminels de guerre: Marsoulas', *Les Lettres Françaises*, 16 December 1944.

D'Ouince, Rene, 'A nos lecteurs', *Études*, January 1945.

Duras, Marguerite, Hiroshima mon amour (Paris: Gallimard, 1960).

Dutourd, Jean, *Au Bon Beurre* (Paris: Gallimard, 1952).

Emmenecker, Jean, 'Socialisme et contre-révolution', *Temps Présent*, 31 August 1945.

Ézine, J.-L., *Les Écrivains sur la sellette* (Paris: Seuil, 1981).

Ferrière, A., *Libération de l'homme* (Geneva: Editions du Mont-Blanc, 1944).

Fessard, Gaston, SJ, *France, prends garde de perdre ta liberté* (Paris: Editions du Témoignage Chrétien, 1945).

Flower, J. E., *Literature and the Left in France* (London: Macmillan, 1983).

Franck, Bernard, 'Grognards et hussards', *Les Temps Modernes*, December 1952.

Friedmann, Georges, *La Crise du progrès: Esquisse d'histoire des idées 1895–1935* (Paris: Gallimard, 1936).

Fumet, Stanislas, 'Charles de Gaulle, ami de *Temps Présent*', *Temps Présent*, 26 August 1944.

Gadoffre, Gilbert (ed.), *Vers le style du XXe siècle* (Paris: Seuil, 1945).

Galtier-Boissière, Jean, *Mon Journal pendant la grande pagaïe* (Paris: La Jeune Parque, 1950).

Garaudy, Roger, 'Discours de Roger Garaudy', in Roger Garaudy and Georges Cogniot, *Les Intellectuels et la Renaissance Française* (Paris: Éditions du PCF, 1945).

Garaudy, Roger, 'Jean-Paul Sartre, un faux prophète', *Les Lettres Françaises*, 29 December 1945.

Gide, André, 'La Délivrance de Tunis', *Les Lettres Françaises*, 18 November 1944.

Hauriou, André, *Vers une doctrine de la Résistance: le socialisme humaniste* (Algiers: Editions Fontaine, 1944).

Hervé, Pierre, 'Un Socialisme humaniste', *Esprit*, February 1945.

Higgins, Ian (ed.), *Anthology of Second World War Poetry* (London: Methuen, 1982).

Indomitus, *Nous sommes des rebelles* (Paris: coll: 'Defense de l'Homme', 1945).

Kanapa, Jean, 'Les Mots ou le métier d'écrivain', *Poésie 47*, 40 (August–September 1947).

Lacroix, Jean, 'Socialisme et unanimité nationale', *Temps Présent*, 8 December 1944.

Lacroix, Jean, 'Socialisme humaniste', *Esprit*, May 1945.

Lacroix, Jean, *Socialisme?* (Paris: Editions du Livre Français, 1945).

Laurent, Jacques, *La Mort à boire* (Paris: Froissard, 1947).

Laurent, Jacques, 'Pour une stèle au Docteur Petiot', *La Table Ronde*, May 1948.

Laurent, Jacques, *Les Corps tranquilles* (Paris: La Table Ronde, 1958).

Laurent, Jacques, *Au Contraire* (Paris: La Table Ronde, 1967).

Laurent, Jacques, *Les Bêtises* (Paris: La Table Ronde, 1960).

Laurent, Jacques, *Histoire égoïste* (Paris: La Table Ronde, 1976).

Laurent, Jacques, *Le Roman du roman* (Paris: Gallimard, 1977).

Laurent, Jacques, 'Interview with Josyane Savignon', *Le Monde*, 28 February 1986.

Lefebvre, Henri, *Le Matérialisme dialectique* (Paris: P.U.F., 1940).

Lefebvre, Henri, *Le Marxisme* (Paris: P.U.F., 1948).

Lhôte, André, 'Un éternel malentendu', *Les Lettres Françaises*, 28 October 1944.

Lottman, Herbert R., *La Rive gauche* (Paris: Seuil, 1981).

Mandouze, André, 'Nous avons rompu, nous saurons unir', *Témoignage Chrétien*, 9 September 1944.

Marcel, Gabriel, 'Hiérarchie des fidelités', *Temps Présent*, 8 September 1944.

Maritain, Jacques, *Humanisme intégral* (Paris: Aubier, 1936).

Masure, Chanoine Eugène, *L'Humanisme chrétien* (Paris: G. Beauchesne, 1937).

Mercier, Jeanne, 'Le Ver dans le fruit', *Études*, February 1945.

Michel, Henri and Mirkine-Guetzévitch, B., *Les Idées politiques et sociales de la Résistance* (Paris: P.U.F., 1954).

Michel, Henri, *Les Courants de pensée de la Résistance* (Paris: P.U.F., 1962).

Morgan, Claude, *Les 'Don Quichotte' et les autres* (Paris: Editions Roblot, coll. 'Cité Première, 1979).

Morin, Edgar and Gratien, Jean, 'Une Interview d'Elio Vittorini', *Les Lettres Françaises*, 27 June 1946.

Morris, A., 'Attacks on the Gaullist "Myth" in French Literature since 1969', *Forum for Modern Language Studies*, XXI, 1 (January 1985).

Mounier, Emmanuel, 'Refaire la Renaissance', *Esprit*, 1 (October 1932).

Mounier, Emmanuel, 'Faut-il refaire la Déclaration des droits de l'homme?', *Esprit*, December 1944.

Mouroux, Jean, *Le Sens chrétien de l'homme* (Paris: Aubier, 1945).

Nettelbeck, C. W., 'Getting the Story Right: Narratives of World War II in Post-1968 France', *Journal of European Studies*, XV (1985).

Nimier, Roger, *Les Epées* (Paris: Gallimard, 1948).

Nimier, Roger, *Le Hussard bleu* (Paris: Gallimard, 1950).

Nizan, Paul, 'Sur l'humanisme', in J.J. Brochier (ed.), *Paul Nizan, intellectuel communiste 1926–1940*, vol. II (Paris: Maspéro, 1970).

Nizan, Paul, *Les Matérialistes de l'antiquité* (Paris: Editions Sociales Internationales, 1936).

Ory, Pascal, *Les Collaborateurs* (Paris: Seuil, coll. 'Points', 1976).

Peuple et Culture, 1 (March 1983), 'Supplément à *Culture*, no. 4'.

Ponge, Francis, 'Notes premières sur l'homme', *Les Temps Modernes*, October 1945.

Racine, Nicole, *Les Écrivains communistes en France, 1920–1936* (Paris: Editions Sociales Internationales, 1973).

Revue d'Histoire de la Deuxième Guerre Mondiale, October 1964 (on Vichy youth policies).

Revue d'Histoire de la Deuxième Guerre Mondiale, January 1966 (on Catholic movements under the Occupation).

Ricoeur, Paul, *Temps et récit*, vol. I (Paris: Seuil, 1983).

Rioux, J.-P., *La France et la Quatrième Republique*, vol. I (Paris: Seuil, 1981).

Ritaine, E., *Les Stratèges de la culture* (Paris: Presses de la Fondation Nationale des Sciences Politiques, 1983).

Robbe-Grillet, Alain, *Les Gommes* (Paris: Les Éditions de Minuit, 1953).

Robbe-Grillet, Alain, *Pour un nouveau roman* (Paris: Gallimard, 1963).

Roy, Claude, 'Esquisse d'un portrait de Loys Masson', in Loys Masson, *Des Bouteilles dans les yeux* (Paris: Robert Laffont, 1970).

Roy, Claude, *Nous* (Paris: Gallimard).

Saez, J.-P. (ed.), *Peuple et Culture: Histoires et mémoires (Entretiens avec Benigo Cacérès, Joffre Dumazedier, Paul Lengrand, Gabriel Monnet, Joseph Rovan)* (Paris: Peuple et Culture, 1986).

Sagan, Françoise, *Bonjour tristesse* (Paris: Julliard, 1954).

Saliège, Mgr, 'Vocation de la France', *Témoignage chrétien*, 30 September 1944.

Sartre, Jean-Paul, *La Nausée* (Paris: Gallimard, 1938).

Sartre, Jean-Paul, *L'Etre et le néant* (Paris: Gallimard, 1943).

Sartre, Jean-Paul, 'Portrait de l'antisémite', *Les Temps Modernes*, December 1945.

Sartre, Jean-Paul, *Qu'est-ce que la littérature?* (Paris: Gallimard, 1947).

Sartre, Jean-Paul, 'Présentation des *Temps Modernes*', in J.-P. Sartre, *Situations*, vol. II (Paris: Gallimard, 1948).

Sartre, Jean-Paul, 'Réponse à Albert Camus', *Les Temps Modernes*, July 1952.

Sartre, Jean-Paul, *Les Mots* (Paris: Gallimard, 1964).

Sartre, Jean-Paul, *Carnets de la Drôle de Guerre* (Paris: Gallimard, 1985).

Teilhard de Chardin, Pierre, 'Hérédité sociale et l'éducation', *Études*, April 1945.

Teilhard de Chardin, Pierre, *Le Phénomène humain* (Paris: Seuil, 1955).

Teirsky, Ronald, *French Communism, 1920–1972* (New York, London: Columbia University Press, 1974).

Toynbee, W.S., *Adult Education and the Voluntary Associations in France* (Nottingham: Nottingham Working Papers in the Education of Adults, 7, 1985).

Verdier, Robert and Stibbe, Pierre, 'Socialisme humaniste', *Esprit*, April 1945.

Vian, Boris, *J'irai cracher sur vos tombes* (Paris: Éditions du Scorpion, 1946).

Vian, Boris, *L'Écume des jours* (Paris: Gallimard, 1947).
Vian, Boris, *L'Automne à Pékin* (Paris: Éditions du Scorpion, 1947).

GERMANY

Der Theateralmanach 1946–1947: Kritisches Jahrbuch der Bühnenkunst (Munich, 1946).
'Die Wahrheit ohne Legende', *Frankfurter Allgemeine Zeitung*, 26 May 1977.
Adolph, Rudolph, 'Georg Kaiser im Exil', in *Der Theateralmanach 1946–1947. Kritisches Jahrbuch der Bühnenkunst* (Munich, 1946).
Andersch, Alfred, 'Das junge Europa formt sein Gesicht', *Der Ruf*, I, 1 (1946–7).
Andersch, Alfred, *Sansibar oder der letzte Grund* (Olten, Freiburg, 1958).
Andersch, Alfred, 'Deutsche Literatur in der Entscheidung', in Gerd Hoffmans (ed.), *Das Alfred Andersch Lesebuch* (Zurich, 1979).
Arnold, Heinz Ludwig (ed.), *Deutsch Literatur im Exil 1933–1945*, vol. I: *Dokumente* (Frankfurt, 1974).
Aufbau, Heft 8 (1949).
Bahn, Volker, 'Das subventionierte Theater der BRD' (Berlin: Doctoral thesis, 1972).
Bauer, Arnold, 'Verbannte und verkannte Literatur', in Heinz Ludwig Arnold (ed.), *Deutsche Literatur im Exil 1933–1944*, vol. I (Frankfurt, 1974).
Becher, Johannes R., *Publizistik*, vol. II: *1939–1945* (Berlin, Weimar, 1978).
Behr, Walter, 'Gefahren des Darstellungstils', in *Der Theateralmanach, 1946–1947*.
Benn, Gottfried, 'Der Roman des Phänotyp', in Gottfried Benn, *Gesammelte Werke*, vol. IV (Wiesbaden, 1961).
Benz, Wolfgang (ed.), *Die Bundesrepublik Deutschland. Geschichte in drei Bänden*, vol. III: *Kultur* (Frankfurt, 1983).
Berliner Kulturrat (eds), *Eine Kulturmetropole wird geteilt* (Berlin, 1987).
Boveri, Margaret, *Tage des Überlebens* (Berlin, 1945: Munich, 1968).
Braun, Karl-Heinz (ed.), *Subjektivität als Problem psychologischer Methodik* (Frankfurt, New York, 1985).
Brecht, Bertolt, *Arbeitsjournal*, vol. II: *1942–1955* (Frankfurt, 1974).
Daiber, Hans, *Deutsches Theater seit 1945. Bundesrepublik. Deutsche Demokratische Republik. Österreich. Schweiz* (Stuttgart, 1976).
Denkler, H and Prum, K. (eds), *Die deutsche Literatur im Dritten Reich* (Stuttgart, 1976).
Deutsche Bühnenverein (eds), *Was spielten die Theater? Bilanz der Spielpläne in der Bundesrepublik Deutschland 1947–1975* (Cologne, 1978).
Döblin, Alfred, *Die literarische Situation* (Baden-Baden, 1947).
Döblin, Alfred, *Briefe* (Olten and Freiburg, 1970).
Domin, Friedrich, 'Die Not und das Notwendige', in *Der Theateralmanach, 1946–1947*.
Dörge, Georg, *Vom kulturellen Lebensstandard: Versuch einer nüchternen Umschau* (Stuttgart, 1947).

Dregger, Alfred, 'Katastrophen kann man nicht feiern', *Frankfurter Allgemeine Zeitung*, 27 December 1984.

Durzak, M. (ed.), *Deutsche Gegenwartsliteratur* (Stuttgart, 1981).

Endres, Elisabeth, *Die Literatur der Adenauerzeit* (Munich, 1980).

Emmerich, Wolfgang, 'Nullpunkt', in *Kulturpolitisches Wörterbuch Bundesrepublik Deutschland/DDR im Vergleich* (Stuttgart, 1983).

Fest, Joachim, 'Sieg und Niederlage', *Frankfurter Allgemeine Zeitung*, 20 April 1985.

Fiedler, Hans [Döblin, Alfred], *Der Nürnberger Lehrprozess* (Baden-Baden, 1946).

Fritsch, Christian and Winckler, Lutz (eds), *Faschismuskritik und Deutschlandbild im Exilroman* (Berlin, 1981).

Gaiser, Gerd, *Die sterbende Jagd* (Frankfurt, 1957).

Glaser, Hermann, *Kulturgeschichte der Bundesrepublik Deutschland: Zwischen Kapitulation und Wahrungsreform 1945–1948*, vol. I (Munich, 1985).

Grass, Günter, *Kopfgeborten oder die Deutschen sterben aus* (Darmstadt, Neuwied, 1980).

Grass, Günter, *Widerstand lernen* (Darmstadt, Neuwied, 1984).

Grellman, Wilhelm, *Deutsche Dichter der Gegenwart* (Frankfurt, 1972).

Gründgens, Gustaf, *Briefe, Aufsätze, Reden*, ed. Rolf Badenhausen and Peter Gründgens-Gorski (Hamburg, 1967).

Habermas, Jürgen, 'Entsorgung der Vergangenheit', in J. Habermas, *Die neue Unübersichtlichkeit: Kleine politische Schriften*, vol. V (Frankfurt, 1985).

Hallgarten, Georg and Radkau, Joachim, *Deutsche Industrie und Politik von Bismark bis heute* (Frankfurt, 1974).

Haug, Wolfgang Fritz, 'Die neue Deutungskämpfe um Anti/Faschismus. Ein Untersuchung zur neokonservativen Offensive im Spiegel der *Frankfurter Allgemeine*', *Das Argument* 28, 158 (1986).

Haug, Wolfgang Fritz, 'Vergangenheit, die Zukunft werden soll. Über den Historiker-Streit', *Das Argument* 29, 161 (1987).

Hausenstein, Wilhelm, *Licht unter dem Horizont: Tagebücher von 1942 bis 1946* (Munich, 1967).

Heister, Hans Werner and Klein, Hans Günter, *Musik und Musikpolitik im faschistischen Deutschland* (Frankfurt, 1984).

Hermand, Jost, Peitsch, H., and Scherpe, K. R. (eds), *Nachkriegsliteratur in Westdeutschland, 1945–1949: Gattungen, Schreibweisen, Institutionen* (Berlin, 1982).

Hermand, Jost, Peitsch, H., and Scherpe, K. R. (eds), *Nachkriegsliteratur*, vol. II: *Autoren, Sprache, Traditionen* (Berlin, 1984).

Heuss, Theodor, *Aufzeichnungen 1945–1947* (Tübingen, 1966).

Hohenemser, Herbert, 'Introduction', in Eugen Schöndienst, *Geschichte des deutschen Bühnenvereins seit 1945* (Frankfurt, 1981).

Holthusen, Hans Egon, *Der unbehauste Mensch* (Munich, 1951).

Horvat, Dragica, 'Die "junge Generation" auf der Suche nach der neuen Literatur', in Berliner Kulturrat (eds), *Eine Kulturmetropole wird geteilt*.

Hüppauf, Bernd, 'Krise ohne Wandel. Die Kulturelle Situation 1945–1949', in B. Hüppauf, *'Die Mühen der Ebenen'. Kontinuität und Wandel in der deutschen Literatur und Gesellschaft, 1945–1949* (Heidelberg, 1981).

Jonas, Lutz, 'Die Finanzierung der offentlichen Theater in der Bundesrepublik Deutschland' (Mainz: Doctoral thesis, 1972).

Jünger, Ernst, *Gesammelte Werke*, vol. IX (Stuttgart, 1979).

Kahnert, Walter, *Objektivismus: Gedanken uber einer neuen Literaturstil* (Berlin, 1946).

Krauss, Werner, 'Das Ende der Generationgemeinschaft', in W. Krauss, *Literaturtheorie, Philosophie und Politik*, ed. Manfred Naumann (Berlin, Weimar, 1984).

Kröll, Friedhelm, ' "und die ich nicht in die Wolken geschrieben hatte". Warum Alfred Döblin in der westdeutschen Nachkriegsliteratur nicht angekommen ist', in Hermand *et al.*, *Nachkriegsliteratur*, II.

Lange, Horst, 'Bücher nach dem Krieg', in H. Schwab-Felisch (ed.), *'Der Ruf'. Eine deutsche Nachkriegszeitung* (Munich, 1972).

Lange, Wigand, *Theater in Deutschland nach 1945: Zur Theaterpolitik der amerikanischen Besätzungsbehörden* (Frankfurt, 1980).

Langgässer, Elizabeth, . . . *soviel berauschende Vergänglichkeit. Briefe 1926–1950* (Hamburg, 1954).

Literaturmagazin, 7 (1977).

Mann, Klaus, *Mephisto: Roman einer Karriere* (Hamburg, 1980).

Mann, Thomas, 'Deutschland und die Deutschen', in T. Mann, *Werke*, vol. XI (Frankfurt, 1960).

Manthey, Jurgen, 'Zurück zur Kultur', *Literaturmagazin*, 7 (1977).

Martell, Henning, 'Ein Weg ohne Kompass. Neubeginn am Beispiel der Zeitschrift *Der Ruf*', *Kurbiskern*, 2 (1975).

Mayer, Hans, *Deutsche Literatur seit Thomas Mann* (Reinbeck, 1968).

Merrit, Anna J and Merrit, Richard L., *Public Opinion in Occupied Germany: The OMGUS Survey, 1945–1949* (Urbana, Ill.: University of Illinois Press, 1970).

Müller, Henning, 'Theater im Zeichen des Kalten Krieges: Untersuchungen zur Theater- und Kulturpolitik in den Westsektoren Berlins 1945–1953' (Berlin: Doctoral thesis, 1976).

Naumann, Manfred, 'Prolegomena zu einer Werner-Krauss-Biographie', *Sinn und Form*, 35 (1983).

Peitsch, Helmut, 'Wolfgang Weyrauch und der Kahlschlag', in *Stadtansichten: Jahrbuch fur Literatur und kulturelles Leben in Berlin (West)*, 2 (1981).

Peitsch, Helmut, 'Theodor Plieviers *Stalingrad*', in Fritsch and Winckler (eds), *Faschismuskritik und Deutschlandbild im Exilroman*.

Peitsch, Helmut, 'Politisierung der Literatur oder "Freiheit der Geistes"? Materialien zu den Literaturverhältnisse in den Westzones', in Hermand *et al.*, *Nachkriegsliteratur in Westdeutschland, 1945–1949*.

Peitsch, Helmut and Reith, Hartmut, 'Keine "innere Emigration" in die "Gefilde" der Literatur. Literärischpolitische Publizistik im Umkreis der Gruppe 1947–1949', in Hermand *et al.*, *Nachkriegsliteratur*, II.

Peitsch, Helmut, 'Kulturfassade vor der Barbarei?', in Heister and Klein (eds), *Musik und Musikpolitik im faschistischen Deutschlands*.

Peitsch, Helmut, 'Methoden der Medienanalyse am Beispiel von Selbstzeugnissen uber den Faschismus in den Massenmedien der Nachkriegszeit', in Braun (ed.), *Subjektivitat als problem psychologischer Methodik*.

Prinz, Friedrich (ed.), *Trümmerzeit in Munchen: Kultur und Gesellschaft einer deutschen Grossstadt im Aufbruch 1945–1949* (Munich, 1984).

Raddatz, Fritz, 'Die ausgehaltene Realität', in Hans Werner Richter (ed.), *Almanach der Gruppe 47 1947–1962* (Reinbeck, 1962).

Raddatz, Fritz, 'Wir werden weiterdichten, wenn alles in Scherben fällt...', *Die Zeit*, 12 October 1979.

Reich-Ranicki, Marcel, *Deutsche Literatur in Ost und West* (Munich, 1963).

Richter, Hans Werner, 'Literatur im Interregnum', *Der Ruf*, I, 15 (1946–1947).

Richter, Hans Werner, *Almanach der Gruppe 47, 1947–1962* (Reinbeck, 1962).

Rischbieter, Henning, 'Theater', in Benz (ed.), *Die Bundesrepublik Deutschland*, III.

Roberts, David, 'Nach der Apokalypse. Kontinuität und Diskontinuität in deutschen Literatur nach 1945', in Hüppauf (ed.), *'Die Mühen der Ebenen'*.

Rösler, Reinhard, 'Beiträge der Publizistik fur die Entwicklung der Literatur in den westlichen Besätzungszonen Deutschlands während der Jahre 1945–1949' (Rostock: Doctoral thesis, 1980).

Ruhle, Günter, 'Restauration und neue Einheit', *Frankfurter Allgemeine Zeitung*, 23 September 1978.

Sanchez-Blanco, Francisco, 'Ortega y Gasset: Philosoph des Wiederaufbaus? Anmerkungen zu einer unbeachteten Rezeption', in Hermand *et al.*, *Nachkriegsliteratur*, II.

Schäfer, Hans Dieter, 'Die nichtfaschistische Literatur der jungen Generation', in Denkler and Prum (eds), *Die deutschen Literatur im Dritten Reich*.

Schäfer, Hans Dieter, 'Zur Periodisierung der deutschen Literatur seit 1930', *Literaturmagazin*, 7 (1977).

Schnabel, Ernst, 'Form und Stoff künftiger Dichtung', *Die Welt*, 17 May 1946.

Schneider, Michael, 'Wie man einen verlorenen Krieg gewinnt', in M. Schneider, *Die Wiedergutmachen* (Cologne, 1985).

Schonauer, Franz, 'Sieburg & Co. Rückblick auf eine sogenannte konservative Literaturkritik', *Literaturmagazin*, 7 (1977).

Schöndienst, Eugen, *Geschichte des Deutschen Buhnenvereins seit 1945* (Frankfurt, 1981).

Schulze, Hagen, 'Schwierigkeiten mit einem Gedenktag: zum 8 Mai 1945', *Der Tagespiele*, 5 May 1985.

Schwab-Felisch, H. (ed.), *'Der Ruf': Eine deutsche Nachkriegszeitung* (Munich, 1972).

Schwarz, Hans Peter, *Die Ära Adenauer: Gründjahre der Republik 1949–1957* (Stuttgart, 1981).

Seelmann-Eggebert, Ulrich, 'Rhein-Main-Neckar-Gebiet', in *Der Theateralmanach, 1946–1947*.

Sturmer, Michael, 'Keine Angst vor gemischten Gefühlen. Trauer und Bitternis, Aufatmen und Dankbarkeit prägen die Erinnerung an den Tag, als der Krieg su Ende war', *Die Zeit*, 25 January 1985.

Thiess, Frank, *Dichtung und Wirklichkeit* (Wiesbaden, 1952).

Thiess, Frank, 'Innere Emigration', in Arnold (ed.), *Deutsche Literatur im Exil 1933–1945*, I.

Thiess, Frank, 'Abschied von Thomas Mann', ibid.

Trapp, Frithjof, 'Logen- und Parterreplätze. Was behinderte die Rezeption der Exilliteratur?', in Ulrich Walberer (ed.), *10 Mai 1933: Bücherverbrennung in Deutschland und die Folgen* (Frankfurt, 1983).

Trommler, Frank, 'Der "Nullpunkt 1945" und seine Verbindlichkeit für die Literaturgeschichte', *BASIS* 1 (1970).

Trommler, Frank, 'Emigration und Nachkriegsliteratur. Zum Problem der geschichtlichen Kontinuität', in Grimm and Hermand (eds), *Exil und innere Emigration*.

Vormweg, Heinrich, 'Deutsche Literatur 1945–1960: Keine Stunde Null', in Durzak (ed.), *Deutsche Gegenwartsliteratur*.

Vormweg, Heinrich, *Günter Grass* (Reinbeck, 1986).

Walberer, Ulrich (ed.), *10 Mai 1933: Bücherverbrennen in Deutschland und die Folgen* (Frankfurt, 1983).

Weyrauch, Wolfgang (ed.), *Tausend Gramm: Sammlung neuer deutschen Geschichten* (Hamburg, Stuttgart, Baden-Baden, Berlin, 1949).

Widmer, Urs, *1945 oder die 'Neue Sprache'* (Düsseldorf, 1966).

GENERAL

Alvarez, A., 'The Literature of the Holocaust', in A. Alvarez, *Beyond all this Fiddle: Essays 1955–1967* (London: Allen Lane, 1968).

Armes, Roy, *Patterns of Realism* (New York: A. S. Barnes, 1971; London: Tantivy Press, 1971).

Balio, Tino, *The American Film Industry* (Madison: Wisconsin University Press, 1976).

Caute, David, *The Fellow-Travellers: A Postscript to the Enlightenment* (London: Weidenfeld and Nicolson, 1973).

Urwin, Derek W., *Western Europe since 1945: A Short Political History* (London: Longman, 1969).

Index